A TREASURY OF FAVORITE POEMS

To the memory of Veronica Hornblower

A TREASURY
OF FAVORITE POEMS

From the scrapbooks of

Frances Parkinson Keyes

HAWTHORN BOOKS, Inc.
Publishers   *New York*

ACKNOWLEDGMENTS

The editor and publisher herewith render thanks to the following authors, publishers, agents, and copyright owners whose interest, cooperation, and permission to reprint have made possible the publication of this book. All possible care has been taken to trace the ownership of every selection included, and to make full acknowledgment for its use. If any errors have inadvertently occurred, they will be corrected in subsequent editions, provided notification is sent to the publisher.

Our sincere thanks to:

Abingdon Press for permission to reprint "The Lifting Hill," from *In Green Pastures* by Jane Merchant. Originally printed in the *New York Times*. Copyright 1957, 1959, by Abingdon Press. Also for "Prayer for a Very New Angel," from *A Poet Prays* by Violet Allyn Storey. Copyright renewal 1954.

John Ackerson for permission to reprint "I am the United States," originally printed in the *Washington Post*, and "Siena, from a Northern Slope," originally in the *New York Times*.

Mildred K. Allen for permission to reprint "I Gathered Stars" by the late Raymond Kresensky, originally printed in the *New York Times*.

Sara Van Alstyne Allen for permission to reprint "Peacock," originally printed in the *Christian Science Monitor*.

E. M. Almedingen for "The House," originally printed in *The Times Literary Supplement* (London).

America, the National Catholic Weekly Review, for "And They Came in Haste," by Sister Mary Irma.

American Agriculturalist for "Evening" by Nacella Young.

Frances DeVliegar Anderson for "As Lilacs Speak," originally in the *New York Times*.

Appleton-Century-Crofts, Inc. for "His Little Sub" by Elizabeth Bennett, from *Century Magazine*. Copyright, 1908, The Century Company.

Anobel Armour for "Boy, Walking and Whistling," originally in the *New York Herald Tribune*, and "Refusal, with Wisdom," from the *Washington Post*.

Elizabeth Jane Astley for "Butternuts," originally printed in the *New York Herald Tribune*.

The Atlantic Monthly for permission to reprint "Some Cities of Spain," by Frances Parkinson Keyes.

Anna R. Baker for "His Choice," originally printed in the *New York Times*.

Christie Mackaye Barnes for "Norman Conquest," by the late Percy Mackaye, originally printed in the *New York Times*.

Isabel Harriss Barr for "Saint Francis Blessing the Birds," originally in the *New York Times*.

The Basilian Press for permission to reprint "Just For Today," by a Sister of Notre Dame, from the *St. Basil Hymnal*.

Pauline Larimer Binford for "Homecoming" from the *New York Times*.

The estate of the late Don Blanding for "Rainbow Islands."

Elizabeth Bohm for "Victorian Parlor," originally printed in *Poetry* magazine.

Carl J. Bostelmann for "Mazda Miracle," originally in the *New York Times*, and included herein by special permission of the author, all rights reserved.

The Boston Herald for permission to reprint "New England" by the late Ella Forbes and "New England Farmhouses" by the late Roselle Mercier Montgomery.

Milton Bracker for permission to reprint "Alert: London," "A Bouquet of Verses for Paris in the Spring," "Epitaph for a Christmas Gift," "New England Village—1942" and "To Each His Own," all previously published in the *New York Times*.

Bianca Bradbury for "New England," originally printed in the *New York Times*, and "The New Calf" from the *New York Herald Tribune*.

Elspeth Bragdon for "Fed," originally printed in the *New York Times*.

Berton Braley for "Metromania," originally in *The New Yorker*. Copyright by Berton Braley, all rights reserved.

Brandt and Brandt for the two excerpts from *John Brown's Body*, by Stephen Vincent Benét, published by Holt, Rinehart & Winston, Inc. Copyright 1927, 1928, by Stephen Vincent Benét, copyright renewed 1955, 1956, by Rosemary Carr Benét.

The Catholic Poetry Society for "The Wise Mother" by Dorothy Hobson, originally in *Spirit*.

Eleanor A. Chaffee for "Memorandum for St. Peter" and "New England Landscape," originally in the *New York Times*, and "Picture in an Old Frame," originally in *The Diplomat*.

H. Daland Chandler for "See-Saw," originally in the *Bulletin of the Boston Society of Architects* and reprinted by special permission of the author; all rights reserved.

The Christian Science Monitor for permission to reprint "Geography of Lilacs" and "Lullaby for a Vermont Town" by the late Frances Frost.

Leslie Savage Clark for "Still There Is Peace," originally in the *New York Times*.

Stanton A. Coblentz for "Tied Dogs," from *Green Vistas*, copyright by The Wings Press, 1943, and "A Booklover's Shelves," both poems originally printed in the *New York Times*.

Richard N. Coffin for permission to reprint three poems by the late Robert P. Tristram Coffin: "Closed House" and "Wild Briar-Roses," originally printed in the *New York Times*, and "Go to the Barn for Courtesy," originally in *The Christian Science Monitor*.

Miss D. E. Collins for permission to reprint "How Far Is It To Bethlehem?" by Frances Chesterton, from *The Oxford Book of Carols*.

William Collins, Ltd., for permission to use "How Many Miles to Babylon?" from *The Way of Poetry*, an anthology edited by John Drinkwater.

Billie B. Cooper for "Quiet Citizen" and "The Stewards," both originally in the *New York Times*.

Daniel Cory for "Sonnet: To George Santayana," originally in the *Washington Post*.

Coward-McCann, Inc., for the two excerpts from *The White Cliffs*, by Alice Duer Miller. Copyright 1940 by Alice Duer Miller.

Curtis Brown, Ltd., for "Oh, Shucks, Ma'am" and "The Hunter" from *Versus,* copyright 1948 by Ogden Nash, published by Little, Brown & Co., and for "The Unwinged Ones" from *The Private Dining Room,* copyright 1952 by Ogden Nash, originally printed in *The New Yorker.*

The John Day Company for "Texas Bus-Ride" from *No Rain From These Clouds,* by Kenneth Porter. Copyright 1946 by Kenneth Porter. Originally printed in *Poetry* magazine.

Alston Deas and The Poetry Society of South Carolina for permission to reprint "Charleston—Post Confederate."

Ethel DeLiesseline and *Good Housekeeping* for permission to reprint "On Restoring an Old House," originally in the March 1953, issue of *Good Housekeeping.* Copyright 1953 by The Hearst Corporation.

Ethel Barrett deVito for "All That He Is" and "An Old Soldier Dies," both originally in the *New York Times.*

Dodd, Mead & Company and McClelland & Stewart, Inc., for permission to reprint "Failure," "Mary and Gabriel," "The Call" and "The Soldier" from *The Collected Poems of Rupert Brooke.* Copyright 1915 by Dodd, Mead & Company. Copyright 1943 by Edward Marsh.

Dodd, Mead & Company for "Benediction," "Choice," "Tulip Beds in Holland," and "Work," from *Hail, Man!*; *The Hour Has Struck* and *Forward March,* by Angela Morgan.

Doubleday & Company, Inc., for "Christmas" from *Candles That Burn* by Aline Kilmer, copyright 1919 by George H. Doran Company; and for "mehitabel sings a song" from the book *archy and mehitabel* by Don Marquis. Copyright 1927 by Doubleday & Company, Inc.

Doubleday & Company, Inc., and Mrs. George Bambridge, the Messrs. Methuen, and the Macmillan Company of Canada for "The Ladies" and "When Earth's Last Picture Is Painted" from *The Seven Seas* and "What Is The Moral?" from *Soldiers Three,* all by Rudyard Kipling.

Marion Doyle for "Kinship," originally printed in the *New York Sun.*

Marjorie Driscoll for "A Young Reporter's If," originally in *The Matrix.*

Duell, Sloan & Pierce for "The Old Woman with Four Sons" from *A Pocketful of Wry,* by Phyllis McGinley. Copyright 1940 and 1959 by Phyllis McGinley.

R. L. Duffus for "The Map of France," originally printed in the *New York Times.*

E. P. Dutton & Co. for "Hills" from *Death and General Putnam, and 101 Other Poems* by Arthur Guiterman, copyright 1935 by E. P. Dutton & Co., Inc.; and "Winterproof" from *Brave Laughter* by Arthur Guiterman, originally published in the *New York Times,* copyright 1943, by E. P. Dutton & Co.; for "Buckingham Palace" and "Vespers" from *When We Were Very Young,* by A. A. Milne, copyright 1924 by E. P. Dutton & Co.,

Inc., renewal 1952 by A. A. Milne; and for "Stray Roads" from *Singing Drums* by Helen Welshimer, copyright 1937, by Helen Welshimer.

Herbert Elliott for "Ghost Church," originally printed in the *New York Times*.

Faber & Faber, Ltd., and the University of Chicago Press for "Jesus and His Mother" from *The Sense of Movement* by Thom Gunn.

Margaret Fishback for "Fish Out of Water" and "Sum Fun," both originally printed in the *New York Herald Tribune*.

Edsel Ford for "The Fox" from a *Thicket of Sky,* copyright 1961, by Edsel Ford. Originally printed in the *New York Times*.

James Dillet Freeman for "Christmas Eve," originally printed in *Unity*.

Ralph Friedrich for "Advice to Dreamers," originally printed in the *Washington Post*.

The Georgia Warm Springs Foundation for permission to reprint "If I Had Known," by the late Mary Carolyn Davies.

Avery Giles for "Soldier's Prayer," originally in the *New York Times*.

Yetza Gillespie for "All Souls," originally in the *New York Times*.

Harold Willard Gleason for "Quandary," originally in the *New York Times*.

Inez George Gridley for "Country Doctor," originally in the *New York Times*.

Donald Hall for "From the Harvard Yard," originally in *The Times Literary Supplement* (London).

Harper & Brothers for "Scenic" from *The Carpentered Hen* by John Updike. Copyright 1957 by John Updike. Originally in *The New Yorker*.

Alice Hartich for "Harvest," originally in the *New York Herald Tribune*.

Sir Alan Herbert for "Why Not A Book?," originally printed in *The Sunday Graphic*.

Alma Robison Higbee for "Old Postmaster," originally in the *New York Times*.

John Holmes for "Tomorrow You," originally printed in the *New York Herald Tribune*.

Holt, Rinehart & Winston, Inc., for "A Boundless Moment" and "Stopping by Woods on a Snowy Evening" from *Complete Poems of Robert Frost*. Copyright 1923 by Holt, Rinehart & Winston, Inc. Copyright renewed 1951 by Robert Frost.

Holt, Rinehart & Winston, Inc., for three poems taken from "A Shropshire Lad" (Authorized Edition) from *Complete Poems* by A. E. Housman. Copyright 1959 by Holt, Rinehart & Winston.

Roy Temple House for "Heart Ruins," originally printed in the *Boston Transcript*.

Gertie Stewart Howard for "Character Sketch," "Hagar Speaks to Sarah," and "Sarah Speaks to Hagar" from *Lonely Apples,* published by the Kaleidograph Press.

Bruce Humphries, Publishers, for "About Face" and "Formula for Old Age," from *Behind This Door, and Other Poems* by Una W. Harsen. Originally printed in the *New York Times.* Copyright 1947 by Bruce Humphries, Inc.

Edward Hutton for "One Man, One Man Alone," originally printed in *The London Times.*

Clara Hyde for "Editor—Weekly Journal," originally in the *New York Times.*

Leslie Nelson Jennings for "Inmate," originally printed in the *New York Times.*

Geoffrey Johnson for "Birthday Candles," originally in the *New York Times.*

Harry Kemp for "Last Word," originally printed in *The Saturday Review.*

Henry W. Keyes, Jr., for "Epilogue," originally printed in the Harvard University *Sophomore Blue Book, 1924.*

Alfred A. Knopf, Inc., for "Soldier" by William Rose Benet and for "The Holy Women," "The Man In White" and "A Page's Road Song" from *Collected Poems of William Alexander Percy.*

Arthur Kramer for "Woe, Brothers, Woe," originally printed in the *New York Times.*

Philip Lazarus for "The Novelist," originally in *The Atlantic Monthly.*

Ruth Lechlitner for "Second Blossoming," originally in the *New York Times.*

Elias Lieberman for "Salvage," "A Schoolmaster Retires" and "To One Facing Retirement," from *To My Brothers, Everywhere,* copyright E. P. Dutton & Co., 1954, originally printed in the *New York Times.*

Carolyn Wilson Link for "Discovery," from *There Is Still Time.* Originally in the *New York Times.*

R. P. Lister for "The Cow," copyright 1950 by *The New Yorker.* Originally in *The New Yorker.*

Little, Brown & Company for permission to reprint "Immortality" by Emily Dickinson.

Little, Brown & Company for "The Cow," "The Family Court," "Pediatric Reflection" and "Political Reflection" and "The Turtle" from *Many Long Years Ago,* copyright 1931 by Ogden Nash, and "The Termite" from *Good Intentions,* copyright 1942 by Ogden Nash.

The Macmillan Company for "Futility" and "You Ask My Age" by Sister Mary Madeleva, from *The Four Last Things,* copyright 1927 and

1929 by Sister Mary Madeleva; and for "Late Summer, Georgia" from *Ritual For Myself* by Anderson Scruggs. Copyright 1941 by C. Anderson Scruggs.

Marion M. Madsen for "Dog, Sleeping Late," originally in the *New York Times.*

Eugene T. Maleska for "Her Christmas Tree," originally in the *New York Times.*

Margery Mansfield for "Indian Summer," originally in *The Christian Science Monitor,* and "Early Friends," originally in the *New York Herald Tribune.*

Dr. John Masefield and the Society of Authors for "Franklin Delano Roosevelt," originally printed in *The London Times.*

Florence Ripley Mastin for "U. S. Mail," originally in the *New York Herald Tribune.*

McClelland & Stewart, Ltd., for "The Road to Tartary" by Bernard Freeman Trotter.

Julian Messner, Inc., for "Immortality" from *The Happy Wanderer* by Frances Parkinson Keyes. Copyright 1954 by Frances Parkinson Keyes.

Anna Blake Mezquida for "The Lonely House" from *A-Gypsying,* published by Marvin Cloyd.

Minnie Hite Moody for "The Harness Shop," "Now Is The Time" and "Prayer Out Of Georgia," all originally printed in the *New York Times.*

The estate of the late Elizabeth Morrow for permission to reprint her poem, "Saint of the Lost."

Helene Mullins for "After A Hundred Storms" from *Streams from the Source,* published by Caxton Press, 1938. Originally in the *New York Times.*

The *New York Times* for "New England Churchyard" by the late Marguerite Janvrin Adams; "Little Christmas" and "Now Grown Older" by Mazie V. Caruthers; "The Thorn" by Berniece Bunn Christman; "Green Mountain Latitudes" and "New Hampshire Moon" by the late Frances Frost; "Tomorrow" by Edward D. Garner; "A Traveler Departs" by W. H. Gerry; "Prayer for a Night of Snow" by the late Daniel Whitehead Hickey; "Death of a Schoolteacher" by Bernard Hirschberg; "Yellow Rose" by Minnie Case Hopkins; "Evening in England" by Raymond Hosken; "Hint Heavenward" by the late Arthur Wallace Peach; "Cargo Ships" by the late Max Press; "Street of Crosses" by the late Arthur Stringer; "The Psalms of David Are Ended" by the late Mary Atwater Taylor; "Growing Older" by the late Charles Hanson Towne; "Prayer for Thanksgiving" by Eleanor Voswinkel; "On Growing Older" by John Wheatley; and "Pastoral" by Viney Wilder.

The New Yorker for "In the Boston Public Garden" by Saul Gottlieb, copyright 1954; "Denise" by Robert Beverly Hale, copyright 1958; "The Lover's Plea" by J. F. Hendry, copyright 1954; "Insomnia" by Gilbert Highet, copyright 1952; and "Shepherd's Song" by John Robert Quinn, copyright 1954.

Brian O'Higgins for "God Bless The Work."

Louise Guyol Owen for "The Revolting Calory Counter," originally printed in *Gourmet*.

The estate of John Oxenham and the Pilgrim Press for "The Sacrament of Fire" from *The Te Deum and the Sacraments* by John Oxenham. Copyright 1928 by John Oxenham, in renewal 1956 by Erica Oxenham.

George A. Pflaum, Publishers, for "November" by Gertrude Hahn, printed originally in *The Young Catholic Messenger*.

Harry I. Phillips for "The Perplexing Battler," originally in the *Washington Post*.

Laurence Pollinger, Ltd., for "A Night in Perugia" from *The Inheritors* by Richard Church, published by William Heinemann, Ltd. Originally in *The Times Literary Supplement* (London).

Dorothy Quick for "Answer" and "Benediction" (originally in *The Churchman*), "Old Things" (originally in *The Hartford Courant*) "The Red Woods" and "Season of Amber" (originally printed in the *New York Times*), and "Words" (originally in *The Lyric*).

Christina Rainsford for "Held by the Land," originally printed in the *New York Times*.

Henry Regnery Co. for "Wishes" and "Prayer for Difficult Days" by Edgar A. Guest.

Bette Richart for "The Delicate Dream Beyond Chaos," originally in *The Saturday Review*.

Dow Richardson for "Graduation," originally printed in the *New York Times Magazine*.

Frances Rodman for "Epitaph for a Pet" and "For a Six-Year-Old," both originally printed in the *New York Times*.

Anne Round and the R. H. Stearns Co. for "What Is A Student?," originally published in the *Boston Herald*.

Rust Craft Publishers for "God Bless The Little Things" by Margaret Murray.

May Sarton for "In Texas" and "Return to Chartres" from *The Lion and The Rose*, published by Rinehart & Company, 1948. Originally printed in *The Atlantic Monthly*.

C. M. Schmid for "The Fighter," originally printed in the *New York Herald Tribune*.

Charles Scribner's Sons for permission to reprint "The Poet's Testament" from *The Poet's Testament* by George Santayana, copyright 1952 by Charles Scribner's Sons, originally printed in *Time;* for "I Have a Rendezvous with Death," "I Loved . . . ," "Paris," and "Sonnet III" from *Poems* by Alan Seeger, copyright 1916 by Charles Scribner's Sons, renewal copyright 1944 by Elsie Adams Seeger; and for "A Wife" from *The House of Rimmon,* Act IV, Scene II, by Henry van Dyke, copyright 1908 by Charles Scribner's Sons; renewal copyright 1936 by Tertius van Dyke, and for "Work" from *Music and Other Poems* (1904) by Henry van Dyke.

Sidgwick and Jackson for "In Due Season" from *The Collected Poems of John Drinkwater.*

Simon & Schuster for "Love in a City" and "What Can You Do with a Woman's Things?" from *Forsaking All Others,* by Alice Duer Miller, copyright 1931 by Alice Duer Miller.

Hiram Lyday Sloanaker for "Hometown Names," originally in the *New York Times.*

Wilbert Snow for "To Robert Frost," originally printed in the *New York Times.*

Jacob C. Solovay for "Love Sonnet to My Students," originally in the *New York Times.*

Kaye Starbird for "Hill Farm," originally printed in *Vermont Life.*

Charles Wharton Stork for "Mont Saint-Michel," originally in the *New York Times.*

George H. Tatum for permission to reprint "Crape Myrtles in the South," "Evening after Rain" and "Old Garden," by the late Edith Tatum, originally in the *New York Times.*

Maurie Taylor and the *Saturday Evening Post* for "Easy Directions," copyright 1958 by the Curtis Publishing Company.

Inez Clark Thorson for "The Wanderer" originally in the *New York Times.*

Ulrich Troubetzkoy for "The Innkeeper's Cat," originally printed in *The Saturday Review.*

Maud E. Uschold for "Taxco, Mexico," originally printed in the *New York Times.*

Beren Van Slyke for "Country Woman," originally in the *New York Herald Tribune.*

The Viking Press, Inc., for permission to reprint the following:

"Girl's-Eye View of Relatives," "The Customs of the Country," "Landscape with Figurines," and "Love Note to a Playwright," from *Times Three,* by Phyllis McGinley, originally printed in *The New Yorker,* copyright 1959 by Phyllis McGinley; and "Bootless Speculation" from *Merry Christ-*

mas, *Happy New Year*, originally in *The New Yorker*, copyright 1957 by Phyllis McGinley.

"Partial Comfort" and "The Maidservant at the Inn" from *Sunset Gun*; and "Inventory," "Social Note," "The Satin Dress" and "Indian Summer" from *Enough Rope*: all included in *The Portable Dorothy Parker*, copyright 1927, 1944; 1926, 1954 by Dorothy Parker.

"Words from England," originally in *The New Yorker*, copyright 1954 by Donald Hall, and "New England November," copyright 1955 by Donald Hall, from *Exiles and Marriages*.

Harold Vinal for "Hour for Swans," originally in the *New York Times*.

Blanche S. Wagstaff for permission to reprint "Hope."

Marion Ward for *"Les Deux Arts,"* originally in the *New York Times*.

May Williams Ward for "The Bereaved" and "Lightning over a Calm Sea," the latter originally in the *New York Times*.

The Westerners' Foundation for "Louisiana Purchase" by the late Badger Clark, originally printed in the *New York Herald Tribune*.

Irene Aloha Wright for *"El Archivo de Indias,"* originally published in *The Hispanic American Historical Review*.

PREFACE

There is probably nothing that appeals less to the woman who is a professional writer than keeping a diary. By the time she has spent a sufficient number of hours in her workroom, to prevent her next deadline from becoming a menacing monster instead of a goal which she might reasonably hope to attain, she has no inclination to linger at her desk a single superfluous minute; she wants to escape before the feeling of being confined becomes one of being actually chained. She probably has not done much anyway, except write and write and write. Such persons as she has seen have been either professional visitors connected with her work or have represented unwelcome interruptions: distant relatives who have arrived unheralded in the city where she is presently assigned, and who expect to be entertained; solicitors for some good cause who do not realize they are jeopardizing it by begging in person instead of writing nice little notes; workmen who were supposed to mend the roof week before last, when it first began to leak into the study, and who now must have checks before they depart, for otherwise starvation will be staring their innocent children in the face. So the pile of source material has been set aside as carefully as possible, but somehow never carefully enough to prevent disarranging it; the checkbook has been extracted from its drawer, the solicitor and the workmen paid and the distant relative invited to dinner; and, afterward, the writer has endeavored to collect her scattered notes, together with her scattered thoughts. If the deadline is really a menace, somehow she drives herself on and on far into the night; if it has not quite reached that stage, she gives up the struggle for the day. In either case one thing is certain: she does not turn to a diary and record the weather, the interruptions and the deep discouragement which threatens to engulf her, together with the anguished conviction that it would have been easier to break rocks for a living than to write books.

This at least represents my viewpoint in regard to a diary, and I have discovered that it is by no means unique. There is, however, a very satisfactory substitute for one, and that is a scrapbook. It is not half so burdensome, at the end of a long hard day, to paste press clippings, programs, invitations, and so forth on large blank pages as it is to try to think of something with which to cover those pages in writing. When it comes to that, someone else can do the pasting for you, whereas—or so it seems—no one else can do the writing. I have been grateful beyond measure to my husband—or rather, to the man who eventually became my husband—because, when I was only fifteen, he presented me with two beautiful large volumes, bound in red leather and stamped in gold with my initials, and told me that he thought I would find it interesting and rewarding to keep a scrapbook. At the time I was not very well and was feeling rather at loose ends generally. The blank pages of the beautiful volumes invited filling; and presently I was pasting into them, not without nostalgia, invitations, programs, school reports, score pads, visiting cards, and ticket stubs saved from the previous winter, but still scattered helter-skelter in my desk and bureau drawers. Such pasting was the beginning of a fixed habit. Those two beautiful red morocco books have been followed by a long series of others, less elegant as to binding, but enriched with delightful and authentic reminders of what I have been seeing and doing in all parts of the world.

Among the items which have found their way into these many bulky volumes have very naturally been clippings which represented something I had enjoyed reading, as well as those which represented something I had enjoyed doing. Much of the former material was in the shape of verse and, at the beginning, most of this was taken from the *Boston Evening Transcript,* a newspaper which, alas! no longer exists, but which in my youth I read avidly, and which always carried a poem on its editorial page. This custom has happily been carried on by the *New York Times* and has proved another treasure trove, as far as I am concerned. To a lesser degree, almost every other periodical of which I am either a regular or intermittent reader has supplied me with verse, which I have found enjoyable, amusing or inspiring as the case might be; and one day my eldest son, looking over the big scrapbooks to which I have already referred, made a suggestion which seemed a logical sequel to the one made by his father, so many years previously.

"Why don't you keep separate scrapbooks for poetry? Smaller books that you could handle easily, and in which you could refer, without too much trouble, to some special poem that you wanted to read again or perhaps to quote. The way they are now, it's like looking for a needle in a haystack to find any given one of them. And if you liked them well enough to keep them, it stands to reason that you didn't want to bury them. Now here's something really good—" and he started reading aloud to me.

Thus the separate poetry scrapbooks came into being and, eventually, they caught the attention of a publisher who had come to see me about something entirely different, but who happened to notice one of the books in question, which I was indeed using for reference, just as my son had predicted, and which was lying on my desk. "Why don't you make this scrapbook the nucleus of an anthology?" he asked. "Most authors confine themselves to poems which are already famous when they prepare an anthology. Why not have one devoted to some which might have been famous, but which have hitherto been overlooked, because they weren't widely enough distributed in the first place or gathered together in the second? Of course, you could supplement these by some famous poems, if you have any special favorites, but those would be incidental. Also, you might add some you enjoyed as a child, before you began to keep a scrapbook, if you could locate these. Yes, that's what we'll do. We'll start an anthology along those lines. . . ."

The present volume is the result of that conference.

Lack of space has, of course, made it impossible to include all the verse collected in my poetry scrapbooks over a period of more than half a century; but, as the publisher advised, this material has formed the nucleus to which other verse has been added. No additional selection of poems were based on the fact that they were famous; they had to be personal favorites to qualify if the whole were to keep the character at which we were aiming. On the other hand, nothing has been left out because of fear that the very fact of its fame would make someone cry out, "What, that same old thing in another anthology!" Our theory has been that if it were good enough to use many times already, it must be good enough to use at least once more!

With the personal element still in mind, I have preceded each separate section with brief editorial comment, to indicate why or under what circumstances a poem had a special appeal or carried a special message to me. It has been my hope that by doing this, I might make its appeal and its message clearer and more poignant to someone else.

The publisher's suggestion that some poems I had especially enjoyed as a child, before I began to keep a scrapbook, would be of interest proved a valuable one. I bethought me of three volumes, entitled *Open Sesame*, I, II and III, published by Ginn and Company when I was a very little girl and all greatly beloved by me. The part these poems played in my early life is described in the Foreword to Section One of this book. I have also included among my selections the hymns which were familiar to me and beloved by me in my childhood; which I later sang to and with my own children; and which I still feel have an important bearing on the spiritual life of many persons besides myself.

The publisher has also paid me the compliment of suggesting that I should include some of my own poetry in the Anthology. I have felt some natural hesitation about doing this; but I have long wished that I might give more permanent form to "Spanish Cities", which I wrote as blank verse, but which was published, somewhat abbreviated, as a "Poetic Essay", first in the *Atlantic Monthly,* and then in a brochure issued by the Spanish State Tourist Bureau. The abbreviation resulted in the deletion of the lines describing Valencia, except those about its most noble and notable dish, *paella,* which was casually transferred to the section on Madrid. In consequence, many were the protests I received: didn't I know that *paella* was the pride of *Valencia?* How could I have been so careless or so ignorant as not to give credit where credit was really due? Hence, if for no other reason—though, as a matter of fact, there are several others!—I am very glad to have all my original "Spanish Cities" included in this section; and I have also included a few other verses, being guided in my choice by my publisher, my family and my secretarial staff as to which are the best.

The long and tedious task of copying the selected material in standardized typewritten form; of sorting it so that it would take its proper place in the various categories of subject matter; of helping to decide what must be deleted in order to keep the size of the book within bounds; and, finally, of writing to publishers, editors and authors, asking for permission to reprint is a formidable undertaking in itself: all this was originally entrusted to my junior secretary, Veronica Hornblower. For more than two months she devoted her entire time to it, with some kindly help from my lifelong friend, Miss Mary Hale, the librarian of Newbury, Vermont. Then Ronnie, as we called her, developed a little cough which did not seem serious. In fact, she scoffed at the suggestion that she should see a doctor about this, and was very tardily persuaded to do so by our family physician, who is also a personal friend, and who happened to hear the little cough when he telephoned to invite us to dinner one day. Within two months, she was dead of inoperable cancer.

This tragedy has been such a great loss, both personally and professionally, that an entire year has been darkened and complicated by it, and the publication of the anthology, which was already regarded as hers no less than mine, has been greatly retarded. Since work was resumed on it, I have had the efficient and cheerful cooperation of Mrs. Catherine Hairston Tomsyck, who—like Ronnie—has devoted solid months to the task. I am very grateful to her for making possible the continuation of this work.

Some modern poems, which we would have liked very much to include, have been omitted because our budget was so limited and their prices so prohibitive. In some cases, where newspapers and magazines have ceased publication, and their contributors are no longer living, it has been impossible to secure the usual permits; but every conceivable effort has been made to do so. In the case of poems whose authors we do not know, we should be pleased to hear from these authors, and will add their names to their works in future editions if they will communicate with us. In a few cases, it has been impossible to ferret out any information whatsoever as to the whereabouts of the poets whose works I wished to use; in these cases, we have included the poems anyway, with the hope that, wherever their authors are, they may be pleased to see their poems in this book.

I should like to thank Mr. Gustav Davidson, secretary of the Poetry Society of America; Mr. Harold Vinal, editor of *Voices: A Journal of Poetry;* Miss Eleanor Gray of the Academy of American Poets; Miss Anne Speer of *The London Times;* the Poetry Department of the *New York Times;* the League of American Penwomen; the members of the New England Poetry Club; and last but certainly not least, Miss Julia Watterson, formerly Research Secretary to Senator Norris Cotton of New Hampshire, and Mr. Kenton Kilmer of the Library of Congress in Washington, for their invaluable assistance in providing the addresses of poets whom we wished to locate.

If, in spite of the efforts of all of us, someone has seemed to be over-looked, it is hoped that the publisher, the editor, and the editor's faith-ful, conscientious and efficient assistants may all be forgiven.

FRANCES PARKINSON KEYES

Beauregard House
New Orleans, Louisiana

CONTENTS

2—CHILDHOOD DAYS

3—YOUTH

Contents   23

4—YOUNG LOVE

5—FRIENDSHIP AND LOVE, OLDER GROWN

6—MOTHERHOOD

7—OLD AGE

8—DEATH AND IMMORTALITY

9—HYMNS

10—PRAYERS AND POEMS OF RELIGION

11—CHRISTMAS

Contents

12—PHILOSOPHY OF LIFE

13—COURAGE AND PATRIOTISM

14—HUMOR

Contents

15—PEOPLE

16—ANIMALS

17—PLACES

18—HOUSES

19—NATURE

20—SEASONS AND FLOWERS

21—ENVOI

1

OPEN SESAME

When I was a little girl, a three-volumed Anthology entitled OPEN SESAME was brought out by Ginn & Company. The first volume was designed to meet the tastes and understanding of a small child; the second, one somewhat older; the third a teenager. My mother gave me the set in its entirety on my ninth birthday and I devoured it with the avidity which nearly all reading material aroused in my breast. I found, when I began reading aloud to my own children, that they derived the same enjoyment from the collection that I did; and it has been carefully kept, at my country home, in the section of the library devoted to children's books. Last summer, when I began to assemble material for an anthology of my own, this collection was among the first that I reviewed; and I found that my pleasure in it was just as keen as when I first read it. I would rejoice to see it reissued in its entirety, for the children and teenagers of the present day; meanwhile, I have selected as many poems from it as I thought it would be possible to include here, without upsetting the balance of the whole; and in doing so I have also tried to strike an even balance between those I especially loved as a child, and those which now seem to me most worthy of preservation for others, in the light of a wider acquaintance with juvenile literature.

THE OWL AND THE PUSSY-CAT

Edward Lear

The Owl and the Pussy-Cat went to sea
   In a beautiful pea-green boat:
They took some honey, and plenty of money
   Wrapped up in a five-pound note.
The Owl looked up to the moon above,
   And sang to a small guitar,
"O lovely Pussy! O Pussy, my love!
   What a beautiful Pussy you are,—
         You are,
   What a beautiful Pussy you are!"

Pussy said to the Owl, "You elegant fowl!
   How wonderful sweet you sing!
O let us be married,—too long we have tarried:—
   But what shall we do for a ring?"
They sailed away, for a year and a day
   To the land where the Bong-tree grows,
And there in a wood a piggy-wig stood,
   With a ring in the end of his nose,—
         His nose,
   With a ring in the end of his nose.

"Dear Pig, are you willing to sell for one shilling
   Your ring?" Said the piggy, "I will."
So they took it away, and were married next day
   By the turkey who lives on the hill.
They dined upon mince and slices of quince,
   Which they ate with a runcible spoon;
And hand in hand, on the edge of the sand,
   They danced by the light of the moon,—
         The moon,
   They danced by the light of the moon.

THE LOST DOLL

Charles Kingsley

I once had a sweet little doll, dears,
    The prettiest doll in the world;
Her cheeks were so red and so white, dears,
    And her hair was so charmingly curled.
But I lost my poor little doll, dears,
    As I played on the heath one day;
And I cried for her more than a week, dears,
    But I never could find where she lay.

I found my poor little doll, dears,
    As I played on the heath one day;
Folks say she is terribly changed, dears,
    For her paint is all washed away.
And her arms trodden off by the cows, dears,
    And her hair's not the least bit curled;
Yet for *old time's sake,* she is still, dears,
    The prettiest doll in the world.

AN OLD GAELIC CRADLE-SONG

Anonymous

Hush! the waves are rolling in,
    White with foam, white with foam:
Father toils amid the din;
    But baby sleeps at home.

Hush! the winds roar hoarse and deep!
    On they come, on they come!
Brother seeks the lazy sheep,
    But baby sleeps at home.

Hush! the rain sweeps o'er the knowes,
    Where they roam, where they roam:
Sister goes to seek the cows;
    But baby sleeps at home.

CRADLE SONG

From the German. Translated by E. L. Prentiss

Sleep, baby, sleep!
Thy father is watching the sheep!
Thy mother is shaking the dreamland tree,
And down drops a little dream for thee.
    Sleep, baby, sleep!

Sleep, baby, sleep!
The great stars are the sheep,
The little stars are the lambs, I guess;
The bright moon is the shepherdess.
Sleep, baby, sleep!

Sleep, baby, sleep!
And cry not like a sheep,
Else the sheep-dog will bark and whine,
And bite this naughty child of mine.
Sleep, baby, sleep!

Sleep, baby, sleep!
Thy Saviour loves His sheep;
He is the Lamb of God on high,
Who, for our sakes, came down to die.
Sleep, baby, sleep!

SEVEN TIMES ONE

Jean Ingelow

There's no dew left on the daisies and clover,
    There's no rain left in heaven;
I've said my "seven times" over and over,
    Seven times one are seven.

I am old, so old I can write a letter;
    My birthday lessons are done;
The lambs play always, they know no better,—
    They are only one times one.

O Moon! in the night I have seen you sailing
    And shining so round and low;
You were bright, ah bright! but your light is failing,—
    You are nothing now but a bow.

You Moon, have you done something wrong in heaven,
    That God has hidden your face?
I hope if you have, you will soon be forgiven,
    And shine again in your place.

O velvet bee, you're a dusty fellow;
    You've powdered your legs with gold!
O brave marshmary buds, rich and yellow,
    Give me your honey to hold!

O columbine, open your folded wrapper,
    Where two twin turtle-doves dwell!
O cuckoo-pint, toll me the purple clapper
    That hangs in your clear green bell!

And show me your nest, with the young ones in it,—
    I will not steal it away;
I am old! you may trust me, linnet, linnet,—
    I am seven times one today.

HOW THE GATES CAME AJAR

From the Italian

It was whispered one morning in heaven
    How the little child-angel, May,
In the shade of the great, white portal,
    Sat sorrowing night and day.
How she said to the stately warden—
    Him of the key and bar—

"O angel, sweet angel! I pray you,
  Set the beautiful gates ajar—
Only a little, I pray you,
  Set the beautiful gates ajar!

"I can hear my mother weeping;
  She is lonely; she cannot see
A glimmer of light in the darkness,
  Where the gates shut after me.
Oh! turn me the key, sweet angel,
  The splendor will shine so far!"
But the warden answered: "I dare not
  Set the beautiful gates ajar,"—
Spoke low and answered: "I dare not
  Set the beautiful gates ajar!"

Then rose up Mary the Blessed,
  Sweet Mary, Mother of Christ:
Her hand on the hand of the angel
  She laid, and her touch sufficed;
Turned was the key in the portal,
  Fell ringing the golden bar;
And lo! in the little child's fingers
  Stood the beautiful gates ajar!
In the little child-angel's fingers
  Stood the beautiful gates ajar!

"And this key, for further using,
  To my blessed Son shall be given;"
Said Mary, Mother of Jesus—
  Tenderest heart in heaven.
Now, never a sad-eyed mother
  But may catch the glory afar;
Since safe in the Lord Christ's bosom,
  Are the keys of the gates ajar;
Close hid in the dear Christ's bosom,
  And the gates forever ajar!

A MIDSUMMER SONG

R. W. Gilder

Oh, father's gone to market-town: he was up before the day,
And Jamie's after robins, and the man is making hay,
And whistling down the hollow goes the boy that minds the
    mill,
While mother from the kitchen-door is calling with a will,
  "Polly!—Polly!—The cows are in the corn!
      Oh, where's Polly?"

From all the misty morning air there comes a summer
    sound,
A murmur as of waters, from skies and trees and ground.
The birds they sing upon the wing, the pigeons bill and
    coo;
And over hill and hollow rings again the loud halloo:
  "Polly!—Polly!—The cows are in the corn!
      Oh, where's Polly?"

Above the trees, the honey-bees swarm by with buzz and
    boom,
And in the field and garden a thousand blossoms bloom.
Within the farmer's meadow a brown-eyed daisy blows,
And down at the edge of the hollow a red and thorny rose.
  But Polly!—Polly!—The cows are in the corn!
      Oh, where's Polly?

How strange at such a time of day the mill should stop
    its clatter!
The farmer's wife is listening now, and wonders what's the
    matter.
Oh, wild the birds are singing in the wood and on the hill,
While whistling up the hollow goes the boy that minds the
    mill.
    But Polly!—Polly!—The cows are in the corn!
        Oh, where's Polly!

THE WAY FOR BILLY AND ME

James Hogg

Where the pools are bright and deep,
Where the gray trout lies asleep,
Up the river and o'er the lea,
That's the way for Billy and me.

Where the blackbird sings the latest,
Where the hawthorn blooms the sweetest,
Where the nestlings chirp and flee,
That's the way for Billy and me.

Where the mowers mow the cleanest,
Where the hay lies thick and greenest;
There to trace the homeward bee,
That's the way for Billy and me.

Where the hazel bank is steepest,
Where the shadow lies the deepest,
Where the clustering nuts fall free,
That's the way for Billy and me.

Why the boys should drive away
Little maidens from their play,
Or love to banter and fight so well,
That's the thing I never could tell.

But this I know, I love to play,
Through the meadow, along the hay;
Up the water and o'er the lea,
That's the way for Billy and me.

A CHRISTMAS CAROL

Dinah Maria Mulock

God rest ye, merry gentlemen! let nothing you dismay,
For Jesus Christ, our Saviour, was born on Christmas
    Day.

The dawn rose red o'er Bethlehem, the stars shone
        through the gray,
When Jesus Christ, our Saviour, was born on Christmas
    Day.

God rest ye, little children; let nothing you affright,
For Jesus Christ, your Saviour, was born this happy
    night;

Along the hills of Galilee the white flocks sleeping
    lay,
When Christ, the Child of Nazareth, was born on
    Christmas Day.

God rest ye, all good Christians; upon this blessed morn
The Lord of all good Christians was of a woman born.

Now all your sorrows He doth heal, your sins, He takes
    away;
For Jesus Christ, our Saviour, was born on Christmas
    Day.

CHRISTMAS CAROL

Old English

As Joseph was a-walking,
   He heard an angel sing,
"This night shall be the birthnight
   Of Christ our heavenly King.

"His birth-shed shall be neither
   In housen nor in hall,
Nor in the place of paradise,
   But in the oxen's stall.

"He neither shall be rockèd
   In silver nor in gold,
But in the wooden manger
   That lieth in the mould.

"He neither shall be washen
   With white wine nor with red,
But with the fair spring water
   That on you shall be shed.

"He neither shall be clothèd
   In purple nor in pall,
But in the fair, white linen
   That useth babies all."

As Joseph was a-walking,
   Thus did the angel sing,
And Mary's son at midnight
   Was born to be our King.

Then be you glad, good people,
   At this time of the year;
And light you up your candles,
   For His star it shineth clear.

UNDER THE HOLLY-BOUGH

Charles Mackay

Ye who have scorned each other,
Or injured friend or brother,
   In this fast-fading year;
Ye who, by word or deed,
Have made a kind heart bleed,
   Come gather here!
Let sinned against and sinning
Forget their strife's beginning,
   And join in friendship now.
Be links no longer broken,
Be sweet forgiveness spoken
   Under the Holly-Bough.

Ye who have loved each other,
Sister and friend and brother,
   In this fast-fading year:

Mother and sire and child,
Young man and maiden mild,
   Come gather here;
And let your heart grow fonder,
As memory shall ponder
   Each past unbroken vow;
Old loves and younger wooing
Are sweet in the renewing
   Under the Holly-Bough.

Ye who have nourished sadness,
Estranged from hope and gladness
   In this fast-fading year;
Ye with o'erburdened mind,
Made aliens from your kind,
   Come gather here.
Let not the useless sorrow
Pursue you night and morrow,
   If e'er you hoped, hope now.
Take heart,—uncloud your faces,
And join in our embraces,
   Under the Holly-Bough.

EPIPHANY

Bishop Reginald Heber

Brightest and best of the sons of the morning!
   Dawn on our darkness, and lend us Thine aid,
Star of the East, the horizon adorning,
   Guide where our Infant Redeemer is laid!

Cold on His cradle the dewdrops are shining,
   Low lies His head with the beasts of the stall:
Angels adore Him in slumber reclining—
   Maker, and Monarch, and Saviour of all!

Say, shall we yield him, in costly devotion,
   Odors of Edom, and offerings divine—
Gems of the mountain, and pearls of the ocean,
   Myrrh from the forest, and gold from the mine?

Vainly we offer each ample oblation,
   Vainly with gifts would His favor secure,
Richer by far is the heart's adoration,
   Dearer to God are the prayers of the poor.

Brightest and best of the sons of the morning!
   Dawn on our darkness, and lend us Thine aid,
Star of the East, the horizon adorning,
   Guide where our Infant Redeemer is laid!

THE FOUNTAIN

James Russell Lowell

Into the sunshine,
   Full of the light,
Leaping and flashing
   From morn till night!

Into the moonlight,
   Whiter than snow,
Waving so flower-like
   When the winds blow!

Into the starlight,
  Rushing in spray,
Happy at midnight,
  Happy by day!

Ever in motion,
  Blithesome and cheery,
Still climbing heavenward,
  Never aweary;

Glad of all weathers,
  Still seeming best,
Upward or downward
  Motion thy rest;

Full of a nature
  Nothing can tame,
Changed every moment,
  Ever the same;

Ceaseless aspiring,
  Ceaseless content,
Darkness or sunshine
  Thy element;

Glorious fountain!
  Let my heart be
Fresh, changeful, constant,
  Upward like thee!

BEFORE SEDAN

Austin Dobson

Here in this leafy place
    Quiet he lies,
Cold, with his sightless face
    Turned to the skies;
'Tis but another dead;
All you can say is said.

Carry his body hence,—
    Kings must have slaves;
Kings climb to eminence
    Over men's graves;
So this man's eyes are dim;—
Throw the earth over him.

What was the white you touched
    There at his side?
Paper his hand had clutched
    Tight ere he died;—
Message or wish, may be;—
Smooth the folds out and see.

Hardly the worst of us
    Here could have smiled!—
Only the tremulous
    Words of a child;—
Prattle, that has for stops
Just a few ruddy drops.

Look. She is sad to miss,
    Morning and night,
His—her dead father's—kiss,
    Tries to be bright,
Good to mamma, and sweet;
That is all. "Marguerite."

Ah, if beside the dead
    Slumbered the pain!
Ah, if the hearts that bled
    Slept with the slain!
If the grief died;—but no;—
Death will not have it so.

BATTLE HYMN OF THE REPUBLIC

Julia Ward Howe

Mine eyes have seen the glory of the coming of the Lord:
He is trampling out the vintage where the grapes of wrath
    are stored;
He hath loosed the fateful lightning of his terrible swift
    sword;
        His truth is marching on.

I have seen him in the watch-fires of a hundred circling
    camps;
They have builded him an altar in the evening dews and
    damps;
I can read his righteous sentence by the dim and flaring
    lamps.
        His day is marching on.

I have read a fiery gospel, writ in burnished rows of steel:
"As ye deal with my contemners, so with you my grace
    shall deal;
Let the Hero, born of woman, crush the serpent with his
    heel,
        Since God is marching on."

He has sounded forth the trumpet that shall never call
    retreat;
He is sifting out the hearts of men before his judgment
    seat;
Oh, be swift, my soul, to answer him! be jubilant, my feet!
        Our God is marching on.

In the beauty of the lilies Christ was born, across the sea,
With a glory in his bosom that transfigures you and me;
As he died to make men holy, let us die to make men
    free,
        While God is marching on.

HENRY V AT THE SIEGE OF HARFLEUR

William Shakespeare

Once more unto the breach, dear friends, once more;
Or close the wall up with our English dead.
In peace there's nothing so becomes a man
As modest stillness and humility;
But when the blast of war blows in our ears,
Then imitate the action of the tiger:
Stiffen the sinews,—summon up the blood,

Disguise fair nature with hard favored rage;
Then lend the eye a terrible aspect;
Let it pry through the portage of the head,
Like the brass cannon.
Let the brow o'erwhelm it
As fearfully as doth a gallèd rock
O'erhang and jutty his confounded base,
Swilled with the wild and wasteful ocean.
Now set the teeth and stretch the nostril wide,
Hold hard the breath, and bend up every spirit
To its full height!—On, on, you noblest English,
Whose blood is red from fathers of war-proof!
Fathers, that like so many Alexanders,
Have in these parts from morn till even fought,
And sheathed their swords for lack of argument.
Dishonor not your mothers; now attest
That those whom you call fathers did beget you!
Be copy now to men of grosser blood,
And teach them how to war; and you, good yeoman,
Whose limbs are made in England, show us here
The mettle of your pasture: let us swear
That you are worth your breeding, which I doubt not:
For there is none of you so mean and base
That hath not noble lustre in your eyes:
I see you stand like greyhounds in the slips,
Straining upon the start. The game's a-foot;
Follow your spirit, and upon this charge,
Cry, "God for Harry, England, and St. George!"

THE LOST LEADER

Robert Browning

Just for a handful of silver he left us,
    Just for a ribbon to stick in his coat—
Found the one gift of which fortune bereft us,
    Lost all the others, she lets us devote;
They, with the gold to give, doled him out silver,
    So much was theirs who so little allowed:
How all our copper had gone for his service!
    Rags—were they purple, his heart had been proud!
We that had loved him so, followed him, honored him,
    Lived in his mild and magnificent eye,
Learned his great language, caught his clear accents,
    Made him our pattern to live and to die!
Shakespeare was of us, Milton was for us,
    Burns, Shelley, were with us, they watch from their
        graves!
He alone breaks from the van and the freemen,
    He alone sinks to the rear and the slaves!

We shall march prospering, not through his presence;
    Songs may inspirit us, not from his lyre;
Deeds will be done, while he boasts his quiescence,
    Still bidding crouch whom the rest bade aspire;
Blot out his name, then, record one lost soul more,
    One task more declined, one more footpath untrod,
One more devil's-triumph and sorrow for angels,
    One wrong more to man, one more insult to God!
Life's night begins: let him never come back to us!
    There would be doubt, hesitation, and pain,

Forced praise on our part—the glimmer of twilight,
    Never glad confident morning again!
Best fight on well, for we taught him—strike gallantly,
    Menace our heart ere we master his own;
Then let him receive the new knowledge and wait us,
    Pardoned in heaven, the first by the throne!

COURAGE!

Arthur Hugh Clough

Say not, the struggle naught availeth,
    The labor and the wounds are vain,
The enemy faints not, nor faileth,
    And as things have been they remain.

If hopes were dupes, fears may be liars;
    It may be, in yon smoke concealed,
Your comrades chase e'en now the fliers,
    And, but for you, possess the field.

For while the tired waves, vainly breaking,
    Seem here no painful inch to gain,
Far back, through creeks and inlets making,
    Comes silent, flooding in, the main.

And not by eastern windows only,
    When daylight comes, comes in the light;
In front, the sun climbs slow, how slowly!
    But westward, look, the land is bright!

ON HIS BLINDNESS

John Milton

When I consider how my light is spent,
Ere half my days, in this dark world and wide,
And that one talent which 'twere death to hide
Lodged with me useless, though my soul more bent
To serve therewith my maker, and present
My true account, lest he, returning, chide;
"Doth God exact day-labor, light denied?"
I fondly ask; but Patience to prevent
That murmur, soon replies, "God doth not need
Either man's work, or his own gifts; who best
Bear his mild yoke they serve him best; his state
Is kingly; thousands at his bidding speed,
And post o'er land and ocean without rest;
They also serve who only stand and wait."

TO NIGHT

Blanco White

Mysterious night! When our first parent knew
Thee from report divine, and heard thy name,
Did he not tremble for this lovely frame,
This glorious canopy of light and blue?
Yet, 'neath the curtain of translucent dew,

Bathed in the rays of that great setting flame,
Hesperus with the host of heaven came,
And lo! creation widened on man's view.
Who could have thought such darkness lay concealed.
Within thy beams, O sun? or who could find,
While fly and leaf and insect lay revealed,
That to such countless orbs thou mad'st us blind?
Why do we, then, shun death with anxious strife?
If light can so deceive, wherefore not life?

ODE TO A GRECIAN URN

John Keats

Thou still unravished bride of quietness!
    Thou foster-child of silence and slow time!
Sylvan historian, who canst thus express
    A flowery tale more sweetly than our rhyme;
What leaf-fringed legend haunts about thy shape
Of deities, or mortals, or of both,
    In Tempe or the vales of Arcady?
What men or gods are these? What maidens loth?
What mad pursuit? What struggles to escape?
    What pipes and timbrels? What wild ecstasy?

Heard melodies are sweet, but those unheard
    Are sweeter; therefore ye soft pipes, play on—
Not to the sensual ear, but more endeared,
    Pipe to the spirit ditties of no tone!
Fair youth beneath the trees, thou canst not leave
Thy song, nor even can those trees be bare;
    Bold lover, never, never canst thou kiss
Though winning near the goal, yet do not grieve—
    She cannot fade, though thou hast not thy bliss,
Forever wilt thou love and she be fair!

Ah, happy, happy boughs! that cannot shed
    Your leaves, nor ever bid the spring adieu;
And happy melodist, unwearied,
    Forever piping songs forever new;
More happy love! More happy, happy love!
    Forever warm and still to be enjoyed,
Forever panting and forever young;
All breathing human passion far above,
    That leaves a heart high sorrowful and cloyed,
A burning forehead and a parching tongue.

Who are these coming to the sacrifice?
    To what green altar, O mysterious priest,
Lead'st thou that heifer lowing at the skies,
    And all her silken flanks with garlands drest?
What little town by river or sea-shore,
    Or mountain-built with peaceful citadel,
Is emptied of her folk, this pious morn?
And, little town, thy streets forevermore
    Will silent be; and not a soul to tell
Why thou art desolate, will e'er return.

O Attic shape! Fair attitude! with brede
    Of marble men and maidens overwrought,
With forest branches and the trodden weed!
    Thou, silent form, dost tease us out of thought
As doth eternity! Cold pastoral!
When old age shall this generation waste,
    Thou shalt remain in midst of other woe
Than ours, a friend to man, to whom thou say'st,
    "Beauty is truth, truth, beauty,—that is all
        Ye know on earth, and all ye need to know!"

SONNET: ON FIRST LOOKING INTO CHAPMAN'S HOMER

John Keats

Much have I travelled in the realms of gold,
And many goodly states and kingdoms seen;
Round many western islands have I been,
Which bards in fealty to Apollo hold,
Oft of one wide expanse had I been told
That deep-browed Homer ruled as his demesne:
Yet did I never breathe its pure serene
Till I heard Chapman speak out loud and bold:
Then felt I like some watcher of the skies
When a new planet swims into his ken;
Or like stout Cortez, when with eagle eyes
He stared at the Pacific,—and all his men
Looked at each other with a wild surmise—
Silent, upon a peak in Darien.

HOW GOOD ARE THE POOR

Victor Hugo

(*Translation of H. W. Alexander. Abridged.*)

'Tis night—within the close-shut cabin door
   The room is wrapped in shade, save where there fall
Some twilight rays that creep along the floor,
   And show the fisher's nets upon the wall.

In the dim corner, from the oaken chest,
    A few white dishes glimmer; in the shade
Stands a tall bed with dusky curtains dressed,
    And a rough mattress at its side is laid.

Five children on the long, low mattress lie—
    A nest of little souls, it heaves with dreams.
In the high chimney the last embers die,
    And redden the dark room with crimson gleams.

The mother kneels and thinks, and pale with fear,
    She prays alone, hearing the billows shout;
While to wild winds, to rocks, to midnight drear,
    The ominous old ocean sobs without.

Poor wives of fishers! Ah! 'tis sad to say
    "Our sons, our husbands, all that we love best,
Our hearts, our souls, are on those waves away,
    Those ravening wolves that know not ruth, nor rest.

"Terrible fear! we seek the pebbly shore,
    Cry to the rising billows, 'Bring them home.'
Alas! what answer gives their troubled roar
    To the dark thoughts that haunt us as we roam?"

The dawn was whitening over the sea's verge
    As she sat pensive, touching broken chords
Of half remorseful thought, while the hoarse surge
    Howled a sad concert to her broken words.

"Ah! my poor husband! We had five before.
    Already so much care, so much to find,
For he must work for all. I give him more.
    What was that noise? His step? Ah no! the wind.

"That I should be afraid of him I love!
    I have done ill. If he should beat me now
I would not blame him. Does not the door move?
    Not yet, poor man!" She sits, with careful brow,

Wrapped in her inward grief; nor hears the roar
   Of wind and waves that dash against his prow
Or the black cormorant shrieking on the shore.

Sudden the door flies open wide, and lets
   Noisily in the dawn-light scarcely clear,
And the good fisher, dragging his damp nets,
   Stands on the threshold, with a joyful cheer.

" 'Tis thou!" she cries, and eager as a lover,
   Leaps up and holds her husband to her breast;
Her greeting kisses all his venture cover;
   " 'Tis I, good wife!" and his broad face expressed.

How gay his heart that Janet's love made light.
   "What weather was it?" "Hard." "Your fishing?"
      "Bad.
The sea was like a nest of thieves to-night,
   But I embrace thee and my heart is light.

"There was a devil in the wind that blew;
   I tore my net, caught nothing, broke my line.
And once I thought the bark was broken too;
   What did you all the night long, Janet mine?"

She, trembling in the darkness, answered, "I!
   Oh, naught—I sewed, I watched, I was afraid.
The waves were loud as thunder from the sky,
   But it is over." Shyly then she said:—

"Our neighbor died last night; it must have been
   When you were gone. She left two little ones,
So small, so frail—William and Madeleine;
   The one just lisps, the other scarcely runs."

The man looked grave, and in the corner cast
   His old fur bonnet, wet with rain and sea,
Muttered awhile and scratched his head—at last:
   "We have five children, this makes seven," said he.

"Already in bad weather we must sleep
    Sometimes without our supper. Now! Ah well—
'Tis not my fault. These accidents are deep;
    It was the good God's will. I cannot tell.

"Why did He take the mother from those scraps
    No bigger than my fist? 'Tis hard to read.
A learned man might understand perhaps—
    So little, they can neither work nor feed.

"Go fetch them, wife; they will be frightened sore,
    If with the dead alone they waken thus.
That was the mother knocking at our door,
    And we must take the children home to us.

"Brother and sister shall they be to ours,
    And they will learn to climb my knee at even.
When He shall see these strangers in our bowers,
    More fish, more food will give the God of Heaven.

"I will work harder; I will drink no wine—
    Go fetch them. Wherefore dost thou linger, dear?
Not thus are wont to move those feet of thine."
    She drew the curtain, saying, *"They are here!"*

FAREWELL ADVICE

Charles Kingsley

Farewell, dear child, I have no song to give thee.
    No lark could pipe to skies so dull and gray:
But ere we part one lesson I would leave thee.
    For every day.

Be good, sweet maid, and let who will be clever.
Do noble things, not dream them all day long;
And so make life, death, and that vast forever,
One grand, sweet song.

2

CHILDHOOD DAYS

It seems to me that there is usually a considerable basic difference between poetry written especially *for* children and poetry written *about* children and childhood for adults. Hence the two sections with which this anthology opens. The first contains poems taken exclusively from OPEN SESAME, with the former purpose in mind; the second contains poems culled here and there at random and selected in a slightly less arbitrary way, but with special consideration of the latter purpose. Admittedly the poems of Robert Louis Stevenson *could* have gone into the first section, but they did not happen to be in OPEN SESAME, and I was holding fast to that. The poems by A. A. Milne were not written until long after OPEN SESAME was compiled. Work by both authors obviously belongs somewhere in this book, and "Childhood Days" seems to me the best place for them.

PICTURE IN AN OLD FRAME

Eleanor Alletta Chaffee

When I was small,
When I was little,
I used to watch
My grandfather whittle.
Light in his hands
As a bird in flying
(Almost I could hear
The curlews crying),
The clipper took shape,
Its proud sails filling,
And over us all
The gold is spilling. . . .

When I was small,
When I was growing,
I learned that through
A wild gale blowing
The lightest craft
Wears in its being
The gift of courage,
The sense of seeing,
The strength that rides
The long ebb swelling,
With thoughts of home
Too deep for telling.

When I was small,
Two gnarled hands slowly
Shaped wood and word
Into something holy. . . .

HOW MANY MILES TO BABYLON?

Anonymous

How many miles is it to Babylon?
Threescore miles and ten.
Can I get there by candlelight?
Yes, and back again.
If your heels are nimble and light
You may get there by candlelight.

THE STEAM FAMILY

Georgia Wood Pangborn

Somebody lives in the Radiator;
I hear them moving about.
A man with a stick knocks hard and quick,
And children whistle and shout.
And a baby cries in the Radiator—
The baby of Mrs. Steam;
And then she sings such pretty things
That I go to sleep and dream—
Of the baby that lives in the Radiator,
The baby of Mrs. Steam.

HIS LITTLE SUB

Elizabeth Bennett

There was a little Boston child
Of ways controlled, of temper mild,
For all that psychic thought extends
He used for therapeutic ends.

He did not have the stomach-ache,
The whooping-cough he did not take;
"No functional disorders act,"
Said he, "on my subconscious tract."

Nor did this little fellow fret
If what he wished he did not get;
His mental poise he'd quickly find
By treating his subconscious mind.

And when his mother cried, "I am
Displeased to find you stealing jam,"
He answered from the pantry shelf,
"Mamma, 't was my subconscious self."

No matter what his mother said
(She was a woman Boston-bred),
Still, for his irritating prank
That child received a conscious spank.

BED IN SUMMER

Robert Louis Stevenson

In winter I get up at night
And dress by yellow candle-light.
In summer, quite the other way,
I have to go to bed by day

I have to go to bed and see
The birds still hopping on the tree,
Or hear the grown-up people's feet
Still going past me in the street.

And does it not seem hard to you,
When all the sky is clear and blue,
And I should like so much to play,
To have to go to bed by day?

MY SHADOW

Robert Louis Stevenson

I have a little shadow that goes in and out with me,
And what can be the use of him is more than I can see.
He is very, very like me from the heels up to the head;
And I see him jump before me, when I jump into my bed.

The funniest thing about him is the way he likes to grow—
Not at all like proper children, which is always very slow;
For he sometimes shoots up taller like an India-rubber ball,
And he sometimes gets so little that there's none of him at all.

He hasn't got a notion of how children ought to play,
And can only make a fool of me in every sort of way.
He stays so close beside me, he's a coward you can see;
I'd think shame to stick to nurse as that shadow sticks to me!

One morning, very early, before the sun was up,
I rose and found the shining dew on every buttercup;
But my lazy little shadow, like an arrant sleepy-head,
Had stayed at home behind me and was fast asleep in bed.

THE LAND OF COUNTERPANE

Robert Louis Stevenson

When I was sick and lay a-bed,
I had two pillows at my head,
And all my toys beside me lay
To keep me happy all the day.

And sometimes for an hour or so
I watched my leaden soldiers go,
With different uniforms and drills,
Among the bedclothes, through the hills;

And sometimes sent my ships in fleets
All up and down among the sheets;
Or brought my trees and houses out,
And planted cities all about.

I was the giant, great and still,
That sits upon the pillow-hill,
And sees before him, dale and plain,
The pleasant land of Counterpane.

BUCKINGHAM PALACE

A. A. Milne

They're changing guard at Buckingham Palace—
Christopher Robin went down with Alice.
Alice is marrying one of the guard.
"A soldier's life is terrible hard,"

Says Alice.

They're changing guard at Buckingham Palace—
Christopher Robin went down with Alice.
We saw a guard in a sentry-box.
"One of the sergeants looks after their socks,"

Says Alice.

They're changing guard at Buckingham Palace—
Christopher Robin went down with Alice.
We looked for the King, but he never came.
"Well, God take care of him, all the same,"

Says Alice.

They're changing guard at Buckingham Palace—
Christopher Robin went down with Alice.
They've great big parties inside the grounds.
"I wouldn't be King for a hundred pounds,"

Says Alice.

They're changing guard at Buckingham Palace—
Christopher Robin went down with Alice.
A face looked out, but it wasn't the King's.
"He's much too busy a-signing things,"
                                    Says Alice.

They're changing guard at Buckingham Palace—
Christopher Robin went down with Alice.
"Do you think the King knows all about *me?*"
"Sure to, dear, but it's time for tea,"
                                    Says Alice.

EARLY FRIENDS

Margery Mansfield

And you related that my hat was red,
    And how I looked, who was a tawny child.
"It seems a hundred years ago," you said.

But as for me, no years have single-filed
Between me and my friends.
Dear playmates, never think you are exiled
From your old pal. Your thoughts, made part of me,
Are in my present now as much as when
You and I and Robert were but ten
And had some high designs upon a tree.
I think that all the years allowed to Man
Will never disentangle you and me.

THE CHILDREN'S HOUR

Henry Wadsworth Longfellow

Between the dark and the daylight,
When the night is beginning to lower,
Comes a pause in the day's occupations,
That is known as the Children's Hour.

I hear in the chamber above me
The patter of little feet,
The sound of a door that is opened
And voices soft and sweet.

From my study I see in the lamplight,
Descending the broad hall stair,
Grave Alice, and laughing Allegra
And Edith with golden hair.

A whisper, and then a silence:
Yet I know by their merry eyes
They are plotting and planning together
To take me by surprise.

A sudden rush from the stairway,
A sudden raid from the hall!
By three doors left unguarded
They enter my castle wall!

They climb up into my turret
O'er the arms and back of my chair;
If I try to escape, they surround me;
They seem to be everywhere.

They almost devour me with kisses,
Their arms about me entwine
Till I think of the Bishop of Bingen
In his Mouse-Tower on the Rhine!

Do you think, O blue-eyed banditti,
Because you have scaled the wall,
Such an old mustache as I am
Is not a match for you all!

I have you fast in my fortress,
And will not let you depart,
But put you down into the dungeon
In the round-tower of my heart.

And there I will keep you forever,
Yes, forever and a day,
Till the walls shall crumble to ruin,
And moulder in dust away!

THE SUGAR-PLUM TREE

Eugene Field

Have you ever heard of the Sugar-Plum Tree?
   'Tis a marvel of great renown!
It blooms on the shore of the Lollypop Sea
   In the garden of Shut-Eye Town;
The fruit that it bears is so wondrously sweet
   (As those who have tasted it say)
That good little children have only to eat
   Of that fruit to be happy next day.

When you've got to the tree, you would have a hard time
    To capture that fruit which I sing;
The tree is so tall that no person could climb
    To the boughs where the sugar-plums swing!
But up in that tree sits a chocolate cat,
    And a gingerbread dog prowls below—
And this is the way you contrive to get at
    Those sugar-plums tempting you so:

You say but the word to that gingerbread dog
    And he barks with such terrible zest
That the chocolate cat is at once all agog,
    As her swelling proportions attest.
And this chocolate cat goes cavorting around
    From this leafy limb unto that,
And the sugar-plums tumble, of course, to the ground—
    Hurrah for that chocolate cat!

There are marshmallows, gumdrops, and peppermint canes
    With stripings of scarlet and gold,
And you carry away of the treasure that rains
    As much as your apron can hold!
So come, little child, cuddle closer to me
    In your dainty white nightcap and gown,
And I'll rock you away to that Sugar-Plum Tree
    In the garden of Shut-Eye Town.

VESPERS

A. A. Milne

Little Boy kneels at the foot of the bed,
Droops on the little hands little gold head.
Hush! Hush! Whisper who dares!
Christopher Robin is saying his prayers.

God Bless Mummy. I know that's right.
Wasn't it fun in the bath tonight?
The cold's so cold, and the hot's so hot.
Oh! *God Bless Daddy*—I quite forgot.

If I open my fingers a little bit more,
I can see Nanny's dressing-gown on the door.
It's a beautiful blue, but it hasn't a hood.
Oh! *God Bless Nanny and make her good.*

Mine has a hood, and I lie in bed,
And pull the hood right over my head,
And I shut my eyes, and I curl up small,
And nobody knows that I'm there at all.

Oh! *Thank you, God for a lovely day.*
And what was the other I had to say?
I said *"Bless Daddy,"* so what can it be?
Oh! Now I remember it. *God Bless Me.*

Little Boy kneels at the foot of the bed,
Droops on the little hands little gold head.
Hush! Hush! Whisper who dares!
Christopher Robin is saying his prayers.

AWAY IN A MANGER

Anonymous

Away in a manger, no crib for His bed,
The little Lord Jesus lay down His sweet head.
The stars in the bright sky looked down where He lay,
The little Lord Jesus asleep on the hay.

The cattle are lowing, the poor Baby wakes,
But little Lord Jesus, no crying He makes.
I love Thee, Lord Jesus, look down from the sky,
And stay by my cradle 'til morning is nigh.

Be near me, Lord Jesus, I ask Thee to stay,
Close by me forever and love me, I pray.
Bless all the dear children in Thy tender care,
And take us to heaven to live with Thee there.

NOW THE DAY IS OVER

Reverend Sabine Baring-Gould, 1865

Now the day is over,
Night is drawing nigh,
Shadows of the evening
Steal across the sky.
Now the darkness gathers,
Stars begin to peep;
Birds, and beasts, and flowers
Soon will be asleep.

Jesus, give the weary
Calm and sweet repose;
With Thy tenderest blessing
May mine eyelids close.
Grant to little children
Visions bright of Thee;
Guard the sailors, tossing
On the deep blue sea.

Comfort every sufferer
Watching late in pain;
Those who plan some evil

From their sin restrain.
Through the long night watches
May Thine angels spread
Their white wings above me,
Watching round my bed.

When the morning wakens,
Then may I arise
Pure, and fresh, and sinless
In Thy holy eyes.
Glory to the Father,
Glory to the Son,
And to Thee, blest Spirit,
Whilst all ages run.

THE CHILDREN

Harold Applebaum

The children of this time have more to learn
Than you or I. My books were short a war
And history was rapt with the return
Of lasting peace. No meddling with the core
Of atoms—physics stopped with Newton, Math
Came straight from Euclid and a man named Ruth
Made muscled miracles in sport. The wrath
That filled the Thirties and consumed the youth
Of half the world still found me unprepared,
My lessons incomplete. But now the young,
With history beneath their arms, aware
Of atoms and the Götterdämmerung,
Assail the future, question our concern—
They have outgrown our teaching—they will learn.

3

YOUTH

Companions, teachers and mothers all write expansively about youth and, of course, each group interprets it differently. Because I find these different interpretations valuable, as well as provocative, I have tried to give examples of each kind. "Walks in the Rain" and "Winter Walks" are the happy comments of a good companion; "What Is a Student?" is the puzzled question of a teacher; "Graduation" is a cry straight from a mother's heart.

Strangely enough, I have found only one such interpretation coming from a father. I would be interested in learning if there is any reasonable explanation for this.

BOY, WALKING AND WHISTLING

Anobel Armour

Having finished each long chore,
He whistled up a summer score,
Made up of sunlight pouring down
On his lean body, toe to crown,
Made up of how the warm dust feels,
Puffing under bare brown heels,
And of how water, green and cool,
Can turn a farm boy in a pool
Into a creature, brown and free,
Which is what any boy should be!

WHAT IS A STUDENT?

Anne Round

He's a first tuxedo
And a sudden tolerance of dances;
An interest in carburetors,
Perhaps a passion for tweeters
And superheterodyne speakers.

He makes a farce of food budgets;
But it does your heart good
To watch him fill up on;
Ice cream (pistachio), hot dogs, fried clams
And Grandmother's lemon meringue pie.

He's a forgotten lollipop
In a pants pocket;
A sudden awakening to the joys
Of button-down collars, beat-up bucks
And trousers with creases.

He'll turn your head with a sudden smile.
A remarkable way of saying
The right thing at the right time.
He'll comfort you with a pat on the shoulder,
Exasperate you with a scratch
On the new coffee table.

He's growing faster than he ought,
Earning odd job money assiduously;
He's old, he's very young,
And he's all yours for just a
Little while longer.

LOVE SONNET TO MY STUDENTS

Jacob C. Solovay

Although I issue to you stern commands,
And give you homework as habitual blights
That cause you fretful days and cheerless nights,
And press upon your brain like tightened bands;
Although my zeroes, copious as the sands
That swirl on beaches in the stormy light,
Create in you dark havoc out of fright,
And make you seek to fly to other lands;
Remember—O remember that my deeds
Belie the very action of my heart,
As wintry waves conceal the warmer sea.

In future years, among maturer creeds,
And urged by age to a more thoughtful part,
Forget my deeds—but O, forget not me!

TOMORROW YOU

John Holmes

The bell rings, the door shuts,
Weeklies are put away.
I stand by the desk, book open, and think,
"One more day.
They are all mine so far, the absent are only ill,
Or cutting the class; with me in college still."
It is time, and I talk, but whom am I talking to?
Unmarried widow, Dead man. Is it you, Or you?
Recite now, girl whose lover will be drowned.
Answer me, boy whose brother never will be found.
You, silent in the back row, waiting, speak
Before you put on uniform next month, next week.
The question is—the question is, who? Who?
Quick, which one among you am I talking to?
You ought to know. The answer is: it will be
Not the well known, and not those near to me
At first, and not the names I'd miss the most
At first, but the tall guy at the car-stop post
You miss after two weeks, then your roommate's friend,
Then yours, then gaps nothing at all can mend.
Then you. There's nothing at all that I can do.
But the one I'll call on first tomorrow is you.
And wonder which it is I really fear,
The "Here, sir," or the "Sorry, but he isn't here."

WALK IN THE RAIN

Frances Frost

This was a day of straightly falling rain.
Dripping we stood
smiling at one another's sky-wet face
in the deep hemlock wood,

when the young fox came from the thicket, his red fur rainy,
his gold eyes unafraid,
and looked at us and trotted off, intent
on his own dream. Waylaid

by dusk on the hill, we saw the low clouds, swirling
over the mountains, lift
and break to delicate flame, and in violet light
the budding antlers drift

beyond the orchard. And we walked slowly homeward,
having no need to say
except with our eyes that whatever happens tomorrow,
this was a good day.

WINTER WALK

Katherine van der Veer

There was a night
We walked in dark,
Stars rising over us
Spark after spark.

Under our feet
In the bitter weather
Snow had the creak
Of saddle leather.

The road ahead
Was white as rice,
The edge of the river
Fringed with ice.

We caught our breath
As the moon came up,
The valley gleamed
Like a crystal cup.

Radiance caught us
Where we stood
The spell of the night
Was in our blood.

GRADUATION

Dow Richardson

He would have been graduated today;
Here under this blue June sky
We would have sat, his best Aunt Kay
Sitting with us. He would have waved "Hi"
After it was over, and come fast
To our chairs in his long stride,
Pulling along some classmate past
Laughing groups. His mother would have cried.
This was his father's school, and so the man
Who thought him all in all would say,
"That was a fine address. And, Dan . . .
Your cap and gown . . . Good fit . . . nice getup, hey?
Barbara, his sister, would have moved
About him, camera-wise, for what
We all knew certainly would have proved
The best outdoor pose she ever shot.
That is the way it would have been.
For years I've looked ahead to it,
Felt the rare joy in the scene when,
Anticipative, I'd lived it every whit.
Odd that today he stands in some ravine
On a crude, wet path, stiffly in line
With classmates, if you will, young eyes keen
Above a young beard, the design
Of his country's cross for valor new
Upon his tunic. A general stepping back some paces
To salute. This is a graduation, too,
And in some South Sea jungle, of all places!
I say, I would have liked the cap and gown
On him, the sheepskin, the setting where there are
Tall Gothic spires of learning near the town.
But I am proud this other way. I'm prouder . . . far.

BOOTLESS SPECULATIONS

Phyllis McGinley

One fact eccentric I often muse on:
Girls of sixteen won't keep their shoes on.

Girls, at sixteen, for all our strictures,
Are proper as Puritans,
Pretty as pictures.
With waists cinched tightly,
Wearing ponytails,
They move more lightly
Than a ship with sails,
Than roses shaking
The summer dews off—
But why must they always be taking their shoes off?

Girls of sixteen
Have rows and rows
Of fanciful, lean
Capezios.
Helter-skelter,
To the point of scandal,
Their closets shelter
Slipper and sandal,
Glass shoes, gilt shoes,
Shoes with baubles on,
Three-inch-stilt shoes
That everyone wobbles on,
Shoes gone risible,
Shoes for sport,
Shoes without visible
Means of support.

Each maidenly foot is a clad-with-care foot,
But how do they go?
Why, chiefly barefoot.

They never enter
Their entrance halls
But front and center
The footwear falls:
Pumps under sofas;
Brogues on the stairs;
Loathsome loafers
Beneath wing chairs;
Shoes on the landing,
Lost in flight;
On porches standing
Overnight
While, legs-a-taper,
Combing their curls,
Blithely caper
The discalced girls,
Shoeless they chatter their gossip windy
Or barefoot at parties
Dance the Lindy.

For girls, at sixteen, have depths unsounded.
Of sugar and spice
Are they compounded;
Sweetly their powers
Shame doubting Thomases;
They keep late hours
But they keep their promises;
They keep cool heads
For the course they cruise on.
But why in the world can't they keep their shoes on?

GIRL'S-EYE VIEW OF RELATIVES

Phyllis McGinley

First Lesson

The thing to remember about fathers is, they're men.
A girl has to keep it in mind.
They are dragon-seekers, bent on improbable rescues.
Scratch any father, you find
Someone chock-full of qualms and romantic terrors,
Believing change is a threat—
Like your first shoes with heels on, like your first bicycle
It took months to get.

Walk in strange woods, they warn you about the snakes there.
Climb, and they fear you'll fall.
Books, angular boys, or swimming in deep water—
Fathers mistrust them all.
Men are the worriers. It is difficult for them
To learn what they must learn:
How you have a journey to take and very likely,
For a while, will not return.

Turn of the Screw

Girl cousins condescend. They wear
Earrings, and dress like fashion's sample,
Have speaking eyes and curly hair.
And parents point to their example.
But the boy cousins one's allotted
Are years too young for one. Or spotted.

Triolet against Sisters

Sisters are always drying their hair.
   Locked into rooms, alone,
They pose at the mirror, shoulders bare,
Trying this way and that their hair,
Or fly importunate down the stair
   To answer a telephone.
Sisters are always drying their hair,
   Locked into rooms, alone.

In Praise of Aunts

Of all that tribe the young must do
Familial obedience to,
Whom we salute on anniversaries,
Whose names we learn while new in nurseries
Or borrow at baptismal fonts,
The soothingest are aunts.

Aunts are discreet, a little shy
By instinct. They forbear to pry
Into recesses of the spirit
Where apprehensions lie.
Yet, given a tale to hear, they *hear* it.

Aunts spinster pamper us with praise,
And seats for worldly matinees
With coffee after. Married aunts,
Attentive to material wants,
Run rather to the shared comestible,
Taboo or indigestible;
Are lenient but cool;
And let us, if we must, play fool.

Aunts carry no duty in their faces.
Their letters, mailed from far-off places,
Are merely letters meant to read
(Answerable at a moderate speed),

Not cries of need
Or vessels heavy with their hopes.
Aunts also send,
Tucked into casual envelopes,
Money entirely ours to spend.

At night they do not lie awake
Shuddering for our sorrow's sake.
Beneath our flesh we seldom wear
Their skeletons, nor need we stare
Into a looking glass and see
Their images begin to be.
Aunts care, but only mildly care,
About our winter moods,
Postures, or social attitudes,
And whether we've made a friend or dropped one.
All should have aunts, or else adopt one.

The Adversary

A mother's hardest to forgive.
Life is the fruit she longs to hand you
Ripe on a plate. And while you live,
Relentlessly she understands you.

XVIII

A. E. Housman

Oh, when I was in love with you,
Then I was clean and brave,
And miles around the wonder grew
How well did I behave.

And now the fancy passes by,
And nothing will remain,
And miles around they'll say that I
Am quite myself again.

WHEN I WAS ONE-AND-TWENTY

A. E. Housman

When I was one-and-twenty
I heard a wise man say,
"Give crowns and pounds and guineas
But not your heart away;
"Give pearls away and rubies
But keep your fancy free."
But I was one-and-twenty,
No use to talk to me.

When I was one-and-twenty
I heard him say again,
"The heart out of the bosom
Was never given in vain;
"'Tis paid with sighs a-plenty
And sold for endless rue."
And I am two-and-twenty,
And oh, 'tis true, 'tis true!

THE YOUNG MAN

A. E. Housman

Oh see how thick the goldcup flowers
Are lying in field and lane,
With dandelions to tell the hours
That never are told again.
Oh may I squire you round the meads
And pick you posies gay?
—'Twill do no harm to take my arm.
"You may, young man, you may."

Ah, spring was sent for lass and lad,
'Tis now the blood runs gold,
And man and maid had best be glad
Before the world is old.
What flowers today may flower tomorrow,
But never as good as new.
—Suppose I wound my arm right round—
" 'Tis true, young man, 'tis true."

Some lads there are, 'tis shame to say,
That only court to thieve,
And once they bear the bloom away
'Tis little enough they leave.
Then keep your heart for men like me
And safe from trustless chaps.
My love is true and all for you.
"Perhaps, young man, perhaps."

Oh, look in my eyes, then, can you doubt?
—Why, 'tis a mile from town.
How green the grass is all about!
We might as well sit down.
—Ah, life, what is it but a flower?
Why must true lovers sigh?
Be kind, have pity, my own, my pretty,—
"Good-bye, young man, good-bye!"

4

YOUNG LOVE

In reviewing the poems I have chosen for "Young Love", I find that nearly one-half of them belong to the category that we call classics —the largest proportion on any given subject.

It did not surprise me that this section proved to contain more than any other, with one exception. (I'll let the reader guess what the one exception is!) But I confess that the ratio of old to new was much greater than I expected, even allowing for the fact that we were obliged to omit the work of one author whom we wanted very much to include because the cost of doing so was prohibitive.

Is the art of expressing the tender passion in moving terms in danger of becoming lost, like that of illuminating missals? Rupert Brooke and Allen Seeger are among the few modern poets who have stirred me in the same way that Lovelace and Sidney have done (of course it is not fair to count Shakespeare in making a comparison!), and I assume that these two will soon be counted among the classics. However, even if the number of modern poets who write feelingly and beautifully is limited, the output of those who do achieve this is of a very high order. At least I feel that it is.

CHERRY-RIPE

Thomas Campion

There is a garden in her face,
  Where roses and white lilies grow;
A heavenly paradise is that place,
  Wherein all pleasant fruits do grow;
There cherries grow that none may buy
Till 'Cherry-ripe' themselves do cry.

Those cherries fairly do enclose
  Of orient pearl a double row,
Which, when her lovely laughter shows,
  They look like rosebuds fill'd with snow
Yet them no peer nor prince may buy
Till 'Cherry-ripe' themselves do cry.

Her eyes like angels watch them still,
  Her brows like bended bows do stand,
Threat'ning with piercing frowns to kill
  All that approach with eye or hand
These sacred cherries to come nigh,
Till 'Cherry-ripe' themselves do cry.

TO CELIA

Ben Jonson

Drink to me only with thine eyes,
  And I will pledge with mine,
Or leave a kiss but in the cup
  And I'll not look for wine.
The thirst that from the soul doth rise
  Doth ask a drink divine;
But might I of Jove's nectar sup,
  I would not change for thine.

I sent thee late a rosy wreath,
  Not so much honouring thee
As giving it a hope that there
  It could not wither'd be;
But thou thereon didst only breathe
  And sent'st it back to me;
Since when it grows, and smells, I swear,
  Not of itself, but thee!

TO LUCASTA, ON GOING TO THE WARS

Richard Lovelace

Tell me not, sweet, I am unkind,—
    That from the nunnery
Of thy chaste breast and quiet mind
    To war and arms I fly.

True, a new mistress now I chase,
    The first foe in the field;
And with a stronger faith embrace
    A sword, a horse, a shield.

Yet this inconstancy is such
    As you, too, shalt adore;
I could not love thee, dear, so much,
    Loved I not honour more.

TO ALTHEA, FROM PRISON

Richard Lovelace

When Love with unconfinèd wings
    Hovers within my gates,
And my divine Althea brings
    To whisper at my grates;

When I lie tangled in her hair,
　　And fetter'd to her eye,
The birds that wanton in the air
　　Know no such liberty.

When flowing cups run swiftly round,
　　With no allaying Thames,
Our careless heads with roses bound,
　　Our hearts with loyal flames;
When thirsty grief in wine we steep,
　　When healths and draughts are free,—
Fishes that tipple in the deep
　　Know no such liberty.

When linnet-like confinèd, I
　　With shriller throat shall sing
The sweetness, mercy, majesty,
　　And glories of my king:
When I shall voice aloud how good
　　He is, how great should be,—
Enlargèd winds that curl the flood
　　Know no such liberty.

Stone walls do not a prison make,
　　Nor iron bars a cage;
Minds innocent and quiet take
　　That for a hermitage:
If I have freedom in my love,
　　And in my soul am free,—
Angels alone that soar above
　　Enjoy such liberty.

SONNET CXVI

William Shakespeare

Let me not to the marriage of true minds
Admit impediments. Love is not love
Which alters when it alteration finds,
Or bends with the remover to remove:
    O, no! it is an ever-fixed mark,
    That looks on tempests and is never shaken;
    It is the star to every wand'ring bark,
    Whose worth's unknown, although his height be taken.
Love's not Time's fool, though rosy lips and cheeks
Within his bending sickle's compass come;
Love alters not with his brief hours and weeks,
But bears it out even to the edge of doom.
    If this be error and upon me proved,
    I never writ, nor no man ever loved.

SONNET XVIII

William Shakespeare

Shall I compare thee to a summer's day?
Thou art more lovely and more temperate:
Rough winds do shake the darling buds of May,
And summer's lease hath all too short a date:
Sometime too hot the eye of heaven shines,
And often is his gold complexion dimm'd;
And every fair from fair sometimes declines,
By chance or nature's changing course untrimm'd;

But thy eternal summer shall not fade,
Nor lose possession of that fair thou owest;
Nor shall Death brag thou wander'st in his shade,
When in eternal lines to time thou grow'st:
     So long as men can breathe, or eyes can see,
     So long lives this, and this gives life to thee.

SWEET AND TWENTY

William Shakespeare

O mistress mine, where are you roaming?
O, stay and hear; your true love's coming,
   That can sing both high and low:
Trip no further, pretty sweeting;
Journeys end in lovers meeting,
   Every wise man's son doth know.

What is love? 'tis not hereafter;
Present mirth hath present laughter;
   What's to come is still unsure:
In delay there lies no plenty;
Then come kiss me, sweet and twenty,
   Youth's a stuff will not endure.

SYLVIA

William Shakespeare

Who is Sylvia, what is she,
    That all our swains commend her?
Holy, fair, and wise is she;
    The heaven such grace did lend her,
That she might admirèd be.

Is she kind as she is fair?
    For beauty lives with kindness,
Love doth to her eyes repair,
    To help him of his blindness,
And, being help'd inhabits there.

Then to Sylvia let us sing,
    That Sylvia is excelling;
She excels each mortal thing
    Upon the dull earth dwelling:
To her let us garlands bring.

MY TRUE LOVE

Sir Philip Sidney

My true love hath my heart, and I have his,
By just exchange one for another given:
I hold his dear, and mine he cannot miss;
There never was a better bargain driven:
My true love hath my heart, and I have his.

His heart in me keeps him and me in one,
My heart in him his thoughts and senses guides:
He loves my heart, for once it was his own,
I cherish his because in me it bides:
My true love hath my heart, and I have his.

THE PASSIONATE SHEPHERD TO HIS LOVE

Christopher Marlowe

Come live with me and be my Love,
And we will all the pleasure prove
That hills and valleys, dale and field,
And all the craggy mountains yield.

There will we sit upon the rocks
And see the shepherds feed their flocks,
By shallow rivers, to whose falls
Melodious birds sing madrigals.

There will I make thee beds of roses
And a thousand fragrant posies,
A cap of flowers, and a kirtle
Embroider'd all with leaves of myrtle.

A gown made of the finest wool,
Which from our pretty lambs we pull,
Fair lined slippers for the cold,
With buckles of the purest gold.

A belt of straw and ivy buds
With coral clasps and amber studs:
And if these pleasures may thee move,
Come live with me and be my Love.

Thy silver dishes for thy meat
As precious as the gods do eat,
Shall on an ivory table be
Prepared each day for thee and me.

The shepherd swains shall dance and sing
For thy delight each May morning:
If these delights thy mind may move,
Then live with me and be my Love.

SHE WALKS IN BEAUTY

Lord Byron

She walks in beauty, like the night
 Of cloudless climes, and starry skies:
And all that's best of dark and bright
 Meet in her aspect and her eyes:
Thus mellowed to that tender light
 Which Heaven to gaudy day denies.

One shade the more, one ray the less,
 Had held impaired the nameless grace,
Which waves in every raven tress,
 Or softly lightens o'er her face;
Where thoughts serenely sweet express,
 How pure, how dear their dwelling-place.

And on that cheek, and o'er that brow,
 So soft, so calm, yet eloquent,
The smiles that win, the tints that glow,
 But tell of days in goodness spent.
A mind at peace with all below,
 A heart whose love is innocent!

SONNET XLIII

Elizabeth Barrett Browning

How do I love thee? Let me count the ways.
I love thee to the depth and breadth and height
My soul can reach, when feeling out of sight
For the ends of Being and ideal Grace.
I love thee to the level of every day's
Most quiet need, by sun and candle-light.
I love thee freely, as men strive for Right;
I love thee purely, as they turn from Praise.
I love thee with the passion put to use
In my old griefs, and with my childhood's faith.
I love thee with a love I seemed to lose
With my lost saints, I love thee with the breath,
Smiles, tears, of all my life!—and, if God choose,
I shall but love thee better after death.

SONNET XIV

Elizabeth Barrett Browning

If thou must love me, let it be for naught
Except for love's sake only. Do not say
"I love her for her smile—her look—her way
Of speaking gently,—for a trick of thought
That falls in well with mine, and certes brought

A sense of pleasant ease on such a day"—
For these things in themselves, Belovèd, may
Be changed, or change for thee, and love, so wrought,
May be unwrought so. Neither love me for
Thine own dear pity's wiping my cheeks dry,
A creature might forget to weep, who bore
Thy comfort long, and lose thy love thereby!
But love me for love's sake, that evermore
Thou may'st love on, through love's eternity.

SONNET XXXVIII

Elizabeth Barrett Browning

(*From Sonnets from the Portuguese*)

First time he kissed me, he but
    only kissed
The fingers of this hand wherewith
    I write;
And ever since, it grew more clean
    and white.
Slow to world-greetings, quick
    with its "Oh, list,"
When the angels speak. A ring
    of amethyst
I could not wear here, plainer to
    my sight,
Than that first kiss. The second
    passed in height
The first, and sought the forehead,
    and half missed,
Half falling on the hair. O beyond
    meed!
That was the chrism of love, which
    love's own crown,

With sanctifying sweetness, did
    precede.
The third upon my lips was folded
    down
In perfect, purple state; since
    when, indeed,
I have been proud and said, "My
    love, my own."

THE CALL

Rupert Brooke

Out of the nothingness of sleep,
The slow dreams of Eternity,
There was a thunder on the deep:
I came, because you called to me.

I broke the Night's primeval bars,
I dared the old abysmal curse,
And flashed through ranks of frightened stars
Suddenly on the universe!

The eternal silences were broken;
Hell became Heaven as I passed—
What shall I give you as a token,
A sign that we have met, at last?

I'll break and forge the stars anew,
Shatter the heavens with a song;
Immortal in my love for you,
Because I love you, very strong.

Your mouth shall mock the old and wise,
Your laugh shall fill the world with flame,
I'll write upon the shrinking skies
The scarlet splendour of your name.

Till Heaven cracks, and Hell thereunder
Dies in her ultimate mad fire,
And darkness falls, with scornful thunder,
On dreams of men and men's desire.

Then only in the empty spaces,
Death, walking very silently,
Shall fear the glory of our faces
Through all the dark infinity.

So, clothed about with perfect love,
The eternal end shall find us one,
Alone above the Night, above
The dust of the dead gods, alone.

I LOVED . . .

Alan Seeger

I loved illustrious cities and the crowds
That eddy through their incandescent nights.
I loved remote horizons with far clouds
Girded, and fringed about with snowy heights.
I loved fair women, their sweet, conscious ways
Of wearing among hands that covet and plead
The rose ablossom at the rainbow's base
That bounds the world's desire and all its need.
Nature I worshipped, whose fecundity

Embraces every vision the most fair,
Of perfect benediction. From a boy
I gloated on existence. Earth to me
Seemed all-sufficient and my sojourn there
One trembling opportunity for joy.

SONNET III

Alan Seeger

Why should you be astonished that my heart,
Plunged for so long in darkness and in dearth,
Should be revived by you, and stir and start
As by warm April now, reviving Earth?
I am the field of undulating grass
And you the gentle perfumed breath of Spring,
And all my lyric being, when you pass,
Is bowed and filled with sudden murmuring.
I asked you nothing and expected less,
But, with that deep, impassioned tenderness
Of one approaching what he most adores,
I only wished to lose a little space
All thought of my own life, and in its place
To live and dream and have my joy in yours.

HEART RUINS

(*After François Coppée*)

Roy Temple House

My heart was like a Roman palace, grand
With marble walls, with granite choice and rare—
I felt a mob of Vandal passions tear
A rude wide entrance, axe and torch in hand.

I wept, and saw a silent ruin stand
To shelter owls and vipers; here and there
A wan-faced blossom sipped the sluggish air;
But brambles hid the ways my pride had planned.

Thus I sat hardened in a hard-eyed dream;
Through sunless noons, through nights that knew no gleam
But God's dread lightnings, and no sound but groans—

Then you came, with the morning in your face,
And lest our love might lack a lodging-place
I built a cottage of the broken stones.

HOPE

Blanche S. Wagstaff

Love took the light
            And went away.
I walk in darkness
            Day by day . . .

And yet I know
            Though it be far
My path winds somewhere
            To a star . . .

JOHN BROWN'S BODY

Stephen Vincent Benét

(Excerpt)

Love came by from the riversmoke,
      When the leaves were fresh on the tree,
But I cut my heart on the blackjack oak
      Before they fell on me.

The leaves are green in the early Spring,
      They are brown as linsey now,
I did not ask for a wedding-ring
      From the wind in the bending bough.

Fall lightly, lightly, leaves of the wild,
    Fall lightly on my care,
I am not the first to go with child
    Because of the blowing air.

I am not the first nor yet the last
    To watch a goosefeather sky,
And wonder what will come of the blast
    And the name to call it by.

Snow down, snow down, you whitefeather bird,
    Snow down, you winter storm,
Where the good girls sleep with a gospel word
    To keep their honor warm.

The good girls sleep in their modesty,
    The bad girls sleep in their shame,
But I must sleep in the hollow tree
    Till my child can have a name.

I will not ask for the wheel and thread
    To spin the labor plain,
Or the scissors hidden under the bed
    To cut the bearing-pain.

I will not ask for the prayer in church
    Or the preacher saying the prayer,
But I will ask the shivering birch
    To hold its arms in the air.

Cold and cold and cold again,
    Cold in the blackjack limb
The winds of the sky for his sponsor-men
    And a bird to christen him.

Now listen to me, you Tennessee corn,
    And listen to my word,
This is the first child ever born
    That was christened by a bird.

He's going to act like a hound let loose
   When he comes from the blackjack tree,
And he's going to walk in proud shoes
   All over Tennessee.

I'll feed him milk out of my own breast
   And call him Whistling Jack.
And his dad'll bring him a partridge nest,
   As soon as his dad comes back.

THE ROAD TO TARTARY

Bernard Freeman Trotter

O Arab! much I fear thou at Mecca's shrine wilt never be,
For the road that thou art going is the road to Tartary.—Sadi.

I left the dusty traveled road the proper people tread—
Like solemn sheep they troop along, Tradition at their head;
I went by meadow, stream, and wood; I wandered at my will;
And in my wayward ears a cry of warning echoed still:
"Beware! beware!"—an old refrain they shouted after me—
"The road that thou art going is the road to Tartary."

I clambered over dawn-lit hills—the dew was on my feet;
I crossed the sullen pass at night in wind and rain and sleet;
I followed trains of errant thought through heaven and earth and hell,
And thence I seemed to hear again that unctuous farewell,
For there I dreamed the little fiends were pointing all at me:
"The road that thou art going is the road to Tartary."

From all the pious wrangling sects I set my spirit free:
I own no creed but God and Love and Immortality.
Their dogmas and their disciplines are dust and smoke and cloud;
They cannot see my sunlit way; and still they cry aloud,
From church, conventicle, and street, that warning old to me:
"The road that thou art going is the road to Tartary."

I found a woman God had made, the blind world tossed aside—
It had not dreamed the greatness hid in poverty and pride.
I left the world to walk with her and talk with her and learn
The secret things of happiness—and will I now return
To that blind, prudish world that shrugs and lifts its brows at me:
"The road that thou art going is the road to Tartary."

Nay; we will go together, Love—we two to greet the sun.
There are more roads than one to heaven, perhaps more heavens
    than one.
Here on the lonely heights we see things hid from those who tread
Like sheep the dusty trodden way, Tradition at their head.
We sense the common goal of all—in Mecca we shall be,
Though the road that we are going seem the road to Tartary.

CHOICE

Angela Morgan

I'd rather have the thought of you
To hold against my heart,
My spirit to be taught of you
With west winds blowing,
Than all the warm caresses
Of another love's bestowing,
Or the glories of the world
In which you had no part.

I'd rather have the theme of you
To thread my nights and days,
I'd rather have the dream of you
With faint stars glowing,
I'd rather have the want of you,
The rich, elusive taunt of you
Forever and forever and forever unconfessed
Than claim the alien comfort
Of any other's breast.

O lover! O my lover,
That this should come to me!
I'd rather have the hope for you,
Ah, Love, I'd rather grope for you
Within the great abyss
Than claim another's kiss—
Alone I'd rather go my way
Throughout eternity.

REFUSAL, WITH WISDOM

Anobel Armour

Once when tall mountain pines were winter-white
And the hill-path sloped away in crystal,
Sprinkled with earth's own stars, fashioned of snow,
He came to her. His breath curled lazily
And only his smile flamed, warming the day.
The strangeness of his words, quickly spoken
To a hill-girl's ears, made her heart know fear.

There was another land than this he told her;
A land where prairie grasses stretched to distance.
There were no trees, dripping with snow, to hide
The sky or shadow earth. There was just space.
He could not see that hills were part of her,
Nor that tall pines were rooted in her soul.

She would have traded hills for prairie land,
But not to one who could not understand.

A SONG OF MARCO POLO

Theodosia Garrison

Madonna, I have gone the world around,
Fought for blue jewels, marked the azure dyes
Of Tyria. Great wonders I have found—
I have seen nothing lovely as your eyes.
Madonna, I have sailed a hundred seas,
Coasted the flaming gardens of the South,
Plucked roses born of fire. Yet what were these?—
I have seen nothing lovely as your mouth.
Madonna, I have seen a land struck white,
Frozen and ice-locked from a world apart,
Have felt the white death at my throat all night—
I have known nothing cold as is your heart.
Madonna, I have ceased from wandering.

THE LOVER'S PLEA

J. F. Hendry

If you cannot think of me
As I of you, please tell
Me, darling, now, for Hell,
And a welcome there, is much to be
Preferred to reaching Paradise, excited,
Only to find that one was not invited.

DISCOVERY

Carolyn Wilson Link

So this is heartbreak! Well,
It's not as I expected;
No sudden burnished hell,
No heavens bisected;

No devastating rush,
No flood of molten metals;
But the relentless hush
Of falling petals

Deflowers the fairy tree
Of hope; with virent glitter,
The fruits of certainty
Form, small and bitter.

This is too slight a reason
To wither and grow tragic,
What all must face in season:
Life without magic.

AFTER A HUNDRED STORMS

Helene Mullins

After a hundred storms, one storm will rend
The sturdiest tree; after a hundred bleedings,
One cut will make the richest heart run dry.
This is as logical as that the end
Should follow the beginning, and no readings
Of stars are necessary to supply
The ultimate fate of what is daily struck.

I told you this a long, long time ago,
When in a world of danger we were young.
Now let us not attribute to ill luck
Our feeble thinking nor our walking slow,
Nor the dusty ruins we find ourselves among.

FAILURE

Rupert Brooke

Because God put His adamantine fate
Between my sullen heart and its desire,
I swore that I would burst the Iron Gate,
Rise up, and curse Him on His throne of fire.
Earth shuddered at my crown of blasphemy,
But Love was as a flame about my feet;
Proud up the Golden Stair I strode; and beat
Thrice on the Gate, and entered with a cry—

All the great courts were quiet in the sun,
And full of vacant echoes: moss had grown
Over the glassy pavement, and begun
To creep within the dusty council-halls.
An idle wind blew round an empty throne
And stirred the heavy curtain on the walls.

THE LAST SONNET

John Keats

Bright star, would I were steadfast as thou art!
Not in lone splendour hung aloft the night,
And watching, with eternal lids apart,
Like Nature's patient sleepless Eremite,
The moving waters at their priestlike task
Of pure ablution round earth's human shores
Or gazing on the new soft-fallen mask

Of snow upon the mountains and the moors:
No—yet still steadfast, still unchangeable,
Pillow'd upon my fair love's ripening breast,
To feel for ever its soft fall and swell,
Awake for ever in a sweet unrest,
Still, still to hear her tender-taken breath,
And so live ever—or else swoon to death.

FUTILITY

Sister M. Madeleva

I have to dress you in your shroud
　(A crude device, by no means new)
And look on you who are so proud
To worms consigned, to ashes bowed,
To keep my heart from loving you.

I have to call your faults by roll
　(Who once had sought to find them few)
To scrutinize your flaws of soul,
Then memorize and cite the whole
To keep myself from wanting you.

And when I painfully have taught
My mind to scorn you and forget,
I look upon the thing I've wrought
So futilely. It comes to naught.
I love you and I want you yet.

5

FRIENDSHIP AND LOVE, OLDER GROWN

The number of poems on young love which I found I had saved through the years was so great that I had to reduce it over and over again, in order to give it a suitable amount of space in an anthology of general character; and, if in the last analysis I had felt I must sacrifice a few of the highly romantic poems of the sixteenth and seventeenth century, and a few of the more realistic poems belonging to our own times, I should have borne this with resignation. On the other hand, I should have fought until the presses were locked, before eliminating any in the section "Friendship and Love, Older Grown".

Every one of these has some special significance for me, though by no means always the same kind of significance. For contrast, I have included Kipling's cynical *Envoi* ("He Travels Fastest Who Travels Alone"), but for the most part my selections represent "life's own patient journey to a star called understanding." Like my friend, Milton Bracker, whose poem on that subject is among those I have selected, I have found that contentment comes not only with the star but with the journey to find it.

One of the poems in this section recalls an experience which was especially moving to me; so among many which I might have chosen as an example of what happens on such a journey, I have selected this one:

During my husband's campaign for a third term in the United States Senate, there were several days when it looked as if he might be defeated. Had this happened, it would have been the first time, though he had been holding some kind of public office ever since he was twenty-three, and he was then nearly seventy. A broken record would have been a great blow to his pride. Moreover, the circumstances which threatened his success were of peculiarly painful character, in a personal sense. I tried very hard to find ways of encouraging and comforting him, but I felt that nothing I said or did was of any use.

It was just at that time that "Salvage", by Elias Lieberman, was published in the *New York Times* and—scanning the editorial page with even greater attention than usual, for personal reasons—I read it. The impression it made on me was so profound that, not without hesitation, I cut it out and put it on my husband's desk. He did not ordinarily care much for poetry, not nearly so much as I did, and I had to guard against boring him with my enthusiasm. But later that same day, he thanked me for calling the clipping to his attention. The poem was good, he said. Nothing more.

When I went to look for the clipping, intending to put it in my scrapbook, it had disappeared. I did not like to question him about it. He might have thrown it in the wastepaper basket, but did not want to hurt my feelings by saying so; or he might have mislaid it among the many other papers on his laden desk, and this was no time to bother him by asking him to look for it. And very soon I forgot all about it. "The rainbow, caught from days gone by" did indeed proclaim a clearing sky, and we were both triumphantly occupied by other matters.

Six years later he died. As I went through those small personal belongings which always present such a tragic problem after a death in the family,[1] I found the clipping in the wallet he always used. He had kept it where he could refer to it constantly, ever since I had given it to him. It had meant as much to him as it had to me.

[1] In this connection, it may be of interest to the reader to turn to "What Do You Do With A Woman's Things?" on page 175.

THANK YOU NOTE

Anonymous

It was one of those days cast in gray,
Sky and heart and the feel of the day,
And nothing minted of earth or strange
And precious fabric could make it change
Until you sent me a loaf of bread
You made yourself. I saw your head
Over a blue bowl, over a book
Reading the recipe, love in your look,
Strength in your fingers, and your heart
Yielding the secret, golden part
That makes this more than fine spun wheat,
That makes the heart and the gray day sweet,
With the curious leaven one can blend
In a golden loaf of bread for a friend.

ALL THAT HE IS

Ethel Barnett de Vito

A man can never wholly see
The separate things that he may be,
Nor guess the growing scope and reach
Of all the things he is to each:

Brother to one; another's son;
Some one's assurance of work well done;
Hero to one; another's friend;
Refuge where some one's grief may end;
Hearer to one that would be heard;
Speaker when some one needs a word.

A man can never wholly plumb
The things he is to all or some,
Nor ever guess the moon and sun
Of all the things he is to one.

INDIAN SUMMER

Dorothy Parker

In youth, it was a way I had
    To do my best to please,
And change, with every passing lad,
    To suit his theories.

But now I know the things I know,
    And do the things I do;
And if you do not like me so,
    To hell, my love, with you!

WORDS

Dorothy Quick

The venom of word's utterance can be
More deadly than the poison of a snake,
Just as a ripple in the quiet sea
Can leave a tide's disturbance in its wake
So unkind words can fester in the brain
And grow deep-rooted into agony.
For words, once spoken, gather in a train
That sweeps on like a flood's catastrophe.
Never unleash the squalor of a thought
Unworthy, to the forcefulness of speech,
Nor yet betray the tongue which should be brought
To offer all the kindness love can teach.

IF I HAD KNOWN

Mary Carolyn Davies

If I had known what trouble you were bearing.
What griefs were in the silence of your face;
I would have been more gentle, and more caring,
And tried to give you gladness for a space.
I would have brought more warmth into the place,
If I had known.

If I had known what thoughts despairing drew you;
(Why do we never try to understand?)
I would have lent a little friendship to you,
And slipped my hand within your hand,
And made your stay more pleasant in the land.
If I had known.

EVENING

Nacella Young

I've tucked the children in and heard their prayers,
And kissed their small warm cheeks, and said goodnight.
I've picked up overalls, and straightened chairs,
And fixed the door to let in a crack of light.
Now I can tiptoe down the shadowy stairs
To where you sit, alone, with book and pipe.

The kitchen's warm and still, and we two sit
In tired silence, for we need no speech;
I take the paper, look it through a bit,
Nor touch your hand that lies in easy reach.
So sure of love we need not speak of it,
Our hearts answer gently, each to each.

THE DELICATE DREAM BEYOND CHAOS

Bette Richart

See me, then, as a singular fragile lady
Who nevertheless is strong:
Who will never be broken by wars or by rumors of wars,
But who will quietly love you her whole life long.

It is for you, in the lilting peace of summer,
She stands arranging roses, among the rarest
Finding no symbol of that exquisite one
In her blood, matchless and fairest.

It is for you she lights the logs in winter,
For you her bright room sheltered from the cold,
Only for you is her gravity forgotten,
And the kiss contrived, naked and bold.

She is a romantic lady in long blue gown,
Whose brain is naught but the image of her lord.
Her heart's slow deeply passionate understanding
Is tender in every word.

And when the moon strikes terror in her lord's eyes
By meanings ambiguous and wild and shady,
She will open her door and call him in that low voice,
And close his troubled eyes with her lips, this lady.

NOW OLDER GROWN

Mazie V. Caruthers

My dancing shoes are laid upon the shelf
With various oddments of my other self—
That youthful self, carefree and pleasure bent,
Who down the sunlit paths of primrose went—
That part of me, whose lovely yesterdays
Are misted over now with purpling haze.
Down roads beset with care, my sober feet
Walk nowadays, but always life is sweet—
Though shadows lengthen and the days grow long,
Within my constant heart abides its song.
Sometimes I take old memories out, to touch
With tender fingers things that meant so much,
Then close the door on such remembering—
Life cannot always linger at its Spring—
And one who long has worn upon her hand
The thinning circle of a wedding band
Knows that the passing years as guerdon bring
To Autumn love a bounteous harvesting!

SALVAGE[2]

Elias Lieberman

Those days were bright with sun-
    light. Think of them
When rain-black clouds, gray skies
    and leaden feet
Make each device of ours a strategem
To stay the tide of imminent defeat.
Those days were glad with song.
    Reflect on these
When silent hours and dull encom-
    pass you,
When darkness conjures up futilities
And crows, in flocks, caw cynical
    review.

I am a king, remembering a throne;
You are a queen remolding dreams
    from dust;
No beggar's cloak shall mock our glory
    flown;
Our sword of faith still glitters,
    free from rust;
And now a rainbow, caught from
    days gone by,
On curves of hope proclaims a clearing
    sky.

Found in my husband's wallet after his death. The poem was given to him by me.

A WIFE

Henry van Dyke

A wife is one who shares
Her husband's thought, incorporates his heart
With hers in love, and crowns him with her trust.
She is God's remedy for loneliness
And God's reward for all the toil of life.

TWO IN THE CAMPAGNA

Robert Browning

I wonder do you feel today
    As I have felt since, hand in hand,
We sat down on the grass, to stray
    In spirit better through the land,
This morn of Rome and May?

For me, I touched a thought, I know,
    Has tantalized me many times,
(Like turns of threads the spiders throw
    Mocking across our path) for rhymes
To catch at and let go.

Help me to hold it! First it left
    The yellowing fennel, run to seed
There, branching from the brickwork's cleft,
    Some old tomb's ruin: yonder weed
Took up the floating weft,

Where one small orange cup amassed
    Five beetles,—blind and green they grope
Among the honeymeal: and last,
    Everywhere on the grassy slope
I traced it. Hold it fast!

The champaign with its endless fleece
    Of feathery grasses everywhere!
Silence and passion, joy and peace,
    An ever-lasting wash of air—
Rome's ghost since her decease.

Such life here, through such lengths of hours,
    Such miracles performed in play,
Such primal naked forms of flowers,
    Such letting nature have her way
While heaven looks from its towers!

How say you? Let us, O my dove,
    Let us be unashamed of soul,
As earth lies bare to heaven above!
How is it under our control
To love or not to love?

I would that you were all to me,
    You that are just so much, no more.
Nor yours nor mine, nor slave nor free!
    Where does the fault lie? What the core
O' the wound, since wound must be?

I would I could adopt your will,
   See with your eyes, and set my heart
Beating by yours, and drink my fill
   At your soul's springs, your part my part
In life, for good and ill.

No. I yearn upward, touch you close,
   Then stand away. I kiss your cheek,
Catch your soul's warmth, I pluck the rose
   And love it more than tongue can speak—
Then the good minute goes.

Already how am I so far
   Out of that minute? Must I go
Still like the thistle-ball, no bar,
   Onward, whenever light winds blow,
Fixed by no friendly star?

Just when I seemed about to learn!
   Where is the thread now? Off again!
The old trick! Only I discern—
   Infinite passion, and the pain
Of finite hearts that yearn.

SECOND BLOSSOMING

Ruth Lechlitner

Now that the hunger born of Spring
Burned in her blood no longer,
Now that fruit
Drew its sweet milk no more from hidden root
Nor bent the heavy bough, no urgent thing
Stirred in her flesh: so must the heart grow wise,
Serene, with Summer's ending, as the skies.

But when from some high portal
Marching, the great winds blew their flaming trumpets
Till each calm hill
Rose from a burning valley to fulfill
Its dream of second blossoming, the mortal
Cry of her own dream broke against the earth
With the sharp agony of second birth.

Compassionate, she knew
In this too perfect and suspended hour
(For second dreams are brief)
Tenderness for the green, unfallen leaf.
Trembling, she touched the aster's starry blue;
And plucked the last red dahlia, petal tossed,
From the dark fingers of the reaching frost.

TO EACH HIS OWN

Milton Bracker

These things I may not see: a cup of space
Scooped by a man in transit from the moon
And scrapings from a cratered lunar place
Shown in a spade, or sifted with a spoon.

The gossamer—or grit—of Saturn's rings,
The fiery spatter or the icy spill
Of the unsampled planetary springs—
I will not know such textures.
Others will.

Nor need I be propelled beyond the sky
To share the triumph of that sure ascent
By youth, who was myself. Time-tethered, I
Ask no extension; no! Term me content
With love's own patient journey to a star
Called understanding. It is where we are.

PARTIAL COMFORT

Dorothy Parker

Whose love is given over-well
Shall look on Helen's face in hell,
Whilst they whose love is thin and wise
May view John Knox in paradise.

FORGIVENESS

Anonymous

Through the long twilight hours, I sought in vain
To banish thoughts of you, and re-create
The image of an ideal I had known;
But I was powerless to combat Fate;
And love for you was far too deeply sown
To be uprooted painlessly, and thrown
Into the dusk and dreariness, alone.
If I have sinned, think not the worst of me,
But strive to visualize what once I was.
Weigh carefully my foibles, bit by bit,

And sift what seem the better from the base;
And in the mercy of your heart—permit
Your judgment to be one of kindly grace.
I think that God, being Love, will most forgive
Those who for love's sweet sake have shattered all
Their principles; and broken laws man-made.
I, at my best, would torture no frail thing
For some small sin it scarce had realized.
How much more tenderly the Great God Love,
Being higher a million million times than I,
Would pity me in my mortality!

FULFILMENT

Thomas S. Jones, Jr.

You are the quiet at the end of the day,
   You are the peace no storms may ever mar,
You are the light that can not fade away—
   Lost be the path in darkness, you the star.

Once as a dream that youth had held unreal,
   Now as a dream more real than all things true;
You only—yet the symbol and the seal
   Of dreams eternal that shall come through you.

L'ENVOI

Rudyard Kipling

What is the moral? Who rides may read.
   When the night is thick and the tracks are blind,
A friend at a pinch is a friend indeed,
   But a fool to wait for the laggard behind:
Down to Gehenna or up to the Throne
He travels the fastest who travels alone.

White hands cling to the tightened rein,
   Slipping the spur from the booted heel,
Tenderest voices cry, 'Turn again,'
   Red lips tarnish the scabbarded steel,
High hopes faint on a warm hearth-stone—
He travels the fastest who travels alone.

One may fall but he falls by himself—
   Falls by himself with himself to blame;
One may attain and to him is the pelf,
   Loot of the city in Gold or Fame:
Plunder of earth shall be all his own
Who travels the fastest and travels alone.

Wherefore the more ye be holpen and stayed—
   Stayed by a friend in the hour of toil,
Sing the heretical song I have made—
   His be the labour and yours be the spoil.
Win by his aid and the aid disown—
He travels the fastest who travels alone.

6

MOTHERHOOD

I feel very strongly that there could not possibly be any more fitting way to introduce this special section of the Anthology than with Rupert Brooke's beautiful poem, "Mary and Gabriel", which—for some reason that I have never been able to understand—is less well-known than many of his that are less sensitive and perceptive. It seems to me that he has interpreted, as no one else out of Holy Writ has done, one of the greatest and most significant moments of Mary's life as a Mother—the other two, of course, being at Bethlehem and on Calvary. Since Mary is the Blessed and Supreme Mother of us all, these are the moments when lesser mothers feel most closely akin to her and most ardently desire to find, in exalted expression, the sentiments for which they themselves have no adequate words.

Another poem I have chosen, "Jesus and His Mother", by Thom Gunn, gives us a different and sadder aspect of her maternity; and the priest's prayer to Mary at the time of his mother's death seems appropriate to use with these.

Phyllis McGinley's poems have been a source of joy to me ever since I first began to read them, as they have been to thousands of others; but I believe great numbers of her followers think of her as a poet whose wisdom is so impregnated with wit that they are more conscious of the second quality than of the first. Now that I myself am an old woman with no daughters at all, I am very conscious, despite my proud possession of three sons, how much wisdom there is in her poem, "The Old Woman with Four Sons".

MARY AND GABRIEL

Rupert Brooke

Young Mary, loitering once her garden way,
Felt a warm splendour grow in the April day,
As wine that blushes water through. And soon,
Out of the gold air of the afternoon,
One knelt before her: hair he had, or fire,
Bound back above his ears with golden wire,
Baring the eager marble of his face.
Not man's nor woman's was the immortal grace
Rounding the limbs beneath that robe of white,
And lighting the proud eyes with changeless light,
Incurious. Calm as his wings, and fair,
That presence filled the garden.
                                        She stood there,

Saying, "What would you, Sir?"
                                        He told his word,
"Blessed art thou of women!" Half she heard,
Hands folded and face bowed, half long had known,
The message of the clear and holy tone,
That fluttered hot sweet sobs about her heart;
Such serene tidings moved such human smart.
Her breath came quick as little flakes of snow.
Her hands crept up her breast. She did but know
It was not hers. She felt a trembling stir
Within her body, a will too strong for her
That held and filled and mastered all. With eyes
Closed, and a thousand soft short broken sighs,
She gave submission; fearful, meek, and glad. . . .
She wished to speak. Under her breasts she had
Such multitudinous burnings, to and fro,
And throbs not understood; she did not know
If they were hurt or joy for her; but only
That she was grown strange to herself, half lonely,

All wonderful, filled full of pains to come
And thoughts she dare not think, swift thoughts and
    dumb,
Human, and quaint, her own, yet very far,
Divine, dear, terrible, familiar. . . .
Her heart was faint for telling; to relate
Her limbs' sweet treachery, her strange high estate,
Over and over, whispering, half revealing,
Weeping; and so find kindness to her healing.
'Twixt tears and laughter, panic hurrying her,
She raised her eyes to that fair messenger.
He knelt unmoved, immortal; with his eyes
Gazing beyond her, calm to the calm skies;
Radiant, untroubled in his wisdom, kind.
His sheaf of lilies stirred not in the wind.
How should she, pitiful with mortality,
Try the wide peace of that felicity
With ripples of her perplexed shaken heart,
And hints of human ecstasy, human smart,
And whispers of the lonely weight she bore,
And how her womb within was hers no more
And at length hers?
             Being tired, she bowed her head;
And said, "So be it!"
             The great wings were spread
Showering glory on the fields, and fire.
The whole air, singing, bore him up, and higher,
Unswerving, unreluctant. Soon he shone
A gold speck in the gold skies; then was gone.

The air was colder, and grey. She stood alone.

JESUS AND HIS MOTHER

Thom Gunn

My only son, more God's than mine,
Stay in this garden ripe with pears.
The yielding of their substance wears
A modest and contented shine:
And when they weep in age, not brine
But lazy syrup are their tears.
"I am my own and not my own."

He seemed much like another man,
That silent foreigner who trod
Outside my door with lily rod:
How could I know what I began
Meeting the eyes more furious than
The eyes of Joseph, those of God?
I was my own and not my own.

And who are these twelve laboring men?
I do not understand your words:
I taught you speech, we named the birds,
You marked their big migrations then
Like any child. So turn again
To silence from the place of crowds.
"I was my own and not my own."

Why are you sullen when I speak?
Here are your tools, the saw and knife
And hammer on your bench. Your life
Is measured here in week and week
Planed as the furniture you make.
And I will teach you like a wife
To be my own and all my own.

Who like an arrogant wind blown
Where he pleases, does without content?
Yet I remember how you went
To speak with scholars in furred gown.
I hear an outcry in the town;
Who carries the dark instrument?
"One all his own and not his own."

Treading the green and nimble sward,
I stare at a strange shadow thrown.
Are you the boy I bore alone,
No doctor near to cut the cord?
I cannot reach to call you Lord,
Answer me as my only son.
"I am my own and not my own."

AND BE HER MOTHER, JUST AS SHE WAS MINE

(A priest on the death of his mother)

Anonymous

No mighty panegyric do I say
      But just the sobbing of my Rosary
To tell Thee, Lady, that I lost today
      My Mother, who was all the world to me!

I recommend her, Lady, to Thy care,
      Be good to her, she was a child of Thine.
She shared Thy pain, let her Thy glory share
      And be her Mother, just as she was mine!

THE WISE MOTHER

Dorothy Hobson

This is her hope: to love, but not
    too much;
To keep the fingers locked together
    tightly
Lest in an off-guard interval they
    clutch
At youth possessively with warping
    touch:
To hold the early sweet allegiance
    lightly
As a blessing only lent by heaven;
    to leave
At liberty the rash young heart and
    brain
To fashion their own life, their own
    death even
(O final gift, O precious to receive)
Free of the sense of having given
    pain.

HAGAR SPEAKS TO SARAH

Gertie Stewart Howard

You were his wife, yet when the dry years fled
Leaving the certainty you were betrayed,
You saw your dream of dreams begin to fade—
And the desire that Abraham coveted
Prone in the dust. Your placid love then led
Your lord to me, the young Egyptian maid;
How I despised you! But was not afraid;
Hope stirred beneath my heart, your hope long
    dead.

But Sarah, even though you cursed and sent
Me far, when I returned to serve, no scorn
Accompanied me, its scathing fire was spent.
I would have kissed your feet that magic morn,
Had you appeared in its bright wonderment,
When Ishmael, my dark eyed son, was born.

SARAH SPEAKS TO HAGAR

Gertie Stewart Howard

You may have deemed our love a star grown cold
When Abraham sought your unguarded tent;
Not so, he came there clothed with my consent
Because no son was ours, and we were old.
Love need be selfless, Hagar, to unbar
The temple doorway. Know you not a wife
Would rather bare her bosom to the knife
Whose aftermath is the unaching scar?

Proud of your fruitfulness, as sanguine youth
Feels not their tread, you scorned my years,
My futile womb. But Hagar, my chagrin
Was not that you bore Ishmael—in truth
Pride's tall defense barred envy's grudging tears—
But that my sacrifice need not have been.

WHEN LOVE MEETS LOVE

Anonymous

When Love meets Love, breast urged to breast,
God interposes
An unacknowledged guest
And leaves a little child among our roses.
We love, God makes. In our sweet mirth
God spies occasion for a birth.
Then is it His, or is it ours?
I know not—He is fond of flowers.

MATERNITY

(*From The White Cliffs*)

Alice Duer Miller

Maternity is common, but not so
It seemed to me. Motherless, I did not know—
I was all unprepared to feel this glow,
Holy as a Madonna's, and as crude
As any animal's beatitude—
Crude as my own black cat's, who used to bring
Her newest litter to me every spring,
And say, with green eyes shining in the sun:
"Behold this miracle that I have done."

THE OLD WOMAN WITH FOUR SONS

Phyllis McGinley

"I have had four sons," said the old woman,
"And no daughters ever.
My sons are kind men, they are kinder than common,
And tall and clever.

"They come often to visit me from the places where they live,
Restless as birds.
Their hands are full of the gifts that men like to give.
Their words are men's words.

"They say 'You look well,' 'Do you need money?' 'The job is fine.'
They chat with the neighbors.
The minds I shaped once are shaped now to a new design
By their wives or their labors.

"They do not come to my room at night, combing their hair,
When we are alone,
To share with me the secrets that women share
In heart and bone.

"Sons do not need you. They are always out of your reach,
Walking strange waters,
Their mouths are not made for small and intimate speech
Like the speech of daughters.

"The lads I bore are my sons still," said the old woman,
"Grown clever and tall,
And they are kind. Oh, they are kinder than common,
But I have no daughter at all."

7

OLD AGE

After some hesitation it was decided to omit Browning's "Rabbi Ben Ezra" because its merits, though noteworthy, did not seem sufficiently great to justify the amount of space it would take up if presented in full, and it does not lend itself to extraction. However, as a woman who can be called "elderly" by others only through courtesy, and does not in the least mind calling herself old, I can heartily agree with part of the claim made in the first verse: I believe it *is* the last of life for which the first is made, and I am quite ready to declare that whether or not the best is yet to come, the present is very good indeed! And I am glad to find that many of the poets whose work I have quoted in full do not believe in retirement, for I do not, either. Slowing down—yes! Idleness—no! It is the quickest way to the grave!

THE LONELY HOUSE

Anna Blake Mezquida

Within my house there are no children's voices;
        No patter of small feet;
No boisterous shouts; no merry, treble laughter;
        No bedtime kisses sweet;
There are no dolls and tops dropped in the hallway—
        My house is very neat.

My house is filled with ivories from China;
        Rich tapestries from Spain;
My house is filled with women's idle-chatter
        Like dripping of soft rain;—
I wonder will my neighbor's little tow-head
        Come visit me again?

YOU ASK MY AGE

Sister M. Madeleva

I am older than dawn
And sunset are.
I can think past the light
Of the oldest star.

The piled-up mountains
And ancient trees,
Timeless rivers
And ageless seas;

East and west winds,
South and north:
I know the hour
That brought them forth.

How old am I?
As days are told,
The earth is younger
Than I am old.

Years cannot measure
Time for me.
Fetch us the clock
Of infinity.

This is the answer
If you would know;
From life I come;
To life I go.

Wherefore I am
More gladly young
Than a child not born,
Than a song not sung;

More young than spring
Before its birth,
Than the dreaming life
In the dreaming earth;

More young than the hosts
Of seraphim
Who sing, "Hosanna,
Elohim."

Older I am
Than any star
And younger than
The angels are.

GROWING OLDER

Charles Hanson Towne

Oh, when our wandering days at length are done,
And we come back to find some simple town,
When the swift race for profit has been run,
And left behind are turrets of renown;
Home, home at last we turn, and find it well
In gentle comfort and soft peace to dwell.

How crowded were the years of youth! How good
To climb the hills that led to Fame's bright way!
Upon some peak of ecstasy we stood,
Shouting "Tomorrow!"—never "Yesterday."
Green were the slopes of Beauty spread afar,
Where we were led by some immortal star.

Tired? Not yet. But we are glad to go
Back to the dream-lit hush of evening hours;
To move through hidden lanes with pace more slow,
And gather only autumn's scentless flowers;
Leaving behind us morning's golden sun,
And the loud tracks where Youth's swift race was run.

HALCYON DAYS

Walt Whitman

Not from successful love alone,
Nor wealth, nor honor'd middle age, nor victories of politics or war;
But as life wanes, and all the turbulent passions calm,
As gorgeous, vapory, silent hues cover the evening sky,
As softness, fulness, rest, suffuse the frame, like fresher, balmier air,
As the days take on a mellower light, and the apple at last hangs really
        finish'd and indolent-ripe on the tree,
Then for the teeming quietest, happiest days of all!
The brooding and blissful halcyon days!

BIRTHDAY CANDLES

Geoffrey Johnson

The candles lit were seven
That crowned my birthday cake;
My young heart sang to heaven
To see them shine and shake—
And then it sighed, desiring
That seventy more were spiring
From the table's polished lake.

"Why want so, why complain so?"
My mother fluted clear,
"I wish they could remain so
And keep us ever here—

You warm against my shoulder
And none a moment older
Than now, my foolish dear."

Candles tonight how many
Would match my years now fled?
I had rather not have any—
Yet burn just one, to shed
The glows of long-lost faces
From far-off childhood places,
Then light me to my bed.

A SCHOOLMASTER RETIRES

Elias Lieberman

Reluctantly he shuts the schoolhouse door,
A life's work ended and a quest begun.
He thinks of texts that he will hunt no more,
Of maps, of charts, designs of problems done.
They will survive as tokens of a chase
That led his boys and girls from dark to light,
The mountain climb of man in time and space
From fens of blindness, high toward peaks of sight.
The sum of all he did and what it means
Cannot be audited; too many lives
Must burgeon still. His recollection gleans
A blur of children, classrooms, humming hives
Where none could tell by any valid measure
Whose gift would be of dross and whose of treasure.

TO ONE PLANNING RETIREMENT

Elias Lieberman

No calendar could ever chain
A youthful soul within
The body's time-beset domain
Since time itself began.

Nor could the seconds, minutes, hours,
Whose jagged wings can tear
The petal-perfect garden flowers,
Destroy young souls with fear.

Reject the call of fancied ease,
The passive mien of age,
Forget those dusty properties
Of an abandoned stage.

An actor, trained by life, will play
With never flagging art
The script composed by each new day
As his authentic part.

ABOUT FACE

Una W. Harsen

This is no time to let age have its way,
To sit serene and idle in the sun
And watch the shadows of the afternoon
Draw to the twilight of the closing day.

We must renew the tasks we thought were done,
Set hand again to plow and wheel and lathe,
Force tired feet to climb the upward path,
Turn weary eyes to face the rising sun.

The past—it is a story that is told.
The future lies within our steadfast keeping;
Today belongs to toil, not sighs and weeping.
This is our day—we who are growing old.

THE TWO OLD WOMEN

Anonymous

Two neighboring crones, antique and gray,
Together talked at close of day.
One said, with brow of wrinkled care,
"Life's cup, at first, was sweet and fair;
On our young lips, with laughter gay,
Its cream of brimming nectar lay;
But vapid when it grew, and stale
And tiresome as a twice-told tale;
And here, in weary age and pain,
Its bitter dregs alone remain."

The other, with contented eye,
Laid down her work, and made reply;
"Yes, life was bright at morning tide,
Yet when the foam and sparkle died,
More rich methought and surer, too,
Its well-connected essence grew;
Even now, though low its spirit drains,
And little in the cup remains,
There's sugar at the bottom still—
And we may taste it, if we will."

ON GROWING OLDER

John Wheatley

Behind glass walls my fancies move,
Seeking an inexpressible love;
Outside, and in its headstrong way,
The world spins faster every day.

The formulated wish, the prayer,
Are compromised and prisoned here,
Baffled, frustrate, bitter, vain,
Like wasps upon a windowpane.

The symbols of a canceled hour
Are words without the poet's power,
Significant like the winds that blow
From whence to where we do not know.

My symbols are the vital tree
Whose roots are bound, whose leaves are free,
The cyclic sun, the patient rain
That falls to die and rise again.

In three dimensions I have made
Protest against a masquerade.
Now for the truth; I fear to pass
Through the broken wall of glass.

THANKS IN OLD AGE

Walt Whitman

Thanks in old age—thanks ere I go,
For health, the midday sun, the impalpable air—for life, mere life,
For precious ever-lingering memories (of you my mother dear—you
        father—you, brothers, sisters, friends,)
For all my days—not those of peace alone—the days of war the same,
For gentle words, caresses, gifts from foreign lands,
For shelter, wine and meat—for sweet appreciation,
(You distant, dim unknown—or young or old—countless, unspecified,
        readers belov'd,
We never met, and ne'er shall meet—and yet our souls embrace, long,
        close and long;)
For beings, groups, love, deeds, words, books—for colors, forms,
For all the brave strong men—devoted, hardy men—who've forward
        sprung in freedom's help, all years, all lands,
For braver, stronger, more devoted men—(a special laurel ere I go, to
        life's war's chosen ones,
The cannoneers of song and thought—the great artillerists—the fore-
        most leaders, captains of the soul:)
As soldier from an ended war return'd—As traveler out of myriads, to
        the long procession retrospective,
Thanks—joyful thanks!—a soldier's, traveler's thanks.

FORMULA FOR OLD AGE

Una W. Harsen

Age should be sweet and mellow with content
Not crabbed, gnarled like a misshapen tree,
Should hold out but lightly its infirmity,
Now that the strength and fire of youth are spent.
Age should have beauty gleaned from happy years,
Reaping rich harvest from the golden past,
Not weeping that bright summer does not last;
Calm in the peace that follows after tears.
Age should have strength to seek, to guide, to lift
The weak, the faltering, the stricken ones,
Strength and sweet sympathy whose music runs
Like a glad hymn of praise for life's good gift.

8

DEATH AND IMMORTALITY

When I first submitted to my Editor my selections for this part of the Anthology, he said in a warning voice, "Remember that comparatively few of your readers will remember World War I with any clarity. I suggest that it might be better to delete most of the material which deals with it."

I disagreed with him on several scores. I believe that a good many of my readers still remember World War I all too vividly. Moreover, I believe that a good many of those who do not are interested in the effect it had on the thinking and activities of this sad era, and that it is illogical to assume otherwise. Certainly we are still interested in the battle-lore of times so far in the past that there is no one still living to remember them. The Editor did not object, I reminded him, to my inclusion of "Before Sedan" on the grounds that Sedan might hardly be so much as a name to the present generation, and he admitted that I had a point. I could make the same point in regard to "The Burial of Sir John Moore". However, in an effort to prove my willingness to take advice, I have reduced the number of poems about World War I to three, and one of them, "The Man in White", does need some explanation.

World War I, as is very generally known, was much more productive of songs than World War II. (Where, for instance, do we find parallels for "Tipperary", "The Long, Long Trail", "Over There", etc.) It was also much more productive of rumors which rose to the rank of legends. Chief among these was the widely circulated story of a white figure, with attributes of divinity, which appeared to the wounded the night after a battle, when they still lay where they had fallen, and walked among them, murmuring words of comfort, cheer and faith. I myself have heard expressions of indignation from French soldiers who were sceptically assured that they *thought* they saw such a figure, but that it was only a feverish hallucination. They *knew* they had seen it, they assured me, and nothing could shake them from this conviction; they not only saw it, they spoke with it. Without exception, they referred to this figure as *Le Camarade Blanc*—The White Comrade. No one doubted that it was a celestial vision.

William Alexander Percy, the author of "The Man in White", obviously shared this conviction.

Death on the battlefield and immortality are closely connected in the minds of almost everyone; but immortality takes many different forms. I have tried to indicate this in my selections.

THE BURIAL OF SIR JOHN MOORE AT CORUNNA

Charles Wolfe

Not a drum was heard, not a funeral note,
   As his corpse to the rampart we hurried;
Not a soldier discharged his farewell shot
   O'er the grave where our hero we buried.

We buried him darkly at dead of night,
   The sods with out bayonets turning;
By the struggling moonbeam's misty light
   And the lantern dimly burning.

No useless coffin enclosed his breast,
   Not in sheet or in shroud we wound him;
But he lay like a warrior taking his rest,
   With his martial cloak around him.

Few and short were the prayers we said,
   And we spoke not a word of sorrow;
But we steadfastly gazed on the face that was dead,
   And we bitterly thought of the morrow.

We thought, as we hollow'd his narrow bed
   And smoothed down his lonely pillow,
That the foe and the stranger would tread o'er his head,
   And we far away on the billow!

Lightly they'll talk of the spirit that's gone
   And o'er his cold ashes upbraid him,—
But little he'll reck, if they let him sleep on
   In the grave where a Briton has laid him.

But half of our heavy task was done
    When the clock struck the hour for retiring:
And we heard the distant and random gun
    That the foe was sullenly firing.

Slowly and sadly we laid him down,
    From the field of his fame fresh and gory;
We carved not a line, and we raised not a stone,
    But we left him alone with his glory.

THE MAN IN WHITE

William Alexander Percy

(Ambulance drivers from the Front tell that to the grievously
wounded, alone on the battlefield, the hallucination often comes
of a man in white who comforts them.)

"Soldier, knowest thou the land
    The land that's home to thee?"
"Stranger, with the voice not strange,
    Why do you lean to me,
A wounded man, and put a word
    That mocks my memory?"

"Soldier, I am from that land,
    The land that's home to thee."
"O stranger with the gentle hands,
    Now let your pity be.
You have no word what land is mine,
    Your closed eyes cannot see
As mine, as mine, the land of lands,
    The land where I would be."

"I see a field of apple trees
 That top a furrowed hill,
A little house, a little room,
 A flowered window sill.
A woman with a face like thine,
 But eyes more sweet and still,
Who prays across the gathered dusk
 To guard her child from ill."

"My God, my God, I fear to look
 Lest there be no man by!
If this be but a fever dream
 O let me sleep and die
And never know a blessed ghost
 From home had heard my cry."

"See me, touch me, let thy head
 On my bosom weigh.
This, the kiss your mother sent,
 That on your lips I lay."
"Yes—it is hers—no other drives
 The awful pain away—
I think—that I could fall asleep—
 If you—would only—stay."

"Rest thee, rest thee on my breast,
 Let the deep sleep come.
Rest thee, rest thee, soldier lad,
 Time is past to roam.
Waking, I shall still be near,
 And we shall be at home."

I HAVE A RENDEZVOUS WITH DEATH

Alan Seeger

I have a rendezvous with Death
At some disputed barricade,
When Spring comes back with rustling shade
And apple-blossoms fill the air—
I have a rendezvous with Death
When Spring brings back blue days and fair.

It may be he shall take my hand
And lead me into his dark land
And close my eyes and quench my breath—
It may be I shall pass him still.
I have a rendezvous with Death
On some scarred slope of battered hill
When Spring comes round again this year
And the first meadow-flowers appear.

God knows 'twere better to be deep
Pillowed in silk and scented down,
Where Love throbs out in blissful sleep,
Pulse nigh to pulse, and breath to breath,
Where hushed awakenings are dear . . .
But I've a rendezvous with Death
At midnight in some flaming town,
When Spring trips north again this year,
And I to my pledged word am true,
I shall not fail that rendezvous.

THE SOLDIER

Rupert Brooke

If I should die, think only this of me:
    That there's some corner of a foreign field
That is forever England. There shall be
    In that rich earth a richer dust concealed;
A dust whom England bore, shaped, made aware,
    Gave, once, her flowers to love, her ways to roam,
A body of England's, breathing English air,
    Washed by the rivers, blest by suns of home.

And think, this heart, all evil shed away,
    A pulse in the eternal mind, no less
        Gives somewhere back the thoughts by England given;
Her sights and sounds; dreams happy as her day;
    And laughter, learnt of friends; and gentleness,
        In hearts at peace, under an English heaven.

AN OLD SOLDIER DIES

Ethel Barnett de Vito

She saw, those last days, when he stormed death's portal,
He would go down with all his armor on,
Godlike—almost too godlike to be mortal,
She thought, Who could live up to such a man?
His fearlessness, as he lay telling stories,
His coolness that denied the ailing flush,
Almost he might be planning further glories:
To conquer this last foe in one swift rush.

How could she wake a need for her at length?
Her role: to wait, to do as she was bid.
Shaken with grief she tried to match his strength
Until he said, "Bend close," and when she did
To hear the final word he would confide,
"I am afraid of death," he said, and died.

SOLDIER

William Rose Benet

My father was a soldier; he obeyed
what others, wrong too often, had to say;
and when he was afraid, he was afraid
    in a stern lonely way.

The speculation of his eagle mind
hovered above their ignorance of him;
and he was just and generous and kind
    and whimsical and grim.

He had an erudition hard to match,
a pride upon whose point he often ran,
quicksilver wisdom difficult to catch,
    the ironic mask of Man,

the eye austere, the tart and witty tongue,
the thought that knew men's actions all unsure;
but even in age his heart was warm and young
    and his intention pure.

About his mouth there was a smiling hid
that gorgon death could never turn to stone;
and when they lowered down the coffin lid
    I heard a trumpet blown.

DEATH OF A SCHOOLTEACHER

Bernard Hirshberg

No floral cortege followed to his grave,
The whistling wind whispered the litany;
He went his lonely way from memory;
A "pause of silence" none in honor gave;
But if you closer peered, then wave on wave,
Host of disciples paced invisibly
The city streets; unto eternity
His heart their lifelong pilgrim road would pave;
He'd ever have it so, for he had taught
A man was measured for what cause he fought;
He gave them strength to press to higher goal,
Transcending grief and anguish of the soul;
He'd sought to mold each child a stalwart oak—
In freedom's cause that neither bent nor broke.

QUANDARY

Harold Willard Gleason

A silent, sun-brown man, he spent his days
Amid the murmur of unnumbered wings,
Watching with quiet eye the human ways
Of honey-bees . . . For him they bore no stings,
Sensing the sympathetic kindliness
He felt for drone workers; hand or head
They lit on, never vicious . . . In distress
She wondered how to tell them he was dead . . .

THE POET'S TESTAMENT

George Santayana

I give back to the earth what the earth gave,
All to the furrow, nothing to the grave,
The candle's out, the spirit's vigil spent;
Sight may not follow where the vision went.

I leave you but the sound of many a word
In mocking echoes haply overheard,
I sang to heaven. My exile made me free,
From world to world, from all worlds carried me.

Spared by the Furies, for the Fates were kind,
I paced the pillared cloisters of the mind;
All times my present, everywhere my place,
Nor fear, nor hope, nor envy saw my face.

Blow what winds would, the ancient truth was mine,
And friendship mellowed in the flush of wine,
And heavenly laughter, shaking from its wings
Atoms of light and tears for mortal things.

To trembling harmonies of field and cloud,
Of flesh and spirit was my worship vowed.
Let form, let music, let all-quickening air
Fulfill in beauty my imperfect prayer.

THE SATIN DRESS

Dorothy Parker

Needle, needle, dip and dart,
Thrusting up and down,
Where's the man could ease a heart
Like a satin gown?

See the stitches curve and crawl
Round the cunning seams—
Patterns thin and sweet and small
As a lady's dreams.

Wantons go in bright brocades;
Brides in organdie;
Gingham's for the plighted maid;
Satin's for the free!

Wool's to line a miser's chest;
Crape's to calm the old;
Velvet hides an empty breast;
Satin's for the bold!

Lawn is for a bishop's yoke;
Linen's for a nun;
Satin for wiser folk—
Would the dress were done!

Satin glows in candle-light—
Satin's for the proud!
They will say who watch at night,
"What a fine shroud!"

A BRIGHT JOURNEY ENDS

Richard Watson Gilder

When fell, today, the word that she had gone,
Not this my thought: Here a bright journey ends,
Here rests a soul unresting; here, at last,
Here ends that earnest strength, that generous life—
For all her life was giving. Rather this
I said (after the first swift, sorrowing pang):
Radiant with love, and love's unending power,
Hence, on a new quest, starts an eager spirit—
No dread, no doubt, unhesitating, forth
With asking eyes; pure as the bodiless souls
Whom poets vision near the central throne
Angelically ministrant to man;
So fares she forth with smiling, Godward face;
Nor should we grieve, but give eternal thanks—
Save that we mortal are, and needs must mourn.

CHARACTER SKETCH

Gertie Stewart Howard

Never an hour for playing,
Her house was kept like new;
No rose-hedge rimmed her garden
Where thyme and parsley grew.
Never a gay print apron
Or a dress that was soft and bright;
Like Martha she was burdened

From dawn till candlelight.
Never a breathless moment,
Watching a sunset sky;
But once when it was fading
She took an hour to die.

WHAT DO YOU DO WITH A WOMAN'S THINGS?

Alice Duer Miller

What can you do with a woman's things
   After a woman is dead?
Not the bracelets and rings and strings
Of pearls, but the small unvalued things—
   What can I do, Wayne said.

What can you do with a woman's dresses,
   After a woman is dead?
Hanging limp in the cedar presses,
They are part of herself, her pretty dresses—
   What can I do, Wayne said.

What can you do with a woman's shoes,
   After a woman is dead?
Shoes that perhaps you helped her choose,
Poor little empty half-worn shoes—
   What can I do, Wayne said.

What can you do with her brush and comb,
   After a woman is dead?
What in God's name can you do with her home
And her loss and her love and her brush and comb—
   What can I do, Wayne said.

THE RUBÁIYÁT OF OMAR KHAYYÁM

Translated by Edward Fitzgerald

(Extract)

Strange, is it not? that of the myriads who
Before us pass'd the door of Darkness through,
Not one returns to tell us of the Road,
Which to discover we must travel too.

I sent my Soul through the Invisible,
Some letter of that After-life to spell:
And by and by my Soul return'd to me,
And answered, "I Myself am Heav'n and Hell."

THE BEREAVED

May Williams Ward

In the next room, in the low chair,
In the soft dark, are you there?

I do not ask it when sun is laid
Through the checkered window in yellow plaid—

Then love that is past seems rich enough
And having had that, I can give you up.

But in the deep dark . . . In the low chair
In the next room, are you there?
I want you there.

ALL SOULS

Yetza Gillespie

If, as the legend tells, the dead return
To their old earth tonight, to drift like leaves
Through branches of mortality, to earn
By memory the thing that each one grieves
Only this night of all the year, I doubt
That any pride reclaims its velvet glove,
The roll of drums; that any heart seeks out
Even the seamless mantle of its love;
Nor that a hand recalls the bitter curve
That fits cold steel. That does not break the rest
Of any of these, nor whether they serve
The thrust or closely sheathe it in the breast . . .
No, this will be a night of little things,
A yellow rose, a shell that sings.

THE LIFTING HILL

Jane Merchant

The hill was a red scar against the sky.
The hill was a red welt upon his heart.
With endless stubborn patience he would try
To fill the gullies and give grass a start
No furious rush of rain could sweep away.
After each gully-washer he was there
To seed the raw and crimson-dripping clay
Again, and yet again; this was his prayer.
Not that the hill was his, or that he had

A soul belonging to him who would view
His work with pride. Some people thought him mad,
And when he died, alone, not many knew.
Not many will recall the man I mean;
But on the lifting hill the grass is green.

IMMORTALITY

Frances Parkinson Keyes

He was a man who never chatted much
And seldom laughed. He'd say, "It looks like rain"—
Or else, "The lawn is drying up again"—
"A thaw is setting in," and other such
Brief homely things: about the placid Dutch
Cattle he bred, about the grass and grain
That grew upon his meadows, and the plain
Where sand had turned to verdure at his touch.

When all the hills were blanketed with snow,
The trees which he had planted glistened green—
Sturdy and straight they stood, row after row,
As steadfast as himself and as serene.

And now I see him, smiling through his vines,
And hear him speaking through his groves of pines.

THE STREET OF CROSSES

Arthur Stringer

Proclaim, lone bugle, as the sun sinks low
On lonelier graves that look on alien foam,
How far past tide and spindrift we still know
They live with us, who rest so far from home.

Proclaim how though like lamps their life went out
And youth and gladness passed into the night
Theirs was the final answer to all doubt,
Theirs was the gift that kept alive the Light.

And when the dawning peace the flags are flown,
With drum and tube the air is tremulous,
More than the homing ranks amid their own,
More than the quick, they will be close to us.

9

HYMNS

Like "Salvage" in the section we have called *Friendship and Love, Older Grown*, "Songs in the Night", which I am using to introduce the hymns included in this section, has a special significance to me: it was not one I found myself. It was one my eldest son sent to me with a notation telling me he was doing so, because his happiest memories of me during his early years at Pine Grove Farm centered around the "children's hour" when I first read aloud to him in the living-room, and then sat beside him when he was in bed, first hearing his prayers, and then singing hymns with him. (As soon as they were old enough, I followed this same procedure with his brothers.) As he became familiar with the hymns I selected, he himself chose the ones among them which meant the most to him. Some which were his favorites, as well as some which were mine, are included in the pages which follow.

SONGS IN THE NIGHT

Mazie V. Caruthers

Like sentinels her little songs
  Surround my bed at night—
('Tis then tomorrow's terrors stalk,
  And unknown peril's fright)—
And with these dragons of the dark
  Wage valiantly their fight.

"The King of Love my Shepherd is"—
  "My faith looks up to Thee"—
"Lead kindly Light!" "In life and death"
  "Oh, Lord, abide with me!"
Such brave old hymns, a shining host,
  My shield and buckler be.

Against the fears that ride the heart
  Steadfast, encompassing,
They call to courage, bring to faith
  A mighty quickening,
As in the night I hear these songs
  My mother used to sing.

CHRISTMAS

Anonymous

Once in Royal David's city
   Stood a lowly cattle shed,
Where a mother laid her baby
   In a manger for His bed.
Mary was that mother mild,
Jesus Christ that little child.

He came down to earth from Heaven,
   Who is God and Lord of all
And his shelter was a stable,
   And his cradle was a stall.
With the poor and mean and lowly,
Lived on earth our Saviour Holy.

And our eyes at last shall see Him
   Through His own redeeming love,
For that child so dear and gentle
   Is our Lord in Heaven above;
And He leads His children on
To the place where He is gone.

Not in that poor, lowly stable,
   With the oxen standing by,
We shall see Him; but in Heaven,
   Set at God's right hand on high,
When, like stars, His children crowned
All in white, shall wait around.

FAIREST LORD JESUS

From the German, 17th century

Fairest Lord Jesus, Ruler of all nature,
      O Thou of God and man the Son,
Thee will I cherish, Thee will I honor,
      Thee, my soul's Glory, Joy and Crown.

Fair are the meadows, fairer still the woodlands,
      Robed in the blooming garb of spring:
Jesus is fairer, Jesus is purer,
      Who makes the woeful heart to sing.

Fair is the sunshine, fairer still the moonlight,
      And all the twinkling, starry host:
Jesus shines brighter, Jesus shines purer,
      Than all the angels heaven can boast.

THE KING OF LOVE MY SHEPHERD IS

H. W. Baker

The King of love my Shepherd is,
Whose goodness faileth never;
I nothing lack if I am His
And He is mine forever.

Where streams of living water flow,
My ransomed soul He leadeth.
And, where the verdant pastures grow,
With food celestial feedeth.

Perverse and foolish oft I strayed,
But yet in love He sought me,
And on His shoulder gently laid,
And home, rejoicing, brought me.

In death's dark vale I fear no ill
With Thee, dear Lord, beside me;
Thy rod and staff my comfort still,
Thy cross before to guide me.

And so through all the length of days,
Thy goodness faileth never;
Good Shepherd, may I sing Thy praise
Within Thy house for ever.

THE SON OF GOD GOES FORTH TO WAR

Bishop Reginald Heber

The Son of God goes forth to war,
A kingly crown to gain;
His blood-red banner streams afar;
Who follows in his train?
Who best can drink his cup of woe,
Triumphant over pain,
Who patient bears his cross below,
He follows in his train.

The martyr first, whose eagle eye
Could pierce beyond the grave,
Who saw his Master in the sky,
And called on him to save;
Like him, with pardon on his tongue,
In midst of mortal pain,
He prayed for them that did the wrong:
Who follows in his train?

A glorious band, the chosen few
On whom the Spirit came,
Twelve valiant saints, their hope they knew,
And mocked the cross and flame;
They met the tyrant's brandished steel,
The lion's gory mane;
They bowed their necks the death to feel:
Who follows in their train?

A noble army, men and boys,
The matron and the maid,
Around the Saviour's throne rejoice,
In robes of light arrayed;
They climbed the steep ascent of heaven
Through peril, toil and pain;
O God, to us may grace be given
To follow in their train.

ONWARD, CHRISTIAN SOLDIERS

Reverend Sabine Baring-Gould

Onward, Christian soldiers,
Marching as to war,
With the cross of Jesus
Going on before!
Christ the royal Master
Leads against the foe;
Forward into battle,
See, His banners go.

Like a mighty army
Moves the Church of God;
Brothers, we are treading
Where the saints have trod;

We are not divided,
All one body we,
One in hope and doctrine,
One in charity.

Crowns and thrones may perish,
Kingdoms rise and wane,
But the Church of Jesus
Constant will remain;
Gates of hell can never
'Gainst that Church prevail;
We have Christ's own promise,
And that cannot fail.

Onward, then, ye people!
Join our happy throng!
Blend with ours your voices
In the triumph song!
Glory, laud, and honor,
Unto Christ the King;
This through countless ages
Men and angels sing.

HOW FIRM A FOUNDATION

Anonymous

How firm a foundation, ye saints of the Lord,
Is laid for your faith in His excellent word!
What more can He say than to you He hath said,
To you who for refuge to Jesus have fled?

"Fear not, I am with thee, oh be not dismayed,
For I am thy God, I will still give thee aid:
I'll strengthen thee, help thee, and cause thee to stand,
Upheld by my righteous, omnipotent hand,

"When through the deep waters I call thee to go,
The rivers of sorrow shall not overflow;
For I will be near thee, thy trouble to bless,
And sanctify to thee thy deepest distress,

"When through fiery trials thy pathway shall lie,
My grace, all sufficient, shall be thy supply;
The flame shall not hurt thee; I only design
Thy dross to consume, and thy gold to refine,

"The soul that on Jesus hath leaned for repose,
I will not, I will not desert to his foes;
That soul though all hell should endeavor to shake,
I'll never, no, never, no never forsake."

O GOD, OUR HELP IN AGES PAST

Isaac Watts

O God, our help in ages past,
  Our hope in years to come,
Our shelter from the stormy blast,
  And our eternal home.

Under the shadow of thy throne
  Thy saints have dwelt secure;
Sufficient is thine arm alone,
  And our defense is sure.

Before the hills in order stood,
  Or earth received her frame,
From everlasting thou art God,
  To endless years the same.

A thousand ages in thy sight
    Are like an evening gone;
Short as the watch that ends the night
    Before the rising sun.

Time, like an ever-rolling stream
    Bears all its sons away;
They fly, forgotten, as a dream
    Dies at the opening day.

Our God, our help in ages past,
    Our hope in years to come,
Be thou our guard while troubles last,
    And our eternal home.

LEAD US, O FATHER

William H. Burleigh

Lead us, O Father, in the paths of peace;
Without thy guiding hand we go astray,
And doubts appall and sorrows still increase;
Lead us through Christ, the true and living Way.

Lead us, O Father, in the paths of truth;
Unhelped by thee, in error's maze we grope,
While passion stains and folly dims our youth,
And age comes on uncheered by faith or hope.

Lead us, O Father, in the paths of right;
Blindly we stumble when we walk alone,
Involved in shadows of a mortal night;
Only with thee we journey safely on.

Lead us, O Father, to thy heavenly rest,
However rough and steep the pathway be,
Through joy or sorrow, as thou deemest best,
Until our lives are perfected in thee.

O MOTHER, DEAR JERUSALEM

Anonymous

O mother dear, Jerusalem,
When shall I come to thee?
When shall my sorrows have an end,
Thy joys when shall I see?
O happy harbor of the saints!
O sweet and pleasant soil!
In thee no sorrow may be found,
No grief, no care, no toil.

No murky cloud o'er-shadows thee,
Nor gloom, nor dark-some night,
But every soul shines as the sun,
For God himself gives light.
There lust and lucre cannot dwell,
There envy bears no sway;
There is no hunger, heat, nor cold,
But pleasure every way.

Thy gardens and thy goodly walks
Continually are green,
Where grow such sweet and pleasant flowers
As nowhere else are seen.
Right through the streets, with silver sound
The living waters flow;
And on the banks, either side,
The trees of life do grow.

There trees for evermore bear fruit,
And evermore do spring;
There evermore the angels are,
And evermore do sing.
Jerusalem, my happy home,
Would God I were in thee!
Would God my woes were at an end,
Thy joys that I might see!

JUST AS I AM, WITHOUT ONE PLEA

C. Elliott

Just as I am, without one plea,
But that Thy blood was shed for me,
And that Thou bid'st me come to Thee,
O Lamb of God, I come, I come.

Just as I am, and waiting not
To rid my soul of one dark blot,
To Thee, whose blood can cleanse each spot,
O Lamb of God, I come, I come.

Just as I am, though tossed about
With many a conflict, many a doubt,
Fightings and fears within, without,
O Lamb of God, I come, I come.

Just as I am, poor, wretched, blind,
Sight, riches, healing of the mind,
Yea, all I need, in Thee to find,
O Lamb of God, I come, I come.

Just as I am, Thou wilt receive,
Wilt welcome, pardon, cleanse, relieve;
Because Thy promise I believe,
O Lamb of God, I come, I come.

Just as I am, Thy love unknown
Has broken every barrier down,
Now to be Thine, yea, Thine alone,
O Lamb of God, I come, I come.

JUST FOR TODAY

A Sister of Notre Dame

Lord, for tomorrow and its needs
    I do not pray;
Keep me, my God, from stain of sin,
    Just for today.

Let me both diligently work
    And duly pray;
Let me be kind in word and deed,
    Just for today.

Let me be slow to do my will,
    Prompt to obey;
Help me to sacrifice myself,
    Just for today.

Let me no wrong or idle word,
    Unthinking say;
Let Thou a seal upon my lips,
    Just for today.

Let me in season, Lord, be grave,
In season gay;
Let me be faithful to Thy grace,
Just for today.

Lord, for tomorrow and its needs,
I do not pray;
But keep me, guide me, love me, Lord,
Just for today.

HOLY, HOLY, HOLY!

Bishop Reginald Heber

Holy, holy, holy! Lord God Almighty!
Early in the morning our song shall rise to Thee;
Holy, holy, holy! merciful and mighty!
God in Three Persons, blessed Trinity!

Holy, holy, holy! all the saints adore Thee,
Casting down their golden crowns around the glassy sea,
Cherubim and seraphim falling down before Thee,
Which wert and art and evermore shalt be.

Holy, holy, holy! though the darkness hide Thee,
Though the eye of sinful man Thy glory may not see,
Only Thou art holy; there is none beside Thee,
Perfect in power, in love and purity.

Holy, holy, holy! Lord God Almighty!
All Thy works shall praise Thy name, in earth, and sky, and sea;
Holy, holy, holy! merciful and mighty!
God in Three Persons, blessed Trinity!

RIDE ON, RIDE ON IN MAJESTY

Henry H. Milman

Ride on, ride on in majesty!
Hark! all the tribes Hosanna cry;
O Saviour meek, pursue thy road,
With palms and scattered garments strewed.

Ride on, ride on in majesty!
In kingly role ride on to die;
O Christ, thy triumphs now begin
O'er captive death and conquered sin.

Ride on, ride on in majesty!
The wingèd squadrons of the sky
Look down with sad and wondering eyes
To see the approaching sacrifice.

Ride on, ride on in majesty!
The last and fiercest strife is nigh;
Bow thy meek head to mortal pain,
Then take, O Christ, thy power and reign.

ALLELUIA, HEARTS TO HEAVEN AND VOICES RAISE

Christopher Wordsworth

Alleluia! Alleluia!
Hearts to heaven and voices raise;
Sing to God a hymn of gladness,
Sing to God a hymn of praise.
He who on the cross as Saviour
For the world's salvation bled,
Jesus Christ, the King of Glory,
Now is risen from the dead.

Now the iron bars are broken,
Christ from death to life is born,
Glorious life, and life immortal,
On this holy Easter morn;
Christ has triumphed, and we conquer
By his mighty enterprise,
We with him to life eternal
By his resurrection rise.

Alleluia! Alleluia!
Glory be to God on high;
Alleluia to the Saviour
Who has won the victory;
Alleluia to the Spirit,
Fount of love and sanctity;
Alleluia! Alleluia!
To the Triune Majesty.

ABIDE WITH ME

Henry F. Lyte

Abide with me! Fast falls the eventide,
The darkness deepens: Lord, with me abide!
When other helpers fail, and comforts flee,
Help of the helpless, O, abide with me!

Swift to its close ebbs out life's little day;
Earth's joys grow dim, its glories pass away;
Change and decay in all around I see;
O thou, who changest not, abide with me!

Not a brief glance, I beg, a passing word,
But as thou dwellest with thy disciples, Lord
Familiar, condescending, patient, free
Come, not to sojourn, but abide with me!

Come, not in terrors as the King of kings,
But kind and good, with healing on thy wings;
Tears for all woes, a heart for every plea;
O friend of sinners, thus abide with me!

Thou on my head in early youth did smile.
And though rebellious and perverse meanwhile,
Thou hast not left me, oft as I left thee;
On to the close, O Lord, abide with me!

I need thy presence every passing hour;
What but thy grace can foil the tempter's power?
Who, like thyself, my guide and stay can be?
Through cloud and sunshine, Lord, abide with me!

I fear no foe, with thee at hand to bless;
Ills have no weight, and tears no bitterness;
Where is death's sting? where, grave, thy victory?
I triumph still, if thou abide with me.

Hold thou thy cross before my closing eyes;
Shine through the gloom and point me to the skies;
Heaven's morning breaks, and earth's vain shadows flee
In life, in death, O Lord, abide with me!

LEAD, KINDLY LIGHT

John Henry Newman

Lead, kindly Light, amid the encircling gloom,
        Lead thou me on.
The night is dark, and I am far from home—
        Lead thou me on.
Keep thou my feet; I do not ask to see
The distant scene—one step enough for me.

I was not ever thus, nor prayed that thou
        Shouldst lead me on;
I loved to choose and see my path; but now
        Lead thou me on.
I loved the garish day, and, spite of fears,
Pride ruled my will; remember not past years.

So long thy power hath blest me, sure it still
        Will lead me on,
O'er moor and fen, o'er crag and torrent, till
        The night is gone;
And with the morn those angel faces smile
Which I have loved long since, and lost awhile.

10

PRAYERS AND POEMS OF RELIGION

Prayer has innumerable aspects. It expresses every form of fear and need, and it should include every type of thanksgiving. Entire volumes are, and should be, devoted to the prayers of saints and other illustrious personages, which may well serve as models to lesser folk; but the lesser folk have their prayers, too, none the less fervent, none the less inspired by faith and permeated with it. Examples of these also fill many worthwhile volumes.

In a book like this, it is feasible to include only a very few of each kind, but I have tried to vary these as much as possible. Henry van Dyke's prayer entitled "Work" has always been one of my own favorites. It has been coupled in my affection with one on the same subject by Brian O'Higgins, ever since a domestic worker in an official family where I often visited brought it to me, printed on an illustrated card, one day when I was autographing books at St. Matthew's Book Stall in Washington. She told me it was her model for the prayer she offered for me every night.

In the corner of the blotter on my desk is a card, on which is printed the prayer of Sir Francis Drake before attacking the Spanish Armada. Since this is not written in verse, it could not be printed in one of the main divisions of this book, but I want to mention it here, partly because it represents a constant challenge, and partly because it was so important to the woman to whose memory this book is dedicated, that a tablet with the prayer inscribed on it has been placed in my garden as a memorial to her. This is the prayer: "Give us to know that it is not the beginning but the continuing of the same until it is *entirely finished* which yieldest true glory."

FOR A VERY NEW ANGEL

Violet Allyn Storey

God, God, be lenient her first night there—
The crib she slept in was so near my bed—
Her blue and white wool blanket was so soft . . .
The pillow hollowed so to fit her head.
Teach me that she'll not want small rooms or me
When she has you and heaven's immensity.

I always left a light out in the hall . . .
I hoped to make her fearless in the dark . . .
And yet she was so small . . . one little light,
Not in the room . . . it scarcely mattered—Hark!
No; no; she seldom cried. God, not too far
For her to see, this first night, light a star!

And, in the morning, when she first woke up,
I always kissed her on the left cheek where
The dimple was . . . And, oh, I wet the brush . . .
It made it easier to curl her hair.
Just . . . just tomorrow morning, God, I pray,
When she wakes up, do things for her my way.

A PAGE'S ROAD SONG

William Alexander Percy

Jesu,
If Thou wilt make
Thy peach trees bloom for me,
And fringe my bridle path both sides
With tulips, red and free,
If Thou wilt make Thy skies as blue
As ours in Sicily,
And wake the little leaves that sleep
On every bending tree—
I promise not to vexen Thee
That Thou shouldst make eternally
Heaven my home;
But right contentedly,
A singing page I'll be
Here, in Thy springtime
Jesu.

PRAYER FOR DIFFICULT DAYS

Edgar A. Guest

Lord, grant our little family
The strength to bear life's tasks together;
Let us brave-hearted servants be,
And give us faith for stormy weather;
Grant us the courage for our tasks,
Whatever toil the morning asks.

Lord, bless our happy circle small,
Let neither care nor loss affright us.
Each evening when the shadows fall,
May love and comradeship unite us.
Though steep the hill and rough the way,
Let us not grumble through the day.

Lord, keep us safe from greed and hate
And all the shams which would destroy us;
Teach us against the whims of Fate
To keep our hearts serene and joyous;
And when the evening comes, content,
Grant us to call the day well spent.

GRANT US, O LORD

Anonymous

Grant us, O Lord, the grace to bear
    The little pricking thorn,
The hasty word that seems unfair,
    The twang of truths well worn,
The jest which makes our weakness plain,
    The darling plan o'erturned,
The careless touch upon our pain,
    The slight we have not earned,
The rasp of care; dear Lord, today
    Lest all these fretting things
Make needless grief, oh, give, we pray,
    The heart that trusts and sings!

SOLDIER'S PRAYER

Avery Giles

God, give me strength to fight the fight,
    And courage to withstand a foe
Whose evil shadow clouds Thy light
    With wanton wickedness and woe.

Give me endurance when the way
    Is weary and the road is rough,
And, whatsoever words I say,
    Ignorance of the word, "enough."

Give me the wit to see the fun,
    That carries fighting men along,
And, if my work be quickly done,
    The grace to greet Death with a song.

PRAYER OUT OF GEORGIA

Minnie Hite Moody

Lord, it is for two colored boys I pray,
Two black boys, young and very far away.
I know, dear Lord, that they are scared to death;
I've seen them run till they were out of breath,
Frightened at simple things, the dancing lights
Of Georgia swamplands on October nights—
The chuck-will's-widow's wail, a hootin' owl—
Be with them Lord. A German on the prowl
Along the Sangro is outside their sphere;

They have known only love, year after year,
And a safe world beneath the mimosa tree,
And in the House, indulgent folk like me.

Lord, war is war, and difficult the task
Of all boys, black or white—I cannot ask
That they be safe or spared; I only know
That they are homesick, lonely boys, and so
Send them some little sign on heavenly wing—
A mule's ears flapping would be just the thing,
And even in thickest battle, so I've heard,
Birds sometimes sing—is there a mockingbird
To lift its voice along the Appian Way?
Lord, let them march where there is good red clay!
I know they'll fight like me if they can see
One speck of Georgia there in Italy.

WORK

Henry van Dyke

Let me but do my work from day to day,
In field or forest, at the desk or loom,
In roaring market-place, or tranquil room;
Let me but find it in my heart to say,
When vagrant wishes beckon me astray,
"This is my work; my blessing, not my doom;
Of all who live I am the one by whom
This work can best be done in my own way."
Then shall I see it, not too great nor small
To suit my spirit and arouse my powers;
Then shall I cheerfully greet the laboring hours,
And cheerfully turn, when the long shadows fall
At eventide, to play and love and rest,
Because I know for me my work is best.

GOD BLESS THE WORK

Brian O'Higgins

God bless the work that lies before your hand,
God's blessing be on all that you have done;
For what is fame or gift or treasure grand,
If His approving smile we have not won?

In body and in soul God keep you strong
To toil for Him and never fail through fear;
This is my wish, for you the whole day long,
God bless you every hour of every year!

LORD OF ALL POTS AND PANS

Anonymous

Lord of all pots and pans and things, since I've not time to be
A saint by doing lovely things, or watching late with Thee,
Or dreaming in the dawnlight, or storming heaven's gates,
Make me a saint by getting meals, and washing up the plates.

Although I must have Martha's hands, I have a Mary mind,
And when I black the boots and shine
Thy sandals, Lord, I find,
I think of how they trod the earth, what time I scrub the floor,
Accept this meditation, Lord, I have not time for more.

Warm all the kitchen with Thy love and light it with Thy peace.
Forgive me all my worrying, and make all grumbling cease.
Thou Who didst feed the multitude and break the sea,
Accept this service that I do; I do it unto Thee.

DEAR LORD AND FATHER OF MANKIND

John Greenleaf Whittier

Dear Lord and Father of mankind,
Forgive our feverish ways!
Remould us in our rightful mind,
In purer lives Thy service find,
    In deeper reverence, praise.

In simple trust like theirs who heard
Beside the Syrian sea
The blessed calling of the Lord,
May we, like they, without a word,
    Rise up and follow Thee.

Drop Thy still dews of quietness,
'Til all our strivings cease;
Take from our souls the strain and stress,
And let our ordered lives confess
    The beauty of Thy peace.

Breathe through the heat of our desire,
Thy coolness and Thy balm,
Let sense be dumb, let flesh retire,
Breathe through the earthquake, sword and fire,
    O still small Voice of calm!

HINT HEAVENWARD

Arthur Wallace Peach

Kind Peter, if you hear before
The gates of heaven lofty
A small dog barking patiently
Or whining softly.

Incline your ear and give him heed,
For he is there entreating
Some word about the little chap
Whom he is seeking.

I think you'd better let him in—
He knows no word like "never"—
Or you will find him at your gate
Barking forever!

. . . MY DOG IS DEAD

Anonymous

A Little Boy Prays for His Dog

Dear God,
  They say my dog is dead;
  He had the softest little head;
  He was so good, he'd always do
  Most anything I told him to.

Kind God,
  Sometimes he'd chase a cat,
  (He wasn't often bad like that),
  And if I called him back, he came
  The minute that I said his name.

Please God,
  If he feels scared up there,
  Won't You please let him sleep somewhere
  Near You? Oh, please take care of him
  I love him so! His name is Tim.

THE EASTERNER'S PRAYER

Anonymous

I pray the prayer the Easterners do
May the peace of Allah abide with you!
Wherever you stay, wherever you go,
May the beautiful palms of Allah grow.
Through days of labor and nights of rest,
The love of good Allah make you blest.
So I touch my heart as the Easterners do—
May the peace of Allah abide with you!
                                        Salaam Alaikum

                        (Peace be unto you.)

PRAYER FOR THANKSGIVING

Eleanor Voswinkel

Accept our thanks, O God, for this great bounty:
For garnered fruits and fields of golden wheat;
Enrich our souls with thoughts of love and sharing,
Curtail our wants, that other men may eat.

In distant homes where hunger still is lurking
And fear is rife, Oh give us eyes to see
The empty hearts and hands, remembering,
In aiding them, we give it unto Thee.

Encompass us with faith and understanding,
That happiness and peace again may reign;
And prove to those who gave their lives so gladly,
In giving all, they have not died in vain.

PRAYER FOR A NIGHT OF SNOW

Daniel Whitehead Hickey

Now in the bleak and frozen night, O Lord,
Loosen the white flakes with a gentle hand,
Sharpen the dark winds lesser than a sword
As they step swiftly down the quiet land.
For I have furry brothers in the fields,
Rabbit and squirrel, chipmunk and the mouse;
Beneath this quarreling sky, the snow it yields,
Give them safe shelter in the forests' house.
Let them find food where snow falls not too deep

Over a thicket of berry, a patch of fern;
Cloak them with comfort and a stretch of sleep.
At daybreak, when the slow horizons burn,
Let all my furry brothers of the night
Stare out, triumphant, on your world of white.

"THE PSALMS OF DAVID . . . ARE ENDED"

Mary Taylor

How very far from ended are the Psalms!
Their martial music marches down the years;
Each lonely passing generation hears
Their sweep and power; their tenderness that calms
The troubled human mind; their blessing falls
Upon the heart bowed down; from flaming sword
To pastures and still waters moves The Word;
Healing or militant its message calls.

A shepherd's thoughts enduring to this day!
Each promise is a prayer, each prayer a song
A lyric loveliness for prop and stay,
A faith unflagging when the road is long.
Words destined for the future as the past,
Our rod and staff as long as life shall last.

BENEDICTION

Dorothy Quick

Saints, in your niches set apart,
Regard the human, sinful heart.
See the weak and erring ways
Unknown to you in all your days.

Saints hewn from marble bright and clean,
Look down upon the scarlet sheen
Of sin, and pray as only you
Throughout the years have learned to do.

Saints, in your holy, haloed place,
Pity and help the human race,
Release them from their sin and fear,
And hide not from your eyes the tear
That you have shed, most tortured one,
Your martyrdom, your pain has won,
The right to weep, the right to give
Your blessing so that men may live.

SAINT OF THE LOST

Elizabeth Morrow

Walking Elysian fields the saints forget
The salt of human tears. What went before
Grows faint and far; the most unfortunate
Cry of the heart falls cold; they heed no more.

Only Saint Anthony can never rest,
Searching the depths for what has slipped or gone,
So long as men pray he must be oppressed
So long as men lose, he must labor on,
His face forever turned from Paradise
Lest he should miss that single sparrow's fall;
He finds the strayed sheep with his faithful eyes;
He holds in sight the lonely prodigal:
Saint of the lost who cannot sleep nor stand
While one child wanders from his mother's hand.

ST. FRANCIS PREACHING TO THE BIRDS

(After Giotto)
Isabel Harriss Barr

This little Saint forever stands
A seraphim in brown
Who holds compassion in his hands
With tonsured head bent down;

While at his bare feet now are gathered,
Upon sheer Umbrian grass,
Attentive, small friends, winged and feathered—
Transparent as stained glass.

Here, sheltering the silent birds,
(He counts the least of these)
Earth-rooted as his simple words,
Sky-reaching, timeless trees.

Like grace which makes the lover blessed
Or joy that never ends
Through hallowed air—an unseen guest—
The Spirit Who is Love descends.

INTO THE WOODS MY MASTER WENT

Sidney Lanier

Into the woods my Master went,
Clean forspent, forspent.
Into the woods my Master came,
Forspent with love and shame.
But the olives they were not blind to Him,
The little green leaves were kind to Him,
The thorn tree had a mind to Him,
When into the woods He came.

Out of the woods my Master went,
And He was well content.
Out of the woods my Master came,
Content with death and shame.
When death and shame would woo Him last,
From out of the trees they drew Him last,
'Twas on a tree they slew Him last,
When out of the woods He came.

AND NOW, O FATHER

Anonymous

And now, O Father, mindful of the love
That bought us, once for all, on Calvary's tree,
And having with us Him that pleads above,
We here present, we here spread forth to Thee
That only offering perfect in Thine eyes,
The one true, pure, immortal sacrifice.

Look, Father, look on His anointed face,
And only look on us as found in Him;
Look not on our misusings of Thy grace,
Our prayer so languid, and our faith so dim;
For lo, between our sins and their reward
We set the Passion of Thy Son our Lord.

And then for those, our dearest and our best,
By this prevailing presence we appeal;
O fold them closer to Thy mercy's breast,
O do Thine utmost for their soul's true weal;
From tainting mischief keep them white and clear,
And crown Thy gifts with strength to persevere.

And so we come; O draw us to Thy feet,
Most patient Saviour, Who canst love us still;
And by this food, so awful and so sweet,
Deliver us from every touch of ill:
In Thine own service make us glad and free,
And grant us never more to part with Thee.

11

CHRISTMAS

Every one of the Christmas poems I have chosen tells its own story. It would be presumptuous, as well as superfluous, for me to add a single word or expression to any of them, and my reasons for choosing them must be as obvious as their meaning.

In selecting the poems about youth, I gave three different viewpoints—that of the companion, that of the teacher and that of the mother. This was because I felt them to be equally important. In selecting the poems about Christmas, I realize that I have given only the viewpoint of the person, young or old, who sees it primarily as a joyous religious festival. This is not because I do not realize that there are many others; but in this case I do not consider that they are all equally important. Even the viewpoint of the very young, excited over their glittering trees and their bulging stockings and their bountiful dinners, loses something if it does not include a vision of the Christ Child; and the viewpoint of the adult who, as Christmas Day approaches, is conscious of nothing but sore feet and a sense of strain, must be very close to losing his birthright for a mess of red pottage.

Now that I am old enough to look back on a great many Christmases, spent in many ways in many lands, I can truthfully say that most of them were happy occasions. (In fact, I can recall only three that were not.) As a child, I was one of a large group of cousins who made merry together at the home of some older relative, given to expansive hospitality. As a young girl, I was the fortunate guest of a noble German family whose celebration began on Christmas Eve and lasted straight through to *Sylvestre Abend,* as they called New Year's Eve. As a young mother, I shared the excitement of three little boys. As a grandmother, I am usually the matriarch of a family gathering that ranges in number from ten to twenty. But two years ago it so happened that I was alone on Christmas Eve, not because no one had asked to have me spend it in company, but because I wanted it otherwise. To be sure, on Christmas Day I gratefully accepted invitations to go out for both dinner and supper. But on Christmas Eve I sat alone with both memories and hopes, in the paneled parlor of the Oxbow, which is the home I love above all others, until it was time to go to Midnight Mass; and that quiet, candle-lighted room seemed permeated not only with the peace that passeth all understanding, but with the true spirit of Christmas. I wish that every elderly woman who dreads a lonely Christmas would try the experiment that I made. I believe she would have a happy surprise. And I also believe, if she should chance to read this book, that she would understand why I chose only one kind of poem about Christmas.

JOY TO THE WORLD! THE LORD IS COME

Isaac Watts

Joy to the world! the Lord is come;
Let earth receive her King,
Let every heart prepare him room,
And heaven and nature sing.

Joy to the earth! the Saviour reigns:
Let men their songs employ.
While fields and floods, rocks, hills and plains
Repeat the sounding joy.

He rules the world with truth and grace,
And makes the nations prove
The glories of his righteousness,
And wonders of his love.

HOW MANY MILES TO BETHLEHEM

Frances Chesterton

How far is it to Bethlehem? Not very far.
Shall we find the stable-room lit by a star?
Can we see the little Child? Is he within?
If we lift the wooden latch, may we go in?
May we stroke the creatures there, ox, ass or sheep?
May we peep like them and see Jesus asleep?
If we touch His tiny hand, will He awake?
Will He know we've come so far, just for His sake?
Great kings have precious gifts, and we have nought,
Little smiles, little tears are all we have brought.
For all weary children Mary must weep.
Here, on His bed of straw, sleep, children, sleep.
God in His Mother's arms, babes in the byre,
Sleep as they sleep who find their heart's desire.

AND THEY CAME WITH HASTE

Sister Mary Irma

And whom do you think the shepherds saw
Kneeling there on the golden straw,
But a Shepherdess in a woolly cap
And woolly mitts
And a lambskin coat
With the wool turned in
Buttoned up to her pretty chin,
And her crook beside her as she bent
Over the crib with eyes intent.

And when they came nearer
And looked there too,
They skipped with joy,
For at once they knew
That the baby Boy
Wrapped up tight in swaddling bands
Save only His head and His waving hands
Was Son of David, the shepherd king,
Shepherd of Shepherds,
Lamb of God.

A star stood over the crib that night,
But all that it saw was a blaze of light.

And the Wise Men saw
A Princess there
In a gown of silk,
With gems in her hair,
And hands like milk,
And a courteous air,
Who lifted to bless them
An Infant King

With a triple crown
And a big seal ring.
And they said: "She comes
From a far country,
Richer than ours;
She is wiser than we;
And Regent she is for her Son the King.
Would we had gifts
More meet to bring!"

And they clapped their hands,
And boys unrolled
The tangy myrrh
And the yellow gold;
And incense rose in a purple cloud,
And the Princess smiled,
And the Prince allowed
The sages to come to His feet and kneel,
And He signed each one
With the sacred seal.
Then Joseph said,
"You must all go home
And tell your friends
Their King has come,"
And all the visitors said good night
And went away,
And the lantern light
Shone on the haloed heads a-nod
Of guardian, Mother, and Son of God.

THE MAID-SERVANT AT THE INN

Dorothy Parker

"It's queer," she said, "I see the light
   As plain as I beheld it then,
All silver-like and calm and bright—
   We've not had stars like that again!

"And she was such a gentle thing
   To birth a baby in the cold.
The barn was dark and frightening—
   This new one's better than the old.

"I mind my eyes were full of tears,
   For I was young, and quick distressed,
But she was less than me in years
   That held a son against her breast.

"I never saw a sweeter child—
   The little one, the darling one!—
I mind I told her, when he smiled
   You'd know he was his mother's son.

"It's queer that I should see them so—
   The time they came to Bethlehem
Was more than thirty years ago;
   I've prayed that all is well with them."

THE EARTH HAS GROWN OLD

Phillips Brooks

The earth has grown old with its burdens of care,
But at Christmas it always is young;
The heart of the jewel burns lustrous and fair,
And its soul, full of music, breaks forth on the air
When the song of the angels is sung.

It is coming, old earth, it is coming tonight!
On the snowflakes which cover thy sod,
The feet of the Christ-child fall gentle and white,
And the voice of the Christ-child tells out with delight
That mankind are the children of God.

O LITTLE TOWN OF BETHLEHEM

Phillips Brooks

O little town of Bethlehem,
How still we see thee lie!
Above thy deep and dreamless sleep
The silent stars go by;
Yet in thy dark streets shineth
The everlasting light;
The hopes and fears of all the years
Are met in thee tonight.

For Christ is born of Mary,
And gathered all above,
While mortals sleep, the angels keep
Their watch of wondering love.
O morning stars, together
Proclaim the holy birth!
And praises sing to God the King
And peace to men on earth.

How silently, how silently,
The wondrous gift is given!
So God imparts to human hearts
The blessing of His heaven.
No ear may hear His coming,
But in this world of sin,
Where meek souls will receive Him still,
The dear Christ enters in.

O holy Child of Bethlehem!
Descend to us, we pray;
Cast out our sin, and enter in;
Be born in us today.
We hear the Christmas angels
The great glad tidings tell;
O come to us, abide with us,
Our Lord Emmanuel!

WHILE SHEPHERDS WATCHED
THEIR FLOCKS BY NIGHT

N. Tate

While shepherds watched their flocks by night, all seated on the
  ground
The angel of the Lord came down, and glory shone around.
"Fear not," said he, for mighty dread had seized their troubled mind;
"Glad tidings of great joy I bring to you and all mankind.

"To you, in David's town, this day is born of David's line
The Saviour, who is Christ the Lord; and this shall be the sign:
The heavenly Babe you there shall find to human view displayed,
All meanly wrapt in swathing bands, and in a manger laid."

Thus spake the seraph; and forthwith appeared a shining throng
Of angels, praising God, who thus addressed their joyful song:
"All glory be to God on high, and to the earth be peace;
Good-will henceforth from heaven to men begin, and never cease."

IT CAME UPON THE MIDNIGHT CLEAR

E. H. Sears

It came upon the midnight clear,
That glorious song of old,
From angels bending near the earth
To touch their harps of gold;
Peace on the earth, good-will to men,
From heaven's all gracious King;
The world in solemn stillness lay
To hear the angels sing.

Still through the cloven skies they come,
With peaceful wings unfurled,
And still their heavenly music floats
O'er all the weary world;
Above its sad and lowly plains
They bend on heavenly wing,
And ever o'er its Babel sounds
The blessed angels sing.

O ye, beneath life's crushing load,
Whose forms are bending low,
Who toil along the climbing way
With painful steps and slow,
Look now! for glad and golden hours
Come swiftly on the wing;
O rest beside the weary road,
And hear the angels sing.

For lo! the days are hastening on,
By prophet bards foretold,
When with the ever circling years
Comes round the age of gold;
When peace shall over all the earth
Its ancient splendors fling,
And the whole world send back the song
Which now the angels sing.

OH COME, ALL YE FAITHFUL

Anonymous

Translated by F. Oakeley

Oh come, all ye faithful, joyful and triumphant,
Oh come ye, oh come ye to Bethlehem;
Come and behold Him, born the King of angels;
Oh come, let us adore Him, oh come, let us adore Him,
Oh come, let us adore Him, Christ the Lord.

God of God, Light of Light,
Lo! He abhors not the Virgin's womb;
Very God, begotten, not created;
Oh come, let us adore Him, oh come, let us adore Him,
Oh come, let us adore Him, Christ the Lord.

Sing, Choirs of Angels, sing in exultation,
Sing, all ye citizens of heaven above;
Glory to God in the highest;
Oh come, let us adore Him, oh come, let us adore Him,
Oh come, let us adore Him, Christ the Lord.

Yea, Lord, we greet Thee, born this happy morning,
Jesus, to Thee be glory given;
Word of the Father, now in flesh appearing;
Oh come, let us adore Him, oh come, let us adore Him,
Oh come, let us adore Him, Christ the Lord.

CHRISTMAS EVE

James Dillet Freeman

There is no star to signal our safekeeping
This Christmas Eve, no angel music to
Ring though the dark and wake us from our sleeping;
The silent night contains no sign from You,
Lord. Yet as once the shepherds and the cattle
Knelt by a stall, tonight we kneel again
And, listening, catch above the noise of battle
Once more a whisper of good will toward men,
Not from the skies, not from an angel chorus,
But in our own heart's still small voice of love
That bids us keep the shining goal before us,
Nor be dismayed, finding no star above—
For You are to be born in our own mind;
There lies the hope of peace for humankind.

CHRISTMAS

Aline Kilmer

"And shall you have a Tree," they say,
"Now one is dead and one away?"
Oh, I shall have a Christmas Tree!
Brighter than ever it shall be;
Dressed out with colored lights to make
The room all glorious for your sake.
And under the Tree a Child shall sleep
Near shepherds watching their wooden sheep.

Threads of silver and ropes of gold,
Scarlet bubbles the Tree shall hold,
And little glass bells that tinkle clear.
I shall trim it alone but feel you near.
And when Christmas Day is almost done,
When they all grow sleepy one by one,
When Kenton's books have all been read,
When Deborah's climbing the stairs to bed,
I shall sit alone by the fire and see
Ghosts of you both come close to me.
For the dead and the absent always stay
With the one they love on Christmas Day.

A CHRISTMAS CROSS

William Boyd Allen

No fir tree in the forest dark
    But humbly bears its cross;
No human heart in God's wide world
    But mourns its bitter loss.

Yet Christmas-tide can clothe the fir
    In splendors all unguessed,
And bring to every suffering heart,
    Its joy, its peace, its rest.

God rest you then, my gentle friend,
    And take your cross away,
Or clothe it with a radiance new,
    On this glad Christmas Day.

HER CHRISTMAS TREE

Eugene T. Maleska

Four is no age to watch when older hands
Take down the worn and brittle evergreen;
Tomorrow tell her dwarfs from wonderlands
Have borrowed it to give a fairy queen
Her Christmas Tree—
Or Old St. Nick has taken it once more
To brighten some poor orphan's winter day.
. . . Four is no age to watch, if thirty-four
Must struggle with his heart to throw away
Her Christmas Tree.

GOD BLESS THE LITTLE THINGS

Margaret Murray

God Bless the little things this Christmastide
All the little wild things that live outside
Little cold robins and rabbits in the snow
Give them good faring and a warm place to go
All the little young things for His sake Who died
Who was a little thing at Christmastide.

WE THREE KINGS OF ORIENT ARE

John H. Hopkins

We three kings of Orient are;
Bearing gifts we traverse afar
Field and fountain, moor and mountain,
Following yonder star.
> O star of wonder, star of night, Star with royal beauty bright,
> Westward leading, still proceeding, Guide us to Thy perfect
> light.

Born a King on Bethlehem's plain,
Gold I bring to crown Him again,
King forever, ceasing never
Over us all to reign.
> O star of wonder, star of night, Star with royal beauty bright,
> Westward leading, still proceeding, Guide us to Thy perfect
> light.

Frankincense to offer have I;
Incense owns a Deity nigh;
Prayer and praising all men raising,
Worship Him, God on high.
> O star of wonder, star of night, Star with royal beauty bright,
> Westward leading, still proceeding, Guide us to Thy perfect
> light.

Myrrh is mine: its bitter perfume
Breathes a life of gathering gloom:
Sorrowing, sighing, bleeding, dying,
Sealèd in the stone-cold tomb.
> O star of wonder, star of night, Star with royal beauty bright,
> Westward leading, still proceeding, Guide us to Thy perfect
> light.

Glorious now behold Him arise,
King and God and Sacrifice;
Alleluia, Alleluia!
Sounds through the earth and skies.

O star of wonder, star of night, Star with royal beauty bright,
Westward leading, still proceeding, Guide us to Thy perfect
light.

LITTLE CHRISTMAS

Mazie V. Caruthers

Ending now the twelve days are.
Faded is the Christmas Star.
And the trio of the Kings
Comes with final offerings.
Soon the crèche, warm-lined with hay,
Where the little Jesus lay—
Mary, with her snood of blue—
Bearded Joseph, gaunt and true—
Shepherds kneeling on the ground,
With their cattle grouped around—
All the symbols of this Day
For a year we'll put away.

But—if by a tree of lights
One has sought that Night of Nights,
As a simple child to find
Old-time faith and peace of mind—
Turned a while from selfish living—
Learned again the joy of giving—
Heard the angels' glad refrain—
Christmas has not been in vain.

12

PHILOSOPHY OF LIFE

Philosophy of life is a term so inclusive that it embraces almost every attitude of mind, from the frankly cynical to the deeply religious. Dorothy Parker has always been a source of delight to me, and her poem, "Inventory," is probably the one that I quote oftener than any other, but this is the second book in which I have given a prominent place to "A Pilgrim's Journey"; and I have found a valuable supplement to it in the poem which ends:

> Stray roads lead to Heaven;
> Those with fearless eyes
> Are the only pilgrims
> Who find Paradise.

Stray roads lead us logically to "Many Roads," which is the title of a poem that points the middle way; and, lest we become too absorbed in progress and direction, it is well to remember that dreams, too, have their proper place in the philosophy of life. It should be a source of encouragement to note that

> No dream endures against a distant day
> But that it falls unnumbered times to earth

and to recall one of the most telling retorts made in the whole realm of poetry:

> 'A dreamer thou,' said the West to the East,
> 'Supine on thy sunbaked sod.
> What recks the world of thy temple and priest?
> A dreamer thou!'—Said the East to the West,
> 'Aye, but I dream of God.'*

* —(All great religions have come from the East.)

231

SOCIAL NOTE

Dorothy Parker

Lady, lady, should you meet
One whose ways are all discreet,
One who murmurs that his wife
Is the lodestar of his life,
One who keeps assuring you
That he never was untrue,
Never loved another one . . .
Lady, lady, better run!

INVENTORY

Dorothy Parker

Four be the things I am wiser to know:
Idleness, sorrow, a friend, and a foe.

Four be the things I'd been better without:
Love, curiosity, freckles, and doubt.

Three be the things I shall never attain:
Envy, content, and sufficient champagne.

Three be the things I shall have till I die:
Laughter and hope and a sock in the eye.

THE RUBÁIYÁT OF OMAR KHAYYÁM

Translated by Edward Fitzgerald

(*Extract*)

Come, fill the Cup, and in the fire of Spring
Your Winter-garment of Repentance fling:
The Bird of Time has but a little way
To flutter—and the Bird is on the Wing.

I sometimes think that never blows so red
The Rose as where some buried Caesar bled;
And every Hyacinth the Garden wears
Dropt in her Lap from some once lovely Head.

Ah, my Beloved, fill the Cup that clears
Today of past Regrets and future Fears:
Tomorrow! Why, Tomorrow I may be
Myself with Yesterday's Sev'n Thousand Years.

Myself when young did eagerly frequent
Doctor and Saint, and heard great argument
About it and about: but evermore
Came out by the same door where in I went.

There was the door to which I found no Key;
There was the Veil through which I might not see:
Some little talk awhile of ME and THEE
There was—and then no more of THEE and ME.

THE HOLY WOMEN

William Alexander Percy

I have seen Mary at the cross
　　And Mary at the tomb
And Mary weeping as she spread her hair
　　In a leper's room.

But it was not in Bethany
　　Or groping up Calvary hill
I learned how women break their hearts to ease
　　Another's ill.

Compassionate and wise in pain,
　　Most faithful in defeat,
The holy Marys I have watched and loved
　　Live on our street.

WORK

A Song of Triumph

Angela Morgan

Work!
Thank God for the might of it,
The ardor, the urge, the delight of it—
Work that springs from the heart's desire,
Setting the brain and the soul on fire—

Oh, what is so good as the heat of it,
And what is so glad as the beat of it,
And what is so kind as the stern command,
Challenging brain and heart and hand?

Work!
Thank God for the pride of it,
For the beautiful, conquering tide of it,
Sweeping the life in its furious flood,
Thrilling the arteries, cleansing the blood,
Mastering stupor and dull despair,
Moving the dreamer to do and dare.
Oh, what is so good as the urge of it,
And what is so glad as the surge of it,
And what is so strong as the summons deep,
Rousing the torpid soul from sleep?

Work!
Thank God for the pace of it,
For the terrible, keen, swift race of it;
Fiery steeds in full control,
Nostrils a-quiver to greet the goal.
Work the Power that drives behind,
Guiding the purposes, taming the mind,
Holding the runaway wishes back,
Reining the will to one steady track,
Speeding the energies faster, faster,
Triumphing over disaster.
Oh, what is so good as the pain of it,
And what is so great as the gain of it?
And what is so kind as the cruel goad,
Forcing us on through the rugged road?

Work!
Thank God for the swing of it,
For the clamoring, hammering ring of it,
Passion of labor daily hurled
On the mighty anvils of the world.
Oh, what is so fierce as the flame of it?

And what is so huge as the aim of it?
Thundering on through dearth and doubt,
Calling the plan of the Maker out.
Work, the Titan; Work, the friend,
Shaping the earth to a glorious end,
Draining the swamps and blasting the hills,
Doing whatever the Spirit wills—
Rending a continent apart,
To answer the dream of the Master heart.
Thank God for a world where none may shirk—
Thank God for the splendor of work!

I HAVE LIVED

Anonymous

I have lived and I have loved;
I have waked and I have slept;
I have sung and I have danced;
I have smiled and I have wept;
I have won and wasted treasure;
I have had my fill of pleasure;
And all these things were weariness,
And some of them were dreariness,
And all these things—but two things—
Were emptiness and pain;
And Love—it was the best of them;
And Sleep—worth all the rest of them.

TOMORROW

Edward D. Garner

There always is tomorrow, and it is
The steed of hope that all men mount at dawn,
To seek anew the road, the path, the door
To the Dream's flowering, as they gallop on.

ADVICE TO DREAMERS

Ralph Friedrich

The excellence of stillness and the great
Reward of silence when the dream has taken
Its sudden flight beyond the ultimate
Dominion of the mind; the heart unshaken,
The eyes unstartled, lest despair awaken
The god's swift anger or the ire of fate—
These shall avail when beauty has forsaken
Awhile the dreamer in his strange estate.

No dream endures against a distant day
But that it falls unnumbered times to earth.
No joy achieves bright immortality
Despite the early splendor of its birth:
The wise are well acquainted with its way;
Theirs is the secret of tranquility.

WISHES

Edgar A. Guest

I'd like to dream a little by the fire,
I've many books I've set aside to read.
An idle day has been my heart's desire.
But still I seem to travel at full speed.
Always the day must have its little deed
Always at night there's somewhere we must go.
The doctors say that rest is what I need
I don't suppose I'll ever get it though.

At times of busy streets I seem to tire,
I've dreamed of poultry of my own to feed,
Hip boots in springtime when the ground's all mire,
But still a cash and carry life I lead.
The country calls me, but I pay no heed,
There are too many city folks I owe,
I'd like a farm where pheasants mate and breed,
I don't suppose I'll ever get it though.

'Tis not to fame or greatness I aspire,
Merely from constant duty I'd be freed.
I'd like to tramp a roadway and inquire.
If strangers would a hungry mortal feed.
I'd like to dig a plot and plant the seed
And spend the summer watching blossoms grow;
I'd like the time to study vine and reed.
I don't suppose I'll ever get it though.

'Tis not in disappointment that I plead;
I live this life as have the fates decreed.
But I would like an easier row to hoe,
I don't suppose I'll ever get it though.

STRAY ROADS

Helen Welshimer

Stray roads lead to Heaven—
You must take a chance
On a moon at midnight,
Or a gypsy dance.

Now and then a fiddler
Plays a tune, gay, sweet,
And an inn with candles
Offers warm retreat.

Sometimes lamps shine brightly,
And a rhyming rain
Falls with dark blue magic
On a window pane.

Stray roads lead to Heaven—
Those with fearless eyes
Are the only pilgrims
Who find Paradise.

IN DUE SEASON

John Drinkwater

The Spring was cold, chill north, chill east
   The grieving skies forbade the May.
Earth, of her Winter weeds released,
   Was sullen yet in April gray;
Bleak airs about the woodland stirred,
And tardy was the nesting bird.

Yet now full-born is Summer seen
   On branches that too long were bare,
Steeping the wilderness in green
   And dropping richness everywhere,
High Summer teeming from a prime
That gave no pledge of Summertime.

The soul has barren seasons, too,
   Or seasons that most barren seem;
Our ways are darkness, and we do
   Less than the phantoms of a dream;
A Summer of the soul is here.

FOUR THINGS

Prudence K. Gearey

These things are beautiful beyond belief:
The pleasant weakness that comes after pain,
The radiant greenness that comes after rain,
The deepened faith that follows after grief,
And the awakening to love again.

THE SMALL TASK

Malvina Lindsay

I wash the dishes—the same dishes,
I washed last night;
I hang up the tea towel and complete my small routine
Of kitchen duties, quietly and passively;
Today I do not hurry or impatiently try to push behind me
The drudgery that perpetually obstructs my path
To rest, to play, to deeds of fame and high renown.

I take mechanically each little duty as it comes,
Thankful for work,
The kindest and most comforting friend in sorrow,
With its firm but gentle whispering
"Life must go on—it is your part to carry it forward;"
And so I pick up all the trailing ends and mend the wedges,
Seeing these obscure figments pattern into something big.

I perform the petty task in home or office,
With a new dignity;
For all tasks now are equal at this perilous time
When freedom of the human spirit hangs in balance,
And I at least am blest to go in quietude and safety,
To do my stint, and to find in its absorption
A temporary Lethe from the fear and evil that prevail.

I carry on willingly the everyday endeavor,
For it is now a symbol
Of all that we have gained as women of the race,
And kept alive through all the tortuous years behind us,
As we have sought to give the world more comfort, peace and beauty;
And in these cups I wash, I know that somehow is preserved
That dream of better things that cannot, must not, fail to come to
   fruit.

LES DEUX ARTS

Marion Ward

The artist has the hillside for his prod,
The poet nothing but the mind's swift thunder;
The artist has the colors mixed by God,
The poet nothing but the tintless wonder
Of thought. And yet the memory retains
To the cold end words that no canvas owns;
The eye that drank the galleries entrains
At death, remembering the sturdy tones
Of one lean line that reached its inner night:
A quatrain or sonnet or a song
Sustains a spirit moving into flight.
Paintings possess us once, but not for long.
The brightest pictures dull when we are old,
But the dark words of poets turn to gold.

IMMORTALITY

Emily Dickinson

My life closed twice before its close;
    It yet remains to see
If Immortality unveil
    A third event to me,

So huge, so hopeless to conceive,
    As these that twice befell.
Parting is all we know of heaven,
    And all we need of hell.

THE LADIES

Rudyard Kipling

I've taken my fun where I've found it;
    I've rogued an' I've ranged in my time;
I've 'ad my pickin' o' sweet'earts,
    An' four o' the lot was prime.
One was an 'arf-caste widow,
    One was a woman at Prome,
One was the wife of a *jemadar-sais*,[1]
    An' one is a girl at 'ome.

Now I aren't no 'and with the ladies,
    For, takin' 'em all along,
You never can say till you've tried 'em,
    An' then you are like to be wrong.

[1] Head-groom.

There's times when you'll think that you mightn't,
    There's times when you'll know that you might;
But the things you will learn from the Yellow an' Brown,
    They'll 'elp you an 'eap with the White!

I was a young un at 'Oogli,
    Shy as a girl to begin;
Aggie de Castrer she made me,
    An' Aggie was clever as sin;
Older than me, but my first un—
    More like a mother she were—
Showed me the way to promotion an' pay,
    An' I learned about women from 'er.

Then I was ordered to Burma,
    Actin' in charge o' Bazar,
An' I got me a tiddy live 'eathen
    Through buyin' supplies off 'er pa.
Funny an' yellow an' faithful—
    Doll in a teacup she were,
But we lived on the square, like a true-married pair,
    An' I learned about women from 'er.

Then we was shifted to Neemuch
    (Or I might ha' been keepin' 'er now),
An' I took with a shiny she-devil,
    The wife of a nigger a Mhow;
'Taught me the gipsy-folks *bolee*,[2]
    Kind o' volcano she were,
For she knifed me one night 'cause I wished she was white,
    And I learned about women from 'er.

Then I come 'ome in the trooper,
    'Long of a kid o' sixteen—
Girl from a convent at Meerut,
    The straightest I ever 'ave seen.

2 Slang.

Love at first sight was 'er trouble,
　She didn't know what it were;
An' I wouldn't do such, 'cause I liked 'er too much
　But—I learned about women from 'er.

I've taken my fun where I've found it,
　An' now I must pay for my fun,
For the more you 'ave known o' the others
　The less will you settle to one;
An' the end of it's sittin' and thinkin',
　An' dreamin' Hell-fires to see;
So be warned by my lot (which I know you will not),
　An' learn about women from me!

What did the Colonel's lady think?
　Nobody never knew.
Somebody asked the sergeant's wife,
　An' she told 'em true.
When you get to a man in the case,
　They're like as a row of pins—
For the colonel's lady an' Judy O'Grady
　Are sisters under their skins!

EAST AND WEST

(All religions have come from the east)

Anonymous

"A dreamer thou" sneered the West to the East
　"Supine on sun-parched sod
　　"Naught recks the world of thy temple and priest,
　　"A dreamer thou!"
Smiled the East to the West;
　"Aye—but I dream of God."

EACH IN HIS OWN TONGUE

Anonymous

"A fire mist and a planet, a crystal and a cell,
A jellyfish and saurian and caves where the cavemen dwell.
Then a sense of law and beauty, and a face turned from the sod.
Some call it Evolution, others call it God.

"A haze on the far horizon, the infinite, tender sky,
The ripe, rich tints of the cornfield and the wild geese sailing high
And all over upland and lowland the charm of the goldenrod.
Some of us call it Autumn, others call it God.

"Like tides on a crescent sea beach, when the moon is new and thin,
Into our hearts high yearnings come welling and surging in,
Come from the mystic ocean whose rim no foot hath trod.
Some of us call it longing, others call it God.

"A picket frozen on duty, a mother starved for her brood,
Socrates drinking the hemlock, and Jesus on the rood;
And millions who, humble and nameless, the straight, hard pathway
    plod.
Some call it consecration, others call it God."

A PILGRIM'S JOURNEY

Anonymous

I must go forth upon a pilgrim's journey
Along a strange and dimly hidden road;
I cannot see what joy or care
Is waiting for me there
Nor can I tell its length or test my load.
But this I know,
That faith will light my journey,
And mercy share the burden I must bring;
That love divine will ever tread the road with me,
And lead the pilgrim to the palace of the King.

The road I'll take upon my pilgrim's journey
May tread its way thro' sunny valleys fair;
May lie in gloom, may even lead
Where danger waits for me,
And I may find both joy and sorrow there.
But this I know,
That faith will light my journey,
And mercy share the burden I must bring;
That love divine will ever tread the road with me,
And lead the pilgrim to the palace of the King.

13

COURAGE AND PATRIOTISM

The charming poem, "For a Six-Year-Old", with which I have begun this section, poses a problem to much older persons as well. War is not the only test of patriotism; courage is shown under many circumstances, unconnected with shot and shell. Therefore, while presenting several poems telling the varied aspects of major wars, I have also chosen some personal aspects of courage when conflict was of an entirely different nature.

And, again, in this section as in those devoted to *Friendship and Love, Older Grown* and *Prayers,* I have included a poem which has a special significance to me personally. At a time when I was hesitating to take a step which for me would be a rather rash one, but which would mean a great gain, both materially and spiritually, if I could do so without disaster, I found a small package, wrapped in plain paper, lying on my desk, when I came home after a long disheartening day's work. Everything I had tried to do had turned out wrong and my courage was at a very low ebb. Far from feeling that I ought to be more daring than ever before, I felt there was no use in trying to do much of anything, and I opened the package without much interest. It contained an unpretentious volume of verse, entitled POEMS OF NEVADA. On one page, a sheet of pink scratch-paper with the letterhead, "United States Senate", was clipped to a poem headed "Action". This type of scratch-paper was then distributed to all ninety-six Senators; there was nothing in the least distinctive about it, and there was no message on the sheet before me. But I instantly knew who had clipped it to that poem, and why!

The next day I unhesitatingly took the step that had seemed to me so rash, and it marked a turning point in my career as a writer.

I was deeply interested later on to find much the same sentiments expressed in "Last Word" that I had found in "Action", and take pleasure in presenting these two poems in sequence, as I have done in several other cases where the same subject is treated by different authors, each shedding a new radiance on it.

FOR A SIX-YEAR-OLD

Frances Rodman

How shall I tell you what the years have taught—
That courage does not always march to airs
Blown by a bugle: is not always wrought
Out of the fabric ostentation wears.

Courage is sometimes frail as hope is frail:
A fragile shoot between two stones, that grows
Brave toward the sun though warmth and brightness fail,
Striving and faith the only strength it knows.

How shall I tell you of the world you face
Strident with sound of weapons and of hate,
Make you aware now of the narrowing space
Between the hope of mortal and his fate?
How shall I tell you this, whose only words
Were learned in love: how give you eyes to see
And ears to hear, who follow the flight of birds
Across a sky where clouds drift slow and free?

How teach you courage who have known no fear,
How fashion armor for one so small, so dear?

ACTION

Sam P. Davis

Better to sink with tempests raging o'er
Masts all dismantled and hull gaping wide
Than rest and rot on some unclouded shore
The idle plaything of the listless tide.

Better the grime of battle on the brow,
With grim defeat to crush thy dying hand
Than through long years of peace to tyrant bow
Or dwell a captive in a strangers land.

Better the castle with beleaguered gate,
By battle's lightning shivered in a day
Than peaceful walls in pomp of sullen state,
Through centuries sinking to a dull decay.

Better resolve to win thy heart's desire,
And striving bravely, die in the endeavor
Than have the embers of some smothered fire
Lie smouldering in thy saddened soul forever.

LAST WORD

Harry Kemp

The Captain who puts boldly out to sea
And does not skirt the cowardly coast, has led
Ever, Man's long advance: speak not to me
Of cautious charts and old men's proverbs said
To drag against the soaring ecstasy.
Without God's fools where would the Present be?—
Bridegrooms who took Disaster to their bed
And gave the world a golden progeny!

To woo Destruction with so fair a face
Is better than to rot in one sure place:
Sometimes a Cause is nothing till it's lost.
For all this soon-dreamed, passing life of ours
And fear of thorns that guard consummate flowers,
Give me the man who does not count the cost!

HIS CHOICE

Anna R. Baker

Given Hamlet's choice—to be or not to be—
He chose unerringly the vital first;
He chose erodent hunger, stinging thirst
Rather than milk and honey; chose the free
Upfling of billows in a lively sea,
Not waves that gently break but never burst.
His choice was made, let come the best or worst,
To taste of life before eternity.

So living, careless of the alternate death,
He slept, but not to dream hypnotic dreams,
Rowed up, not down, the rapid-fretted streams
Shouting with confidence his shibboleth.
And the final flood that quenched his lantern's beams
He fought to the last harsh, unrelenting breath.

INVICTUS

William Ernest Henley

Out of the night that covers me,
   Black as the pit from pole to pole,
I thank whatever gods may be,
   For my unconquerable soul.

In the fell clutch of circumstance
   I have not winced nor cried aloud.
Under the bludgeonings of chance
   My head is bloody but unbowed.

Beyond this place of wrath and tears
   Looms but the horror of the shade,
And yet the menace of the years
   Finds and shall find me unafraid.

It matters not how straight the gate
   How charged with punishments the scroll,
I am the master of my fate,
   I am the captain of my soul.

FROM THE WHITE CLIFFS

Alice Duer Miller

The English love their country with a love
Steady, and simple, wordless, dignified;
I think it sets their patriotism above
All others. We Americans have pride—
We glory in our country's short romance.
We boast of it, and love it. Frenchmen, when
The ultimate menace comes, will die for France
Logically as they lived. But Englishmen
Will serve day after day, obey the law,
And do dull tasks that keep a nation strong.
Once I remember in London how I saw
Pale shabby people standing in a long
Line in the twilight and the misty rain
To pay their tax. I then saw England plain.

ALERT: LONDON

Milton Bracker

There go the guns. The shocked and trembling air
Assails the windows; strident terror sings
Within my heart. Above, unseen, somewhere
Huge hummingbirds with rigid, bloodless wings
Are prowling, probing, readying to strike.
Where will it be? And who will die tonight?—
I ask myself, uneasy and unlike
These veterans who find the tension slight.

Again the loaded guns. I dare not smile
Yet comfort surges from their dogged boom,
For they talk back like heroes, proudly, while
I hunch, damp-fingered, in the blacked-out room.
There go the guns! As if I'd knelt and prayed,
New faith infects me. I am unafraid.

JOHN OF GAUNT'S SPEECH ON ENGLAND
(FROM RICHARD II)

William Shakespeare

This royal throne of kings, this scepter'd isle,
This earth of majesty, this seat of Mars,
This other Eden, demi-paradise;
This fortress built by Nature for herself
Against infection and the hand of war;
This happy breed of men, this little world,
This precious stone, set in the silver sea,
Which serves it in the office of a wall,
Or as a moat defensive to a house,
Against the envy of less happier lands;
This blessed plot, this earth, this realm, this England . . .
. . . That England, that was wont to conquer others,
Hath made a shameful conquest of itself.
Ah, would the scandal vanish with my life,
How happy then were my ensuing death!

CONCORD HYMN

Ralph Waldo Emerson

By the rude bridge that arched the flood,
Their flag to April's breeze unfurled,
Here once the embattled farmers stood,
And fired the shot heard 'round the world.

The foe long since in silence slept;
Alike the conqueror silent sleeps;
And Time the ruined bridge has swept
Down the dark stream which seaward creeps.

On this green bank, by this soft stream,
We set this day a votive stone;
That memory may their deeds redeem,
When, like our sires, our sons are gone.

Spirit, that made those spirits dare
To die, and leave their children free,
Bid Time and Nature gently spare
The shaft we raise to them and thee.

THE BIVOUAC OF THE DEAD

Theodore O'Hara

The muffled drum's sad roll has beat
The soldiers' last tattoo,
No more on life's parade shall meet

That brave and fallen few.
On Fame's eternal camping ground
Their silent tents are spread
And Glory guards with solemn round,
The bivouac of the dead.

No rumor of the foe's advance,
Now swells upon the wind,
No troubled thought at midnight haunts
Of loved ones left behind;
No vision of the morrow's strife
The warrior's dream alarms;
No braying horn or screaming fife
At dawn shall call to arms.

Their shivered swords are red with rust,
Their plumed heads are bowed;
Their haughty banner, trailed in dust,
Is now their martial shroud,
And plenteous funeral tears have washed
The red stains from each brow,
And the proud forms, by battle gashed,
Are free from anguish now.

The neighing troop, the flashing blade,
The bugle's stirring blast,
The charge, the dreadful cannonade,
The din and shout are past;
No war's shrill note, no cannon's peal,
Shall thrill with fierce delight
Those breasts that never more may feel
The rapture of the fight.

Like the fierce northern hurricane
That sweeps his great plateau,
Flushed with the triumph yet to gain,
Came down the serried foe.
Who heard the thunder of the fray
Break o'er the field beneath,

Knew well the watchword of that day
Was "Victory or Death".

Long has the doubtful conflict raged
O'er all that stricken plain,
For never fiercer fight had waged
The vengeful blood of Spain.
And still the storm of battle blew,
Still swelled the gory tide;
Not long our stout old chieftain knew,
Such odds his strength could bide.

'Twas in that hour his stern command
Called to a martyr's grave,
The flower of his beloved land,
The nation's flag to save.
By rivers of their father's gore
His firstborn laurels grew,
And well he deemed the sons would pour
Their lives for glory, too.

Full many a norther's breath has swept
O'er Angostura's plain—
And long the pitying sky has wept
Above the mouldering slain.
The raven's scream, the eagle's flight
Or shepherd's pensive lay,
Alone shall wake each sullen height
That frowned o'er that dread fray.

Sons of the Dark and Bloody Ground,
You must not slumber there,
Where stranger steps and tongues resound
Along the heedless air.
Your own proud land's heroic soil
Shall be your fitter grave;
She claims from War his richest spoil,
The ashes of her brave.

Thus, 'neath the shaded turf they rest
Far from the gory field,
Borne to a Spartan mother's breast
On many a bloody shield;
The sunshine of their native sky
Smiles sadly on them here,
And kindred eyes and hearts watch by
The heroes' sepulchre.

Rest on, embalmed and sainted dead,
Dear as the blood ye gave;
No impious footsteps here shall tread
The herbage of your grave;
Nor shall your glory be forgot
While Fame her record keeps,
Or Honor points the hallowed spot
Where Valor proudly sleeps.

Yon marble minstrel's voiceless stone
In deathless song shall tell,
When many a vanquished age hath flown,
The story how ye fell;
Nor wreck, nor change, nor winter's blight,
Nor Time's remorseless doom,
Shall dim one ray of glory's light
That gilds your deathless tomb.

NEW ENGLAND VILLAGE, 1942

Milton Bracker

Here are the hills, the river and the school,
The grange, the stores, three churches.
Down a way
You'll find the drowsing station, where the rule
Is two trains up, and two trains down, each day.

St. Andrew's churchyard rests an ancient guild
Of Howlands, Wathleys, Winegars and Lains
Who, by their way of living, helped to build
The mood of peace the village still retains.

Yet look again, lest you conclude the world
Spins past these homes. No leafy street but one
Bright window has a little flag unfurled,
With every star of blue an absent son.

Loving its own, but loving freedom more,
This tiny village, too, has gone to war.

NORMAN CONQUEST

Percy Mackaye

Like that young major, dead, who led in vain
The living at St. Lo to victory,
Mortal, a corpse: immortal, a brave man,
Irradiating the immensity

Of valor to his fellows,—even so
Our inward challenge urges each of us
To slough our mortal sloth, unshard the glow
Of our real being, and victorious
Blast out the Huns of Hatred in ourselves
From taking sanctuary in our hearts,
Snuggling to be suckled where the Devil delves
To make of us his demon-counterparts.
Inward, not outward, throbs the eternal war
Where each is his own Norman Conqueror.

CARGO-SHIPS

Max Press

A braver sight I never hope to see
Than the tramp steamers, with their flags unfurled,
Moving on, on into the teeth of death—
The dirty little ships that saved the world.

HOME-COMING

Pauline Larimer Binford

At first he had not wanted much to go,
To leave his mother and the kids alone;
Since Dad had died, they counted on him so,
As though at eighteen he were fully grown,

As for Korea—just a pinkish blob
Upon the dime-store globe—he'd never thought
He would be needed there to do a job.
He could not understand just why they fought.
And now his mother and the kids are there
Just where he left them in the crowded station.
A flag is draped, and someone says a prayer
And speaks about a posthumous citation.
His little brother pats a brave bronze star,
And wonders: "Is Korea so far?"

ULYSSES

Alfred, Lord Tennyson

It little profits that an idle king,
By this still hearth, among these barren crags,
Matched with an aged wife, I mete and dole
Unequal laws unto a savage race,
That hoard, and sleep, and feed, and know not me.
I cannot rest from travel; I will drink
Life to the lees. All times I have enjoyed
Greatly, have suffered greatly, both with those
That loved me, and alone; on shore, and when
Through scudding drifts the rainy Hyades
Vext the dim sea. I am become a name;
For always roaming with a hungry heart
Much I have seen and known,—cities of men
And manners, climates, councils, governments,
Myself not least, but honoured of them all,—
And drunk delight of battle with my peers,
Far on the ringing plains of windy Troy.
I am a part of all that I have met;
Yet all experience is an arch wherethrough

Gleams that untravelled world whose margin fades
For ever and for ever when I move.
How dull it is to pause, to make an end,
To rust unburnished, not to shine in use!
As though to breathe were life! Life piled on life
Were all too little, and of one to me
Little remains; but every hour is saved
From that eternal silence, something more,
A bringer of new things; and vile it were
From some three suns to store and hoard myself,
And this gray spirit yearning in desire
To follow knowledge like a sinking star,
Beyond the utmost bound of human thought.
This is my son, mine own Telemachus,
To whom I leave the sceptre and the isle,—
Well-loved of me, discerning to fulfill
This labour, by slow prudence to make mild
A rugged people, and through soft degrees
Subdue them to the useful and the good.
Most blameless is he, centred in the sphere
Of common duties, decent not to fail
In offices of tenderness, and pay
Meet adoration to my household gods,
When I am gone. He works his work, I mine.
There lies the port; the vessel puffs her sail;
There gloom the dark, broad seas. My mariners,
Souls that have toiled and wrought, and thought with me—
That ever with a frolic welcome took
The thunder and the sunshine, and opposed
Free hearts, free foreheads,—you and I are old;
Old age hath yet his honour and his toil.
Death closes all; but something ere the end,
Some work of noble note, may yet be done,
Not unbecoming men that strove with Gods.
The lights begin to twinkle from the rocks;
The long day wanes; the slow moon climbs; the deep
Moans round with many voices. Come, my friends,
'Tis not too late to seek a newer world.
Push off, and sitting well in order smite

The sounding furrows; for my purpose holds
To sail beyond the sunset, and the baths
Of all the western stars, until I die.
It may be that the gulfs will wash us down;
It may be we shall touch the Happy Isles,
And see the great Achilles, whom we knew.
Though much is taken, much abides; and though
We are not now that strength which in old days
Moved earth and heaven, that which we are, we are,—
One equal temper of heroic hearts,
Made weak by time and fate, but strong in will
To strive, to seek, to find, and not to yield.

14

HUMOR

I know it is customary in presenting a parody to preface it "With Apologies to So-and-So".

I feel no apology is due Kipling for "A Young Reporter's 'If'". I believe he would have enjoyed it as much as I have. (And furthermore, I believe it will strike a responsive chord in the breast of anyone who has written for a daily paper!) I also believe that Henry Wadsworth Longfellow would have enjoyed "The Horse's Version of Paul Revere's Ride".

In the book which the inimitable Bennett Cerf calls *Out On A Limerick,* he ascribes the authorship of many of the limericks he has chosen to some particular persons, myself among them. Alas! I should love to claim this one as original—or rather, the version of it which I always quote and which I prefer to the one with the slight change which Mr. Cerf makes in it; but I did not write it. I heard it many years ago, and found it so applicable to many situations of which I was the victim that I adopted it, but with no false pretenses. As a matter of fact, I believe it is very difficult to give with assurance of accuracy the origin of a limerick. But if there are any among these I have chosen with a proven authorship, I hope the writer will communicate with me and let me give him, in the next edition, the credit line now missing.

'well boss mehitabel the cat'

Don Marquis

well boss mehitabel the cat
has been wooing
the muse no pun please
and i am privileged
to present her song just
as she sang it to
several of her dubious
feline friends in the alley
last night as follows

there s a dance or two
in the old dame yet
believe me you
there s a dance or two
before i m through
you get me pet
there s a dance or two
in the old dame yet

life s too dam funny
for me to explain
it s kicks or money
life s too dam funny
it s one day sunny
the next day rain
life s too dam funny
for me to explain

but toujours gai
is my motto kid
the devil s to pay

but toujours gai
and once in a way
let s lift the lid
but toujours gai
is my motto kid

thank god i m a lady
and class will tell
you hear me sadie
thank god i m a lady
my past is shady
but wotthehell
thank god i m a lady
and class will tell

A YOUNG REPORTER'S "IF"

Marjorie Driscoll

If you can keep your head, when all around you
The city room is swiftly going mad.
When frantic bosses stand in line to hound you,
And you can't find those notes you know you had;
When seven leg men call, by fits and snatches,
And each one gives the corpse a different name,
If you can fill in all the missing patches
And keep the copy rolling just the same.

If you can stand long hours when, bored and weary,
You're glad to see an obit come your way;
If you can make a Must Go yarn less dreary,
And write the weather forecast, day by day;

If you can take three lines and build a story
That's good enough to hold the banner line;
If you can dodge the phrase that's old and hoary,
And find—and spell—the right word every time;

If you can guess just what your boss is thinking,
And write the lead he wants, without a clue;
If you can hear him panic, without blinking,
Because you know he has his worries, too;
With deadlines coming closer every minute,
If you can do the job they think you can,
Yours is Page One and everything that's in it,
And, what is more, you'll be a rewrite man.

THE HORSE'S VERSION OF
THE RIDE OF PAUL REVERE

Anonymous

Listen, my jockeys, and you shall hear
How I carried my master, Paul Revere,
From the Charles bank, at the midnight hour,
When the lights flashed out in the belfry tower.
The British had landed! Paul gave me a pat
And said, "Well, Bess, old gal that's that."

And off we sped through the country wide—
And maybe I didn't give Paul a ride!
But honest, I had to laugh at the folk
We waked, who said, "What's this, a joke?"
And one old party, a Cambridge squire,
In nightgown and helmet, yelled, "Where's the fire?"

And of course, as I couldn't talk, you know,
I just whinnied, "You tell 'em Paul; let's go!"
Then away we flew, through village and town.
I don't know the route but it's all set down
In Longfellow's poem, I simply said:
"We'll make the grade if I don't drop dead."

Well, I didn't, and when that ride was done,
And Paul said, "Bess, there's Lexington,"
And I saw a stall and a pile of hay,
Well, I just lay down and I passed away.
And when I woke up next day and heard
What the minutemen had done—my word!
I wobbled up and gave three horse cheers
For that ride of mine—and Paul Revere's!

THE HAPPY FARMER BOY

Anonymous

I'd like to be a boy again, without a woe or care,
With freckles scattered on my face and hayseed in my hair.
I'd like to rise at four o'clock and do a hundred chores,
Saw the wood and feed the hogs and lock the stable doors,
And herd the hens and watch the bees and take the mule to drink,
And teach the turkeys how to swim so that they wouldn't sink,
And milk about a hundred cows and bring the wood to burn,
And stand out in the sun all day and churn and churn and churn,
And wear my brother's cast-off clothes and walk four miles to school,
And get a licking every day for breaking some old rule,
And then get home again at night and do the chores some more,
And milk the cows and feed the hogs and curry mules galore,

And then crawl wearily upstairs to seek my little bed,
Hear dad say, "That worthless boy! He isn't worth his bread!"
I'd like to be a boy again—a boy has so much fun.
His life is just a round of mirth from rise to set of sun.
I guess there's nothing pleasanter than closing stable doors
And herding hens and chasing bees and doing evening chores!

SEE-SAW

H. Daland Chandler

Ictinus and Callicrates—
No architects were quite like these;—
To them one day said Pericles:
    There's the Acrop,
    On which atop,
    No one than us is any keener
    To pour libations to Athena.
        Thereupon
    They batted out the Parthenon,
    (And being, as they were, fastidious,
    For decor called on brother Phidias.)

Today we've chucked all this a milo,
To live in glassy cubes on stilts,
Under a concrete orange-peel or in a silo,
(Amenities mechanized, the spirit wilts,)
    No matter what you think or say,
    The Parthenon is here today;
    Those U. N. buildings—wonder how
    They'll rank a hundred years from now?
        How will the Lever building rate
        In 20 hundred 58?
Callicrates and friend Ictinus,—
Will they have dwindled to a minus?

And will you find the halo fits
Harrison and Abramovitz?
(And yet perhaps 'twill still be these:
Ictinus and Callicrates!)

THE REVOLTING CALORY COUNTER

Louise Guyol Owen

Oh, I could be in the height of fashion,
Slender and trim and tiny of waist—
If I would keep to a simple ration
Of food that's lacking in charm and taste:
On watery soups and the duller fruits,
And various sugar substitutes;
Lettuce with lemon and not much salt—
Coffee as black as a prison vault—
The horrible milk that's known as skim . . .
And I would be slim, slim, slim!

But I turn my eyes from the glass of fashion.
Hereafter I'll look, not out, but in.
I shall give rein to a simple passion
For all the foods that won't keep me thin.
I'm going to spend the whole of my salary
On the grand, seductive, fattening calory:
Roasts of pork with a rich brown glaze;
Broccoli doused in hollandaise;
Baked potatoes dripping with butter;
New-made doughnuts so hot they sputter;
Chocolate cake as sweet as a dream . . .
And cream—cream—CREAM!
And never say "diet" again to me
Until the day I omit the "t"!

DIET RIOT

Jean Sartwell

I'm fed up with
The vitamin.
To which I've stuck
When thick or thin.

As for good food,
There's little I'd rate
Above the lowly
Carbohydrate.

I'm tired of counting
Calories
By which well-padded
Salaries

Are made by many
A dietician:
The whole affair
Is not my dish an'

Stirs in me
Sheer lassitude
I'll just relax
And have some: Food.

FATHER WILL SETTLE THE BILL[1]

Anonymous

Allow me to look at your dress goods,
And trimmings to match, if you please;
'Tis easy to make a selection
From elegant patterns like these;
This poplin is quite to my fancy,
But here is a prettier still,
I cannot do better than take it . . .
AND FATHER WILL SETTLE THE BILL.

I wish you would do me the favor
To let me examine that ring,
How nicely it looks on my finger,
I must have the beautiful thing . . .
I scarcely feel able to buy it,
Yet now on a venture I will;
I cannot resist the temptation,
AND FATHER WILL SETTLE THE BILL.

FATHER WILLIAM

Lewis Carroll

"You are old, Father William," the young man said,
"And your hair has become very white;
And yet you incessantly stand on your head—
Do you think, at your age, it is right?"

---

[1] The menacing song above, published in 1870 when Macy's, an infant of twelve, had not yet shed its strictly cash light on Cleveland, whence the ditty came. We do not condone (and never did) this cold-hearted, light-fingered treatment of Father. February 29th, to Macy customers, does not mean just an extra day to run up bills and terrorize the Old Man. Ah, no. Leap Year finds us, as usual, true to cash and Father. Since the poem was published, Macy's has reversed its long-time policy and now extends credit to reliable customers. It is to be hoped, however, that Father is still protected somehow.

"In my youth," Father William replied to his son,
"I feared it might injure the brain;
But now that I'm perfectly sure I have none,
Why, I do it again and again."

"You are old," said the youth, "as I mentioned before,
And have grown most uncommonly fat;
Yet you turned a back somersault in at the door—
Pray, what is the reason for that?"

"In my youth," said the sage, as he shook his gray locks,
"I kept all my limbs very supple
By the use of this ointment—one shilling the box—
Allow me to sell you a couple?"

"You are old," said the youth, "and your jaws are too weak
For anything tougher than suet;
Yet you finished the goose, with the bones and the beak;
Pray, how did you manage to do it?"

"In my youth," said his father, "I took to the law,
And argued each case with my wife;
And the muscular strength which it gave to my jaw,
Has lasted the rest of my life."

"You are old," said the youth; "one would hardly suppose
That your eye was as steady as ever;
Yet you balanced an eel on the end of your nose—
What made you so awfully clever?"

"I have answered three questions, and that is enough,"
Said his father; "Don't give yourself airs!
Do you think I can listen all day to such stuff?
Be off, or I'll kick you downstairs!"

LOVE NOTE TO A PLAYWRIGHT

Phyllis McGinley

Perhaps the literary man
    I most admire among my betters
Is Richard Brinsley Sheridan,
    Who, viewing life as more than letters,
Persisted, like a stubborn Gael,
In not acknowledging his mail.

They say he hardly ever penned
    A proper "Yrs. received & noted,"
But spent what time he had to spend
    Shaping the law that England voted,
Or calling, on his comic flute,
The tune for Captain Absolute.

Though chief of the prodigious wits
    That Georgian taverns set to bubblin',
He did not answer Please Remits
    Or scoldings from his aunts in Dublin
Or birthday messages or half
The notes that begged an autograph.

I hear it sent his household wild—
    Became a sort of parlor fable—
The way that correspondence piled,
    Mountainous, on his writing table,
While he ignored the double ring
And wouldn't answer *any*thing;

Not scrawls from friends or screeds from foes
    Or scribble from the quibble-lover
Or chits beginning "I enclose

Manuscript under separate cover,"
Or cards from people off on journeys,
Or formal statements from attorneys.

The post came in. He let it lie
   (All this biographers agree on.)
Especially he did not reply
   To things that had R.S.V.P. on.
Sometimes for months he dropped no lines
To dear ones, or sent Valentines;

But, polishing a second act
   Or coaxing kings to license Freedom,
Let his epistles wait. In fact,
   They say he didn't even read'm.
The which, some mornings, seems to me
A glorious blow for Liberty.

Brave Celt! Although one must deplore
   His manners, and with reason ample,
How bright from duty's other shore,
   This moment, seems his bold example!
And would I owned in equal balance
His courage (and, of course, his talents),

Who, using up his mail to start
   An autumn fire or chink a crevice,
Cried, "Letters longer are than art,
   But *vita* is extremely *brevis!*"
Then, choosing what was worth the candle,
Sat down and wrote *The School for Scandal*.

HERE'S TO THE MAIDEN

Richard Brinsley Sheridan

Here's to the maiden of bashful fifteen
   Now to the widow of fifty;
Here's to the flaunting extravagant queen,
   And here's to the housewife that's thrifty.
      Let the toast pass,
      Drink to the lass,
      I'll warrant she'll prove
      An excuse for the glass.

Here's to the charmer whose dimples we prize,
   Now to the damsel with none, Sir,
Here's to the girl with a pair of blue eyes,
   And now to the nymph with but one, Sir.

Here's to the maid with a bosom of snow,
   Now to her that's as brown as a berry,
Here's to the wife with a face full of woe,
   And now to the damsel that's merry.

For let her be clumsy, or let her be slim,
   Young or ancient, I care not a feather,
So fill up a bumper, nay, fill to the brim,
   And let us e'en toast 'em together,
      Let the toast pass,
      Drink to the lass,
      I'll warrant she'll prove
      An excuse for the glass.

THE NOVELIST

Philip Lazarus

His first attempt, reviewers say,
Shows evidence that any day
He may bring to the printed page
The foremost novel of his age.
His second try, when it's complete,
Is hailed with blurbs far more discreet
In which he's urged to shun the herd
And, incidentally, write a third.
His third, as you correctly reckoned,
Falls short of both the first and second.
Embittered, battered, shaken, bluer,
He then becomes a book reviewer.

AMBITION

Anonymous

I would I
    were beneath a
    tree,
A-sleeping in the
    shade,
With all the bills
    I've got to
    pay
PAID!

I would I were on
yonder hill,
A-basking in the
sun,
With all the work
I've got to
do
DONE!

I would I were
beside the sea,
Or sailing in a boat,
With all the things
I've got to
write
WROTE!

THE LAWYERS' INVOCATION TO SPRING

H. H. Brownell

Whereas on certain boughs and sprays
Now divers birds are heard to sing,
And sundry flowers their heads upraise,
Hail to the coming on of Spring!

The songs of those said birds arouse
The memory of our youthful hours,
As green as those said sprays and boughs,
As fresh and sweet as those said flowers.

The birds aforesaid—happy pairs—
Love 'mid the aforesaid boughs, enshrines
In freehold nests; themselves, their heirs,
Administrators, and assigns.

Oh! busiest term of Cupid's court,
Where tenderest plaintiffs actions bring—
Season of frolic and of sport,
Hail, as aforesaid, coming Spring!

WOE, BROTHERS, WOE!

Arthur Kramer

Alarmed, perplexed, befuddled,
We contemplate the realm,
Our normal ways are muddled;
Confusions overwhelm;
We groan of crescent prices,
Of obstacles to peace,
And crisis after crisis
Impends, without surcease.
And now—though desolated
Enough, Lord knows—our hurts
Are further acerbated:
I speak, of course, of skirts.

Ay, pull that lofty hemline down!
Long has it waved on high,
And many an eye has danced to see
A flash of nether thigh.
Below it bloomed a comely calf
To study and appraise.
No longer shall that contour form
A pleasance for our gaze!

For fashion has decreed it,
And that, my lads, is that.
And each and all will heed it,
Else I ingest my hat.
What though with scorn we flay them?
What though we beg and weep?
As well expect to stay them
As panic-stricken sheep!
No wheedling, no derision
Will move one stubborn she—
Thus passes from our vision,
Alas, the nylon'd knee.

I think that I shall never see
A poem lovely as a knee.
A knee that from an easy chair
Invites the charmèd eye to stare;
A knee that cheers the saddest cuss
As it ascends an omnibus;
A knee whose pert circumference
Can mock a lawyer's eloquence;
Whose puissant primeval curve
Can cause a cleric's eye to swerve.
Poems are made by fools like Gray,
Herrick, Swinburne, Keats and Gay,
Dowson, Sidney, Suckling, Cotton,
Spenser, Meredith, Lovelace, Wotton,
Whitman, Hardy, Burns and Blunt,
Drayton, Dryden, Beaumont, Hunt,
Pope and Byron, Jonson, Horace,
Shelley, Congreve, Crabbe and Morris
Heine, Waller and Calverley—
And I doubt that any of them
Could have made a knee.

But fashion thunders "Longer!"
As I have said above,
And her ukase is stronger
Than lucre or than love.

To no avail our tears now;
Our goose is with the cook;
To duller, drabber years now
It is our lot to look—
Until, one day, when, restless
And bored, and seeking sport,
She yawns, "These skirts are zestless;
I think I'll make 'em short."

EASY DIRECTIONS

Maurie Taylor

When telling me how I can get there,
Leave nothing to gamble or guess.
I won't be upset
If directions I get
Assume I'm a moron or less.

So give me some street names to cling to
Or draw me a map I can scan.
And be quite explicit—
You, maybe, can't miss it,
But, brother, believe me—I can.

GUEST YOU ARE WELCOME HERE

Anonymous

Be at your ease
Get up when you're ready
Go to bed when you please.
Happy to share with you such as we've got
The leaks in the roof and the soup in the pot
You don't have to thank us or laugh at our jokes,
Sit deep and come often, you're one of the folks.

EPITAPH FOR A CHRISTMAS GIFT

(Or Lament of a Solid-Color Man)

Milton Bracker

Dear friend, I cannot tell a lie:
I do not like a patterned tie!
I cannot simulate a tingle
When necktie colors merge and mingle
Or when they tint inspiring scenes
Like Eisenhower in his teens,

Ergo, I have no use at all
For ties that sound a bugle call
Or show a racehorse in a stall
Or show a fullback with the ball—

*(And even less do I have use
If back is plaid and ball is puce.)*

I do not care how Sigmund Freud
Assays the fact that I'm annoyed;
I'd rather wear a borrowed bow-tie
Or simply run around with no tie;
The four-in-hands that some guys do wear,
I never was intended *to* wear.

The ties with fishes, scale to scale,
The ties with devils, tail to tail,
The ties with hunters, hunting quail,
The ties with females, hunting male.

But if such horrors must be seen,
What's wrong with *brown,* or *blue,* or *green?*

SUM FUN

Margaret Fishback

Farewell to francs and liras, too . . .
I'm glad I need no longer do
Titanic mental acrobatics
To cope with daily mathematics.

Nor do I feel disposed to cry
At bidding pounds and pence goodbye.
Our dollar system's much more deft,
Except—I have no dollars left!

INSOMNIA

Gilbert Highet

Midnight:
kill the light.

One:
thoughts still run.

Two:
what can I do, what can I do?

Three:
all asleep but me.

Four:
something breathing under the door.

Five:
the window comes alive.

Six:
sleep and waking mix.

Seven:
at least, still living.

Eight:
up, a little late.

Nine:
fine, thanks, fine.

WHY NOT A BOOK?

Sir Alan Herbert

'Browned off,' you say, 'and blue'
'There's not enough to do?'
          Well, try a book.
Books do not wake the child
Or make the neighbors wild—
Books do not bark or bite,
Or need a walk at night,
          So try a book.
No tax—no licence fee—
No valve—no battery,
A book needs no repair,
A book is always there—
          Best friend a book.
You worry, or you weep—
You're sick—you cannot sleep—
          Well, try a book.

LIMERICKS

Anonymous

There was a young lady of Kent
Who said that she knew what it meant
When men asked her to dine,
Gave her cocktails and wine:
She knew what it meant—but she went!

There was a young lady in Niger,
Who went for a ride on a tiger.
They returned from the ride
With the lady inside,
And the smile on the face of the tiger.

There was a young lad of Quebec,
Who was buried in snow to his neck.
When asked, "Are you friz?"
He replied, "Yes, I is,
But we don't call this cold in Quebec."

There was a young man named Ignatius,
Who lived in a garret quite spacious.
When he went to a dance,
He always wore pants,
But when in that garret—Good Gracious!

There was a young man so benighted,
He never knew when he was slighted;
He'd go to a party
And eat just as hearty
As if he had been really invited.

There was a young man of Madrid,
Who was slapped in the face by a kid.
He said, "I would be glad
To wallop that lad,
I'll be damned if I don't," and he did!

There was a young lady of Lynn,
Who was so exceedingly thin,
That when she assayed
To drink lemonade,
She slid through the straw and fell in!

There was a young lady named Gleedle,
Who in church once sat down on a needle.
Though firmly imbedded,
It was happily threaded,
And was promptly pulled out by the beadle.

There was a young maid of Siam,
Who said to her boy friend, Khayyam,
"If you kiss me, of course,
You'll have to use force,
But thank goodness, you're stronger than I am!"

There was a young lady named Florence,
Who for kissing expressed great abhorrence.
But when she'd been kissed
And found out what she'd missed,
She cried 'til the tears came in torrents.

A tutor who tooted a flute
Tried to teach two young tooters to toot.
Said the two to the tutor,
"Is it harder to toot, or
To tutor two tooters to toot?"

There was a young fellow named Paul,
Who fell in the spring in the fall.
'Twould have been a sad thing
Had he died in the spring,
But he didn't, he died in the fall.

There was a young lady of Jodhpur,
Whose parents decided to drop her.
So she went to Ostend
With a gentleman friend,
And the rest of the story's improper.

Said a sporty young person named Groat,
Who owned a black racehorse of note,
"I consider it smart
To dine *a la carte,*
But my horse always takes table d'oat."

There was an old man of Nantucket,
Who kept his spare cash in a bucket,
But his daughter, named Nan,
Ran away with a man,
And as for the bucket, Nantucket.

Paw followed the pair to Pawtucket,
Both Nan and the man and the bucket.
Said he to the man,
"You're welcome to Nan,"
And as for the bucket, Pawtucket.

Msgr. Ronald Knox, for a bet, induced a newspaper to print this classified advertisement:

"An Anglican curate in want
Of a second-hand portable font,
Would exchange for the same
A portrait (in frame)
Of the Bishop-elect of Vermont."

There was a fair maid whose maneuver
Was to get her portrait in the Louvre.
But they sent it away
On the very first day—
And it's now in a dive in Vancouver.

There was a young lass named Harrison
Who longed for the love of a Saracen.
But she had to confine her
Intent to a Shriner,
Who suffers, I fear, by comparison.

From Number Nine, Penwiper Mews,
There is really abominable news:
They've discovered a head
In the box for the bread,
But nobody seems to know whose.

THE UNWINGED ONES

Ogden Nash

I don't travel on planes.
I travel on trains.
Once in a while, on trains,
I see people who travel on planes.
Every once in a while I'm surrounded
By people whose planes have been grounded.
I'm enthralled by their air-minded snobbery,
Their exclusive hobnobbery.
They feel that they have to explain
How they happen to be on a train,
For even in Drawing Room A
They seem to feel déclassé.

So they sit with portentous faces
Clutching their attaché cases.
They grumble and fume about how
They'd have been in Miami by now.
By the time that they're passing through Rahway
They should be in Havana or Norway,
And they strongly imply that perhaps,
Since they're late, the world will collapse.
Sometimes on the train I'm surrounded
By people whose planes have been grounded.
That's the only trouble with trains;
When it fogs, when it smogs, when it rains,
You get people from planes.

THE HUNTER

Ogden Nash

The hunter crouches in his blind
'Neath camouflage of every kind,
And conjures up a quacking noise
To lend allure to his decoys.
This grown-up man, with pluck and luck
Is hoping to outwit a duck.

POLITICAL REFLECTION

Ogden Nash

Like an art-lover looking at the Mona Lisa in the Louvre
Is the New York *Herald-Tribune* looking at Mr. Herbert Houvre.

FAMILY COURT

Ogden Nash

One would be in less danger
From the wiles of the stranger
If one's own kin and kith
Were more fun to be with.

PEDIATRIC REFLECTION

Ogden Nash

Many an infant that screams like a calliope
Could be soothed by a little attention to its diope.

OH SHUCKS, MA'AM, I MEAN EXCUSE ME

Ogden Nash

The greatest error ever erred
Is a nice girl with a naughty word.
For naughty words I hold no brief,
They fill my modest heart with grief,
But since it's plainer every day,
That naughty words are here to stay,
At least let's send them back again
To where they come from: namely, men.
For men, although to language prone,
Know when to leave the stuff alone;
The stevedore, before each damn,
Stops to consider where he am;
The lumberjack is careful, too,
Of what he says in front of who;
And if surrounded by the young,
The taxi driver curbs his tongue.
The reason men speak softly thus is
That circumstances alter cusses,
And naughty words scream out like sirens
When uttered in the wrong environs.
But maidens who restrict their hips
Place no such limits on their lips;
Once they have learned a startling Verb,
No tactful qualms their heads disturb;
They scatter Adjectives hither and thence
Regardless of their audience,
And cannot hold a Noun in trust
But have to out with it, or bust,
And that's why men creep into crannies
When girls play cribbage with their grannies,
And nervous husbands develop hives
When ministers call upon their wives,

And fathers tie themselves in knots
When damsels stoop to caress their tots,
For who knows what may not be heard
From a nice girl with a naughty word?
One truth all womankind nonplusses:
That circumstances alter cusses.

15

PEOPLE

Nearly all of these poems are about people I know . . . the country doctor, the village postmaster, the small-town editor, the old-fashioned farmer, the new paper boy, the daredevil pilot, the consecrated bibliophile. Though I never actually met Stephen Vincent Benét's "Mary Lou", I have met her prototype over and over again, and I recognized her instantly when I encountered her in *John Brown's Body*. In like measure I recognized Phillips' "Perplexing Battler". Walt Whitman did not even need to name Lincoln for me or anyone else to recognize him. Robert Frost embodied everything that is best in my own best-loved state; but these last years I have seen him most clearly as he looked standing at the rostrum at the Capitol. I saw Franklin D. Roosevelt there, too, when he told us all we had nothing to fear but fear itself. He was right.

And Santayana? Listen, I have lived in Avila myself, long happy months at a time, but I learned about it first with Santayana in *People and Places*. And Andrea del Sarto? I have found him and his Lucretia in so many galleries that I have lost count of the number. We have been friends ever since I was ten years old!

COUNTRY DOCTOR

Inez George Gridley

The doctor was an angry man.
It was a common sight
To see him leave his lighted door
To battle in the night.

He fought the storms, he fought the roads,
His daily chore was strife.
He had a running feud with Death
That lasted all his life.

Sometimes Death raced him up the branch
And beat him to a shack;
But sometimes when Doc hollered "Wait!"
Life fluttered and came back.

So many times he rolled his sleeves
And waded in the fray.
Because of that good angry man
I am alive today.

EDITOR—WEEKLY JOURNAL

Clara Hyde

With printer's ink he welds the town together
Commenting on farm produce and the weather,
The births and deaths, arrivals in the square,
Though gossiped everywhere when they occur,
Add to his weekly stint a homey glow;
Small town folk read what they already know.
They find his mixed feed rations, prices noted
Are right as rain, at every fence rail quoted.
The Sunday sermon and the brand new roof
The church is wearing, all are ample proof
His editorial comments are well grounded.
Upon such matters is our nation founded.
Although a sack of apples, a fat hen,
May pay a year's subscription, always when
The country's mind is measured, as a gage,
His peers will scan the Weekly Journal's page.

OLD POSTMASTER

Alma Robison Higbee

For sixty years he shared their joys and sorrows,
He was the eyes and literate hands for all,
He ordered their pills and garden catalogues,
Read letters from boys who never wrote at all,
His office was the place to go for solace,
By the stove in the sawdust box, kind met with kind,

There he dispensed philosophy and logic
And the wise counsel of a seasoned mind.
He who loved them all and brought them solace
Heard, one night, his final call alone,
The carrier found his windows blind and darkened
And the rusty, friendly stove as cold as stone.

QUIET CITIZEN

Billy B. Cooper

He spent his life in doing daily chores;
In plowing fields and planting them to grain;
He fed his stock and safely sheltered it
From winter storms and summer sun and rain.
He rose at daylight, eager to be out
About his work, and with the setting sun
He could recount a dozen finished tasks
And in his heart could call his work well done.

He reared his four boys quietly, without
Apparent effort, and the boys became
Tall, upright men whose neighbors found them fair
In all their dealings, honoring his name.
He made his simple mark in life, nor cared
For fame or fortune; he walked hand in hand
With nature, and his tranquil years were spent
Shaping the destiny of prairie land.

STEWARDS

Billy B. Cooper

He's always liked a stormy sky
At daybreak; thunder overhead,
With dark clouds forming, windy, high,
He watches from his ailing bed,
Recalling briefly, with a sigh,
Forgotten years; the stock he's led
To shelter; rubbing yearlings dry,
And leaving all secure and fed.

On sunny days there is no need
To give a thought to morning chores;
His sons will water well and feed
Each hungry mouth. The open doors
Attest the ease with which, indeed,
He is excelled. His spirit soars
In gentle pride that his own seed
Sustains the earth which he adores.

HILL FARM

Kaye Starbird

A man, to be a man, must live his life
The way he sees it . . . not as others see it;
And there are men who will not compromise
With progress . . . looking on it as opinion
Rather than truth.

Up on the lost hill farms
Beyond the metal silos and macadam,
Now and again you come upon a man
Who puts his faith in what has gone before him,
Trusting the lone and difficult survival
That served his father and his father's father
To serve him, too.

He reached a crossroads once
Perhaps; a year or season when he wondered
About the towns or where the railroads went
Or how it felt to sleep 'til eight. But that
Was long ago and never might have happened.
Yet—if, indeed, it did—habit is sometimes
Stronger than wonder, and a man sometimes
Stronger than either, when at last he chooses
The road that he must take.

Winters are long
Up in the north, and days begin in darkness.
Mornings, the white snow eddies round the barn
And ice is frozen in the drinking troughs,
Where the few cows and solitary horse
Wait for the sound of footsteps, breathing steam.
After the winter ends, and crows return
To flap and caw behind the sugarhouse
And spring comes late and never all at once . . .
Even when pear trees blossom in the wood
And peepers cry at evening from the river,
A frost can kill the slowly-greening garden
Or kill the apple crop.

Summer will come
This year and next, as always, and will never
Be long enough to mend the roofs and fences
And hoe and harrow; never long enough
To swing the scythe and rake the hay and draw it
Into the mow, between the rainstorms needed
To grow the grain and fill the drying well.

Then suddenly, some wide gold day, the summer
Changes to autumn, with the crops to harvest
And wood to cut and stack inside the woodshed
Against another winter.

Old ways die,
But on the lost hill farms beyond the signboards,
Beyond the metal silos and macadam,
Now and again you come upon a man
Who lives his life as men before him lived it,
Trusting the past the way he trusts the winter
To end in spring . . . spring when the April promise
Of one small blade of grass coming alive
Assures him all dark meadows will survive.

NEW PAPER BOY

Abigail Cresson

Each house stands in a pocket of the dark;
No one is up; the sky is gray and low;
Frowning, he slowly guides his bike along.
This is serious business. He must go
Trudging up steps, the crumpled route list clutched
In one brown paw. While, very carefully,
And half aloud, he reads each number out,
Before he dares to make delivery.
But, when he finishes at last, his heart
Grows lighter than the empty canvas bag
That flaps behind him as his pedals spin
And takes the wind as proudly as a flag.
Gay as a robin now, he makes for home;
His whistle shrills to meet the rising sun.
He balances; lets go the handlebars—
The first of his first real job is done!

U. S. MAIL

Florence Ripley Mastin

Storm is a dragon leveling the spires
Of tall New Hampshire, titans out of foam
Trample the Florida keys, electric fires
Leap upon Denver from the mountain home.

An earthquake shudders at the Golden Gate,
A monstrous fog creeps up Manhattan Bay,
And off Cape Hatteras, lying in wait,
Water spouts rear menacing necks of gray.

Young pilots scrutinize the low and high
On the weather map, the dots of clear and rain,
Observe the arrowed winds—then casually
Their mail ships cross a continent again.

ON A BOOKLOVER'S SHELVES

Stanton A. Coblentz

Gaze at these shelves—the man beneath shines clear.
These volumes, like confessionals, contain
The readings of the spirit's atmosphere,
The autograph of his selective brain
Transports and longings, as upon a chart,
Are here made visible; he keeps a trust
With song, romance and drama, music, art,
Travel or flower-lore—a lifelong list!

Turn from the clean new pages—peer beyond
At those dog-eared and scrawled with many a note,
There, mirrored like a landscape in a pond,
Reflections of his clouds and summits float,
Time's last recording angel surely looks
Not at man's deeds alone, but at his books.

JOHN BROWN'S BODY

Stephen Vincent Benét

(*Excerpt*)

Cudjo, the negro, watched from the pantry
The smooth glissades of the dancing gentry,
His splay-feet tapping in time to the tune
While his broad face beamed like a drunken moon

. . . .

Cudjo watched and measured and knew them,
Seeing behind and around and through them
With the shrewd, dispassionate, smiling eye
Of the old-time servant in days gone by.
He couldn't read and he couldn't write,
But he knew Quality, black or white,
And even his master could not find
The secret place in the back of his mind
Where witch-bones talked to a scarlet rag
And a child's voice spoke from a conjur-bag.
For he belonged to the hidden nation,
The mute, enormous confederation
Of the planted earth and the burden borne
And the horse that is ridden and given corn.
The wind from the brier-patch brought him news
That never went walking in white men's shoes

And the grapevine whispered its message faster
Than a horse could gallop across a grave,
Till, long ere the letter could tell the master,
The doomsday rabbits had sold the slave.

He was faithful as bread or salt,
A flawless servant without a fault,
Major-domo of Wingate Hall,
Proud of his white folks, proud of it all.
They might scold him, they might let him scold them,
But there was a bond, and the bond would hold,
On either side until both were cold.

.   .   .   .

Fat Aunt Bess is older than Time
But her eyes still shine like a bright, new dime,
Though two generations have gone to rest
On the sleepy mountain of her breast.
Wingate children in Wingate Hall,
From the first weak cry in the bearing-bed
She has petted and punished them, one and all,
She has closed their eyes when they lay dead.
She raised Marse Billy when he was puny,
She cared for the Squire when he got loony,
Fed him and washed him and combed his head,
Nobody else would do instead.
The matriarch of the weak and the young,
The lazy crooning, comforting tongue.
She has had children of her own,
But the white-skinned ones are bone of her bone.
They may not be hers, but she is theirs,
And if the shares were unequal shares,
She does not know it, now she is old.
They will keep her out of the rain and cold.
And some were naughty, and some were good,
But she will be warm while they have wood,
Rule them and spoil them and play physician
With the vast, insensate force of tradition,

Half a nuisance and half a mother
And legally neither one nor the other,
Till at last they follow her to her grave,
The family-despot, and the slave.

[—Curious blossom from bitter ground,
Master of masters who left you bound,
Who shall unravel the mingled strands
Or read the anomaly of your hands?
They have made you a shrine and a humorous fable,
But they kept you a slave while they were able,
And yet, there was something between the two
That you shared with them and they shared with you,
Brittle and dim, but a streak of gold,
A genuine kindness, unbought, unsold,
Graciousness founded on hopeless wrong
But queerly living and queerly strong. . . .]

There were three stout pillars that held up all
The weight and tradition of Wingate Hall.
One was Cudjo and one was you
And the third was the mistress, Mary Lou.
Mary Lou Wingate, as slightly made
And as hard to break as a rapier-blade.
Bristol's daughter and Wingate's bride,
Never well since the last child died
But staring at pain with courteous eyes.
When the pain outwits it, the body dies,
Meanwhile the body bears the pain.
She loved her hands and they made her vain,
The tiny hands of her generation
That gathered the reins of the whole plantation;
The velvet sheathing the steel demurely
In the trained, light grip that holds so surely.

She was at work by candlelight,
She was at work in the dead of night,
Smoothing out troubles and healing schisms
And doctoring phthisics and rheumatisms,

Guiding the cooking and watching the baking,
The sewing, the soap-and-candle-making,
The brewing, the darning, the lady-daughters,
The births and deaths in the negro-quarters,
Seeing that Suke had some new, strong shoes
And Joe got a week in the calaboose,
While Dicey's Jacob escaped a whipping
And the jellybag dripped with its proper dripping,
And the shirts and estrangements were neatly mended,
And all of the tasks that never ended.
Her manner was gracious but hardly fervent
And she seldom raised her voice to a servant.
She was often mistaken, not often blind,
And she knew the whole duty of womankind,
To take the burden and have the power
And seem like the well-protected flower,
To manage a dozen industries
With a casual gesture in scraps of ease,
To hate the sin and to love the sinner
And to see that the gentlemen got their dinner
Ready and plenty and piping-hot
Whether you wanted to eat or not.
And always, always, to have the charm
That makes the gentlemen take your arm
But never the bright, unseemly spell
That makes strange gentlemen love too well,
Once you were married and settled down
With a suitable gentleman of your own.
And when that happened, and you had bred
The requisite children, living and dead,
To pity the fool and comfort the weak
And always let the gentlemen speak
To succor your love from deep-struck roots
When gentlemen went to bed in their boots,
And manage a gentleman's whole plantation
In the manner befitting your female station.

This was the creed that her mother taught her
And the creed that she taught to every daughter.

She knew her Bible—and how to flirt
With a swansdown fan and a brocade skirt
For she trusted in God but she liked formalities
And the world and Heaven were both realities.
—In Heaven, of course, we should all be equal,
But until we come to that golden sequel,
Gentility must keep to gentility
Where God and breeding had made things stable,
While the rest of the cosmos deserved civility
But dined in its boots at the second-table.
This view may be reckoned a trifle narrow,
But it had the driving force of an arrow,
And it helped Mary Lou to stand up straight,
For she was gentle, but she could hate
And she hated the North with the hate of Jael
When the dry hot hands went seeking the nail,
The terrible hate of women's ire,
The smoky, the long-consuming fire.
The Yankees were devils, and she could pray,
For devils, no doubt, upon Judgment Day,
But now in the world, she would hate them still
And send the gentlemen out to kill.

The gentlemen killed and the gentlemen died,
But she was the South's incarnate pride
That mended the broken gentlemen
And sent them out to the war again,
That kept the house with the men away
And baked the bricks where there was no clay,
Made courage from terror and bread from bran
And propped the South on a swansdown fan
Through four long years of ruin and stress,
The pride—and deadly bitterness.

THE PERPLEXING BATTLER

H. I. Phillips

The Englishman's a funny foe—
    He fumbles;
At starting he is very slow,
    And stumbles.

The Englishman's the slowest poke—
    He's dopey;
He seems a rather sleepy bloke—
    He's mopey.

He doesn't pack much early lick—
    He's mulish;
He seems to be a little thick
    And foolish.

His timing isn't very good—
    Appalling!
I've never even understood
    Such stalling.

He seems to like to miss the ball
    By inches;
He likes to be against the wall
    In pinches.

He always rates the early razz—
    He's awful;
He doesn't mind it when he has
    His "craw" full.

He staggers all around the ring—
    The blighter;
You'd never think him, from his swing,
    A fighter.

He often hears the cry "Too late!"—
    He misses;
He often hangs around to wait
    For hisses!

He takes it often on the chin,
    This stout boy;
But when he seems to be all in . . .
    Look out, boy!

He lets his arms fall to his side—
    Yes, maybe;
But when they think that he has died,
    Oh, baby!

He staggers, reels and jolly well
    Gets thinner—
But at the end he gets the yell—
    "THE WINNER!"

SONNET

Daniel Cory

To George Santayana in a private hospital in Italy.

The walls dissolve—the strings of memory bend
And vibrate with the latest news of Rome;
The red sun drops behind St. Peter's dome
And I walk in the Pincio with my friend.

Twilight in sky and mind. Is this the end
Of all we loved? Outside the shackled home
Of civilization now strange steel birds comb
The ancient roads the plundering Huns defend.

Master! Your words shine like the evening stars:
"The essence of the Past can never fade."
No shrieking bomb can spoil—no rude hands mar
The structure of the fugue that Time has played.
The walls congeal. We are no more together.
But all this room is filled with Roman weather.

ANDREA DEL SARTO

Called "The Faultless Painter"

Robert Browning

But do not let us quarrel any more,
No, my Lucrezia; bear with me for once:
Sit down and all shall happen as you wish.
You turn your face, but does it bring your heart?
I'll work then for your friend's friend, never fear,
Treat his own subject after his own way,
Fix his own time, accept too his own price,
And shut the money into this small hand
When next it takes mine. Will it? tenderly?
Oh, I'll content him,—but to-morrow, Love!
I am often much wearier than you think,
This evening more than usual, and it seems
As if—forgive now—should you let me sit
Here by the window with your hand in mine
And look a half-hour forth on Fiesole,
Both of one mind, as married people use,
Quietly, quietly, the evening through,

I might get up to-morrow to my work
Cheerful and fresh as ever. Let us try.
To-morrow, how you shall be glad for this!
Your soft hand is a woman of itself,
And mine the man's bared breast she curls inside.
Don't count the time lost, neither; you must serve
For each of the five pictures we require:
It saves a model. So! keep looking so—
My serpentining beauty, rounds on rounds!
—How could you ever prick those perfect ears,
Even to put the pearl there! oh, so sweet—
My face, my moon, my everybody's moon,
Which everybody looks on and calls his,
And, I suppose, is looked on by in turn,
While she looks—no one's: very dear, no less.
You smile? why, there's my picture ready made,
There's what we painters call our harmony!
A common grayness silvers everything,—
All in a twilight, you and I alike
—You, at the point of your first pride in me
(That's gone you know),—but I, at every point:
My youth, my hope, my art, being all toned down
To yonder sober pleasant Fiesole.
There's the bell clinking from the chapel-top;
That length of convent-wall across the way
Holds the trees safer, huddled more inside;
The last monk leaves the garden; days decrease,
And autumn grows, autumn in everything.
Eh? the whole seems to fall into a shape
As if I saw alike my work and self
And all that I was born to be and do.
A twilight-piece. Love, we are in God's hand.
How strange now looks the life he makes us lead;
So free we seem, so fettered fast we are!
I feel he laid the fetter: let it lie!
This chamber for example—turn your head—
All that's behind us! You don't understand
Nor care to understand about my art,
But you can hear at least when people speak:

And that cartoon, the second from the door
—It is the thing, Love! so such thing should be—
Behold Madonna!—I am bold to say.
I can do with my pencil what I know,
What I see, what at bottom of my heart
I wish for, if I ever wish so deep—
Do easily, too—when I say, perfectly,
I do not boast, perhaps: yourself are judge,
Who listened to the Legate's talk last week,
And just as much they used to say in France.
At any rate 'tis easy, all of it!
No sketches first, no studies, that's long past:
I do what many dream of all their lives,
—Dream? strive to do, and agonize to do,
And fail in doing. I could count twenty such
On twice your fingers, and not leave this town,
Who strive—you don't know how the others strive
To paint a little thing like that you smeared
Carelessly passing with your robes afloat,—
Yet do much less, so much less, Someone says,
(I know his name, no matter)—so much less!
Well, less is more, Lucrezia: I am judged.
There burns a truer light of God in them,
In their vexed beating stuffed and stopped-up brain,
Heart, or whate'er else, than goes on to prompt
This low-pulsed forthright craftsman's hand of mine.
Their works drop groundward, but themselves, I know,
Reach many a time a heaven that's shut to me,
Enter and take their place there sure enough,
Though they come back and cannot tell the world.
My works are nearer heaven, but I sit here.
The sudden blood of these men! at a word—
Praise them, it boils, or blame them, it boils too.
I, painting from myself and to myself,
Know what I do, am unmoved by men's blame
Or their praise either. Somebody remarks
Morello's outline there is wrongly traced,
His hue mistaken; what of that? or else,
Rightly traced and well ordered; what of that?

Speak as they please, what does the mountain care?
Ah, but a man's reach should exceed his grasp,
Or what's a heaven for? All is silver-gray
Placid and perfect with my art: the worse!
I know both what I want and what might gain,
And yet how profitless to know, to sigh
"Had I been two, another and myself,
Our head would have o'erlooked the world!" No doubt.
Yonder's a work now, of that famous youth
The Urbinate who died five years ago.
('Tis copied George Vasari sent it me.)
Well, I can fancy how he did it all,
Pouring his soul, with kings and popes to see,
Reaching, that heaven might so replenish him,
Above and through his art—for it gives way;
That arm is wrongly put—and there again—
A fault to pardon in the drawing's lines,
Its body, so to speak: its soul is right,
He means right—that, a child may understand.
Still, what an arm! and I could alter it:
But all the play, the insight and the stretch—
Out of me, out of me! And wherefore out?
Had you enjoined them on me, given me soul,
We might have risen to Rafael, I and you!
Nay, Love, you did give all I asked, I think—
More than I merit, yes, by many times.
But had you—oh, with the same perfect brow,
And perfect eyes, and more than perfect mouth,
And the low voice my soul hears, as a bird
The fowler's pipe, and follows to the snare—
Had you, with these the same, but brought a mind!
Some women do so. Had the mouth there urged
"God and the glory! never care for gain.
The present by the future, what is that?
Live for fame, side by side with Agnolo!
Rafael is waiting: up to God, all three!"
I might have done it for you. So it seems:
Perhaps not. All is as God overrules.
Beside, incentives come from the soul's self;

The rest avail not. Why do I need you?
What wife had Rafael, or has Agnolo?
In this world, who can do a thing, will not;
And who would do it, cannot, I perceive:
Yet the will's somewhat—somewhat, too, the power—
And thus we half-men struggle. At the end,
God, I conclude, compensates, punishes.
'Tis safer for me, if the award be strict,
That I am something underrated here,
Poor this long while, despised, to speak the truth.
I dared not, do you know, leave home all day,
For fear of chancing on the Paris lords.
The best is when they pass and look aside;
But they speak sometimes; I must bear it all.
Well may they speak! That Francis, that first time,
And that long festal year at Fontainebleau!
I surely then could sometimes leave the ground,
Put on the glory, Rafael's daily wear,
In that humane great monarch's golden look,—
One finger in his beard or twisted curl
Over his mouth's good mark that made the smile,
One arm about my shoulder, round my neck,
The jingle of his gold chain in my ear,
I painting proudly with his breath on me,
All his court round him, seeing with his eyes,
Such frank French eyes, and such a fire of souls
Profuse, my hand kept plying by those hearts,—
And, best of all, this, this, this face beyond,
This in the background, waiting on my work,
To crown the issue with a last reward!
A good time, was it not, my kingly days?
And had you not grown restless . . . but I know—
'Tis done and past; 'twas right, my instinct said;
Too live the life grew, golden and not gray,
And I'm the weak-eyed bat no sun should tempt
Out of the grange whose four walls make his world.
How could it end in any other way?
You called me, and I came home to your heart.
The triumph was—to reach and stay there; since

I reached it ere the triumph, what is lost?
Let my hands frame your face in your hair's gold,
You beautiful Lucrezia that are mine!
"Rafael did this, Andrea painted that;
The Roman is the better when you pray,
But still the other's Virgin was his wife"—
Men will excuse me. I am glad to judge
Both pictures in your presence; clearer grows
My better fortune, I resolve to think.
For, do you know, Lucrezia, as God lives,
Said one day Agnolo, his very self,
To Rafael . . . I have known it all these years . . .
(When the young man was flaming out his thoughts
Upon a palace-wall for Rome to see,
Too lifted up in heart because of it)
"Friend, there's a certain sorry little scrub
Goes up and down our Florence, none cares how,
Who, were he set to plan and execute
As you are, pricked on by your popes and kings,
Would bring the sweat into that brow of yours!"
To Rafael's!—And indeed the arm is wrong.
I hardly dare . . . yet, only you to see,
Give the chalk here—quick, thus the line should go!
Ay, but the soul! he's Rafael! rub it out!
Still, all I care for, if he spoke the truth,
(What he? why, who but Michel Agnolo?
Do you forget already words like those?)
If really there was such a chance, so lost,—
Is, whether you're—not grateful—but more pleased.
Well, let me think so. And you smile indeed!
This hour has been an hour! Another smile?
If you would sit thus by me every night
I should work better, do you comprehend?
I mean that I should earn more, give you more.
See, it is settled dusk now; there's a star;
Morello's gone, the watch-lights show the wall,
The cue-owls speak the name we call them by.
Come from the window, love,—come in, at last,
Inside the melancholy little house

We built to be so gay with. God is just.
King Francis may forgive me: oft at nights
When I look up from painting, eyes tired out,
The walls become illumined, brick from brick
Distinct, instead of mortar, fierce bright gold,
That gold of his I did cement them with!
Let us but love each other. Must you go?
That Cousin here again? he waits outside?
Must see you—you, and not with me? Those loans?
More gaming debts to pay? you smiled for that?
Well, let smiles buy me! have you more to spend?
While hand and eye and something of a heart
Are left me, work's my ware, and what's it worth?
I'll pay my fancy. Only let me sit
The gray remainder of the evening out,
Idle you call it, and muse perfectly
How I could paint, were I but back in France,
One picture, just one more—the Virgin's face,
Not yours this time! I want you at my side
To hear them—that is, Michel Agnolo—
Judge all I do and tell you of its worth.
Will you? To-morrow, satisfy your friend.
I take the subjects for his corridor,
Finish the portrait out of hand—there, there,
And throw him in another thing or two
If he demurs; the whole should prove enough
To pay for this same Cousin's freak. Beside,
What's better and what's all I care about,
Get you the thirteen *scudi* for the ruff!
Love, does that please you? Ah, but what does he,
The Cousin! what does he to please you more?

I am grown peaceful as old age to-night.
I regret little, I would change still less.
Since there my past life lies, why alter it?
The very wrong to Francis!—it is true
I took his coin, was tempted and complied,
And built this house and sinned, and all is said.
My father and my mother died of want.

Well, had I riches of my own? you see
How one gets rich! Let each one bear his lot.
They were born poor, lived poor, and poor they died:
And I have labored somewhat in my time
And not been paid profusely. Some good son
Paint my two hundred pictures—let him try!
No doubt, there's something strikes a balance. Yes,
You loved me quite enough, it seems to-night.
This must suffice me here. What would one have?
In heaven, perhaps, new chances, one more chance—
Four great walls in the New Jerusalem,
Meted on each side by the angel's reed,
For Leonard, Rafael, Agnolo and me
To cover—the three first without a wife,
While I have mine! So—still they overcome
Because there's still Lucrezia,—as I choose.

Again the Cousin's whistle! Go, my Love.

O CAPTAIN! MY CAPTAIN!

(*Abraham Lincoln*)

Walt Whitman

O Captain! my Captain! our fearful trip is done,
The ship has weather'd every rack, the prize we sought is won,
The port is near, the bells I hear, the people all exulting,
While follow eyes the steady keel, the vessel grim and daring;
     But O heart! heart! heart!
     O the bleeding drops of red,
     Where on the deck my Captain lies,
     Fallen cold and dead.

O Captain! my Captain! rise up and hear the bells;
Rise up—for you the flag is flung—for you the bugle trills,
For you bouquets and ribbon'd wreaths—for you the shores a-crowding,
For you they call, the swaying mass, their eager faces turning;

Here Captain! dear father!
The arm beneath your head!
It is some dream that on the deck,
You've fallen cold and dead.

My Captain does not answer, his lips are pale and still,
My father does not feel my arm, he has no pulse nor will,
The ship is anchor'd safe and sound, its voyage closed and done,
From fearful trip the victor ship comes in with object won:

Exult O shores, and ring O bells!
But I with mournful tread,
Walk the deck my Captain lies,
Fallen cold and dead.

TO ROBERT FROST

Wilbert Snow

The twist and tone of sharp New England speech,
New England's rocks and ice, its snow and wind,
Its winter Edens, and the farthest reach
Of that cloud-shadowed cliff, New England's mind;
Stone walls whose building wore men to the bone,
The October gold of Vermont's rolling hills,
Forgotten people doomed to live alone,
The clamorous bull-frogs, brooks, and whippoorwills,—

All these you caught in such authentic style
That symbols mushroomed up and stood erect;
Philosophy, with your persuasive smile,
Came clothed in many a Yankee analect;
You gave New England's stony farm a song,
So clear its echo lingers long and long.

FRANKLIN DELANO ROOSEVELT

John Masefield

Honour this man, so stricken in his prime,
So shattered in his life's most kindling years,
That had his spirit not been strong as Time
He could have won no tribute more than tears.

Honour a dauntless soul and golden voice
(None sweeter ever spoke in Christian lands)
Through him, the horror passed, and we rejoice,
Our countries are released, and Freedom stands.

16

ANIMALS

I found, when the time came to consider the sections of this anthology separately, instead of considering the collection as a whole, that the one devoted to animals was overweighted with poems about dogs! I read and reread these poems, hoping to find some that I would be reconciled to discarding, but I was unsuccessful. However, a solution presented itself: I was able to find good reasons for putting some of them in other sections—in *Prayers*, for instance, though that certainly would not have occurred to me in the first place.

As a child and young girl, I always had a pet kitten or a companionable cat, often both. But my husband, who concentrated on cows and, for the time being, taught me to do the same, did not like cats; none of my sons clamored for one and, gradually, they lost their place in my design for living, though I continued to enjoy them when I encountered them in the habitations of my acquaintances. On the other hand, someone either in or connected with my household nearly always owned a dog, and my relations with these animals were friendly. But they were not important to me. Then, comparatively late in life, I very unexpectedly became the proud possessor of my own dog.

It happened in this way: while I was living at The Cottage, near Baton Rouge, on the River Road, writing the book to which I gave that name, Hermann Deutsch, the journalist, who is a good friend of mine, asked me if I would let his dog, Bumps, stay with me at The Cottage while Hermann himself was covering a session of the Louisiana Legislature. He would be staying at a hotel where he could not keep Bumps, and he hated to leave this devoted and fantastically intelligent animal for any length of time at a kennel. Bumps was one of those dogs with which I was already on friendly terms, so I was delighted to welcome him as a guest; and, before long, my interest in him became professional as well as personal, for he provided excellent copy. (Readers of *The River Road* will find his prototype in Fabian's Bellizar.) His mate, Susie, who joined our household as soon as possible after her happy delivery of six beautiful puppies, which of course accompanied her, also furnished valuable source material.

In due time, the legislature completed its work, its members returned to their homes, and the reporters who had covered its activities did likewise. One of the puppies had died and all the others, except one, had been given away; I took it for granted that this one would accompany her parents and their owner on their return to New Orleans. And then I was given a surprise which, at the moment I received it, was also something of a shock; the remaining puppy was a present to me, as a slight token of appreciation for my hospitality to her family. She would be staying on at The Cottage and her name was Lucky.

Of course, the free-will offering of a purebred cocker spaniel by the owner of its parents is nothing short of an accolade, comparable to being decorated with the Legion of Honor. But the canine family had been quite a responsibility and a source of anxiety as well as pleasure, for Bumps, though happily recovered, had been seriously ill and, as I have said, one of the puppies had died. I could not help feeling that the permanent acquisition of a dog, at my time of life, might be as great a mistake as an autumnal love affair would be. I could not have been more wrong. For twelve years, until she peacefully and painlessly died of old age, Lucky was a source of boundless joy to me.

When I went back and forth between Louisiana and New England, Lucky went, too. She was a good traveler, both by train and by car, though she greatly preferred the latter. After we left The Cottage, she adapted herself to our ways at Pine Grove Farm in Haverhill, New Hampshire and at the Oxbow in Newbury, Vermont as readily and as pleasantly as she did to our ways at Compensation in Crowley, Louisiana and at Beauregard House in New Orleans. My grandchildren adored her, and she was very polite to them. When I went abroad, she remained in Louisiana with my faithful retainers, Beverly and Creacy King. They adored her, too, and she was perfectly content with them. She was not a one-woman dog, in the same sense as her granddaughter, Sham, who eventually became the property and the shadow of my senior secretary, Deanie Bullock. Sham's devotion to Deanie was such that she was not aware of anyone else, if Deanie were around; and, when they were separated, her main occupation consisted of watching hopefully for Deanie to come back. Like her great-grandfather Bumps, she was almost fantastically intelligent. When we were at the Oxbow, Deanie and I had a favorite game that we played with her. "Would you care to go to Boston, Sham?" one of us would inquire. Sham, ensconced in the most comfortable chair in the study, would not stir. "Well, would it interest you to go to the races?" would be the next question. Sometimes the drooping eyelids would open a little wider, but not much. "Then what about the Farm?" And Sham would be out of her chair with one leap, wagging her diminutive tail and making joyous circles around us.

Having witnessed this performance and many equally noteworthy, it did not surprise Deanie and me to learn that, during one of our prolonged absences, Sham had written a poem. Ronnie Hornblower —the English junior secretary, also known as "Blowie"—who had only recently joined our staff sent it to us, having acted as amanuensis. It read like this:

> To my dear 'Mum':
> "Can you believe it when I say,
> I hate it when you go away?
> Why must it always be just when—
> You come home, you go again?
> It's very hard for dogs like me
> To understand why this must be.
> I know it's not that you're unkind,
> But being lonely's *such* a bind.
> Yet frankly 'spite my many moans,
> Old 'Blowie' often gives me bones.
> I still can't grasp the way she talks,
> But one good thing—we go for walks.
> Even so it's not the same,
> And won't be till you're home again.
> *Please* hurry back—with love I am,
> Your ever loving doggie—Sham
> lick, lick."

Lucky composed no poems and she did not pine when I left her, but just the same she knew she was my dog, and she hailed my return from my travels with enthusiasm. I might be gone for six months on end, but the morning after my return, she would be waiting patiently outside my door for the sound of the bell which meant I had wakened and was ready for her and for coffee. No day's work was so endless that she did not lie companionably beside my desk, encouraging me to go on; no illness was so long and tedious that she stirred from my bedside without returning to it the minute she had been aired and fed. She knew by instinct if I were troubled and unhappy; I could shut myself away from everyone else, but not from her. She cried until I permitted her to rejoin me.

Like other great ladies, Lucky had her faults. Her attitude was haughty, though never discourteous, to those she did not especially like and, if anyone ventured to take possession of her favorite chair before she could ensconce herself in it, she glared balefully at the intruder and never missed the first chance to reclaim it for herself. She was an indifferent and negligent mother, perhaps because maternity went hard with her and, once, even necessitated a Caesarean section. Her daughter, Susie, the namesake of Lucky's mother and the child of Lucky's first litter, was much more devoted to her little half-brothers and sisters than Lucky was to her own children. She wasn't interested in learning tricks and, indeed, seemed to regard rather scornfully the dogs that performed them. Such antics were beneath the dignity of a really important dog, which she unquestionably was. These minor flaws in her character, if such they should be called, did not impair her value in my eyes. She was infinitely dear to me, and so is her memory. I have never even considered giving her a successor.

Perhaps this tribute to one of the best friends I ever had, or can ever hope to have, will explain why there are so many poems about dogs in this anthology and perhaps some readers will find, without explanation, the reason why each of the other animals presented deserves its place in the collection.

THE INNKEEPER'S CAT

Ulrich Troubetzkoy

The cat climbed into blazing night
along the palm's elliptic stem,
a speck in overwhelming light,
to prowl the roofs of Bethlehem.

Midnight was chill, so he crawled back
by the inn stable where he knew
warm creatures slept, but through a crack
strange radiance made him pause and mew.

A man as splendid as a king
opened the door and let him in;
he saw the gold, he heard them sing,
his fur got prickly on his skin.

He could not hum the hymns he heard,
nor mumble prayers, but in caress,
he tiptoed to the Child and purred,
and rubbed against His Mother's dress.

THE FIGHTER

C. M. Schmid

Our cat came in torn up again.
He's a small cat, but he weighs nine pounds—we weighed him.
He doesn't *have* to fight, if he doesn't want to, does he?
He doesn't even seem to mind being torn up—
Do you suppose he *wants* to fight?

If you want something bad enough you fight for it.
That's it—he *has* to fight.
After all, he does have to fight.
And he doesn't mind the consequences—
He accepts the consequences.
Good cat.

EPITAPH FOR A PET

Frances Rodman

This grief is for the time he chewed the slipper
And took his punishment with hurt surprise
That from all kindness could fall such chastisement;
This tear is for the sorrow in his eyes.
And this, for all the times we had no leisure
To romp with him, and left him lonely there,
Hoping, until the door closed, to be summoned
Scrambling and eager, down the darkened stair.
And this regret is for the many pleasures
So trivial to us, so great to him,
We might have offered, but it was a trouble;
Although it seems, now that our eyes are dim
With the remembering, we might have given
(Having it in our power), more of heaven . . .

MEMORANDUM FOR ST. PETER

Eleanor Alletta Chaffee

If one deserves admittance who bore most
Small miseries, and manhandling now and then,
Open the gate to let in this small ghost
Who, guileless, trusted all his fellow-men.
So little made him glad; a bone, a ball
Tossed in a hurried moment, to be hid
Somewhere most secret near the old stone wall,
With dignity that marked all that he did.
So little made him sad; an angry word
(Little deserved by one who longed to please)
And all the sparkle suddenly would be blurred,
A head pressed urgently against our knees.

I pray you, lift the latch; he will not bark
Until I whistle in the later dark . . .

DENISE

Robert Beverly Hale

Come here, Denise!
Come let us find a little patch of sun
And meditate a measurement of time.

I have outlived five dogs:
Hector and Hercules,
Genghis the golden,
The fashionable Pamplemousse,
And, lately, Hans of Weimar,
Hans of the amber eyes.

You are my last, Denise;
Life is but one dog more,
Denise, my raisin-bread Dalmatian,
Denise of the delicate crossed paws.

DOG, SLEEPING LATE

Marion M. Madsen

Always before he knew the sound
Of meal-in-the-making: with twitching nose
As an arrow, he shot, target-bound
Kitchenward. As a bugle blows,
So loudly, something stirred his dreams:
From anywhere in the house he woke.
But now the circuit is weak, the beams
Seldom get through; no games provoke
His eyes to shine; no words can roll
His head from listening, side to side.
Now in a winter wood no stroll
Renews his hunter-zeal. The tide
Of sleep flows longer, later here
This sunny corner; he can puff
Remembered races; all too clear
His dreams are strenuous enough.

TIED DOGS

Stanton A. Coblentz

Often, when hearing one who rails at fate,
I think of two tied dogs I used to know:
Prince yapped and howled to tell the world his woe;
Rex mutely chewed the rope, and leapt the gate.

THE THORN

Berniece Bunn Christman

What did the beast know
Of wonder and pain
And marks on the soul
For loss or gain?

He came to me, his friend,
With wounded cries
To show the thorn of lead.
I only saw his eyes.

THE FOX

Edsel Ford

I had to shoot a fox today. If he
Had been full-grown and healthy in his hate,
Or flung his fury headlong into me
As my hand tripped the latch that swung the gate
Of death to let him in, I might be proud
That he lies cold beneath the winter stars.
But he was thin and pitiful, and cowed
To see me standing fixed among my scars
With him as my revenge. In his pale eyes
(And this is what I hated most, I think)
Was neither light nor cunning. Too late wise
In knowing even to this ultimate brink
I favored him, I fired—nor could foresee
His dying with such inexorable dignity.

HOUR FOR SWANS

Harold Vinal

It was an hour for swans, in such a dusk
Great birds might seek the waters, something in
The attar of the leaves was that of musk;
We seemed to hear the wings and see the fen
Rise silver from the willows and a faster
Movement of light go by and if we peered
We might have seen those birds of alabaster,
We might have heard their whispers, had we neared.

The waters hardly moved and what went gliding
Was half of cloud and half of moonlight there:
In such a dusk swans might arise from hiding
To drink the fragrant and delicious air
Of summer and against the shadowed, low
Stain of the banks, stand neck to neck in snow.

ODE TO A NIGHTINGALE

John Keats

(Abridged)

Thou wast not born for death, immortal bird!
No hungry generations tread thee down;
Thy voice I heard this passing night was heard
In ancient days by emperor and clown;
Perhaps the self-same song that found a path
Through the sad heart of Ruth, when sick for home,
She stood in tears amid the alien corn;
The same that oft-times hath
Charmed magic casements, opening on the foam
Of perilous seas, in fairy lands forlorn.

Forlorn! The very word is like a bell
To toll me back from thee to my sole self!
Adieu! the fancy cannot cheat so well
As she is famed to do, deceiving elf.
Adieu! Adieu! thy plaintive anthem fades
Past the near meadows, over the still stream,
Up to the hillside; and now 'tis buried deep
In the next valley-glades.
Was it a vision, or a waking dream?
Fled is that music—do I wake or sleep?

PEACOCK

Sara Van Alstyne Allen

Peacock, the dusk will find you
Awkward and ugly in your flight,
Your voice of disenchantment in the night.
But now you walk erect and proud,
The furled beauty of your fan
Lifted above the emerald lawn,
The iridescent feathers on your neck
Ripple like music in the summer sun,
Waking such blue as might be found
In temples by a secret sea where the curved walls
Repeat the water's blue design,
Where a tropic tree, loosing its flowers,
Echoes the silken sound
As you pass over the summer grass.

THE TURTLE

Ogden Nash

The turtle lives 'twixt plated decks,
Which practically conceal its sex.
I often wonder how the turtle,
In such a fix, can be so fertile.

THE TERMITE

Ogden Nash

Some primal termite knocked on wood
And tasted it, and found it good,
And that is why your Cousin May
Fell through the parlor floor today.

THE COW

Ogden Nash

The cow is of the bovine ilk;
One end is moo, the other, milk.

PROFILE

David Morton

Now that the wind has gentled, the three lambs
Stand up on spread, unsteady legs, and stare
At the torn sky, and sniff the dangerous air.

Had I their speech, I'd cry to them: my dears,
Go skip like the scriptural hills . . . be foolish and bold;
Believe that spring is forever . . . run away from the fold.

You may get hurt—you will—but you will skip
That sorriest of fates, come late December:
A sad old sheep, with nothing to remember.

Be off, my dears, be deaf to the old and clever.
This is your spring . . . Believe it is forever.

SHEPHERD'S SONG

John Robert Quinn

Who will watch
My silver sheep
When my shadow
Falls asleep
Deeper than
The dark is deep?

Who will lead
My lambs like foam
To the meadow,
Bring them home,
When I am gold
In the honeycomb?

THE COW

R. P. Lister

Enthroned in quiet simplicity, the cow
Holds court to little birds that strut around
In nervous reverence, and pause to bow
Before they tug their luncheon from the ground.

Above, the splendid canopy of leaves
Protects her from the disrespectful sun;
The caterpillars clamber on its eaves,
And on silk threads the servile spiders run.

The cautious squirrels, wrapped round in cozy fur,
Peer at her shyly round the toadstool's rim,
And grasshoppers, devoutly facing her,
Set up a patriotic noontide hymn,

While she, in spotted calm, sedately lies
With sweet contentment in her queenly eyes.

THE NEW CALF

Bianca Bradbury . .

The mother licked it clean and moved away.
It swayed, and its round new eyes
Held nothing but surprise
At sunlight, and the size
Of the world it tumbled into. Four thin legs
Took it, trembling, after her.
It found the milk and rested on her side.
It staggered off, looked back, returned,
Making sure of warmth and nearness. Then
It wobbled away to see the world,
Stumbled into tansy, sniffed and ferned
Wet edge of the running brook. The old cow lowed,
And ambled down to find it. Only an hour
Had passed since birth,
But the calf had found another mother. There,
Curled by the brook, like a white and heavy flower,
It slept upon the soft, cool cheek of earth.

GO TO THE BARN FOR COURTESY

Robert P. Tristram Coffin

Go to the barn to find good manners,
It is the shortest way, these days
When men are all so busy living,
To learn the bronze and gentle ways.

Horses eat with a decorum,
They make no move of awkwardness,
Their velvet muscles move like music,
They eat their hay with a caress.

There is no sound but has its meaning,
And most of the barn sounds are low,
Even the youngest, hungriest calf
Goes to his supper grave and slow.

Cows have a dignity, a deportment;
They make you sure, they wish you well,
Watch their eyes grow large and tender
When you come, and you can tell.

Quiet, quiet all around you,
Though hunger is here everywhere,
Tenderer than the hay's fragrance
Gentleness fills all the air.

I have been called a barn poet,
And I am very proud to be,
For courtesy and gentle behaviour
Have always been good poems to me.

17

PLACES

Unless I am mistaken, I have selected more poems about *Places* than on any other one subject. This seems to be indicated no less because so many people are interested in Places—though these are very numerous—than because they have to be divided into three groups, as far as their taste in reading are concerned: (1) those who like to read about the places they have visited and enjoyed, and thus awake fond memories; (2) those who like to read about places that they have not visited but have longed to see, and fear they never will; and (3) those who prefer to do all their traveling vicariously while seated in a comfortable armchair. The sum total of these is quite formidable, and I have tried to keep these varied tastes in mind.

It will surprise no one among my acquaintances that I have included so many poems about New England. On the other hand, it may perhaps strike some readers as strange that I have included three poems about Texas and none at all about Missouri and South Dakota, especially when I admit—I hope without endangering my life!—that Texas does not happen to be one of my favorite states, although San Antonio seems to me one of the most fascinating cities in the United States. But I have not come across any particularly arresting poems about Missouri and South Dakota, and every one of these about Texas seems to me in its own way perceptive, vigorous and utterly charming.

Milton Bracker's delightful verses about Paris are admittedly written in lighter vein than most of those I have selected about places. But while they are entirely without malice, they are accurate to an almost devastating degree when it comes to describing aspects of life which have baffled and often enraged the unreconciled stranger in the City of Light. What outsider has not struggled with the Parisian telephone, tangled with a concierge, and despaired of getting potatoes that were not fried? But, on the other hand, is there any limit to the number of outsiders who do not feel, like Mr. Bracker, that they would like to spend a year in Paris? I do not think so! And I think there are also quite a number who would like to spend a year in Seville or Siena or—you choose!

I AM THE UNITED STATES

John Ackerson

You heard me in the purl of a fountain,
Iron-grilled, at New Orleans; in the flow
Of rapid Oregon; in gales that blow
Round Lookout Mountain,
Chanting of my battles long ago.

Now I sound my clarion in chain-lightning
From mouths of my sixty thousand guns,
A whiteness, of a myriad starry suns,
Man's hope that, brightening,
Cleanses earth of Samurai and Huns.

Soon you'll hear my voice in children's laughter;
Superb they are, as daybreak that awaits
From eastern to my western fortress-gates.
I am today, tomorrow, the hereafter.
I am the United States.

THE CUSTOMS OF THE COUNTRY

Phyllis McGinley

Connecticut, with much at stake,
Prefers to call a pool a lake,
But in New Hampshire and beyond
They like to call a lake a pond.

LANDSCAPE WITH FIGURINES

Phyllis McGinley

Vermont has mountains,
Vermont has pines,
Has highways innocent of billboard signs,
Has white front porches, neighborly and wandering,
Where ladies hang laundry
When they feel like laundering.

People in Vermont
Keep their tongues well-throttled,
Have carbonated summertimes that should be bottled,
Have cows like goddesses and cats like pandas.
But they *will* hang their washing
On their front verandahs.

HOMETOWN NAME

Hiram Lyday Sloanaker

How sweet the hometown to the exile's tongue!
Though he may fare forth far, to ancient lands,
Lavish with beauty and exotic lore,
Still, still among such beauties does his mind
Go wandering—he aches and starves and thirsts;
And, idling, where men have praises sung,
He stands hard dispossessed; his truant mind
Flies on an eager journey to his youth
Long gone, and he does say, for instance, "Newton!"
That pretty town he knew long, long ago,
Innocent upon its rolling Iowa plain,
White clapboards in a friendly emerald land;
"Newton"—a name so sweet he drinks it down
From memory's rusty dipper in his hand.

NEW ENGLAND

Bianca Bradbury

This country has a harmony its own,
Of time, and moving tide, and wind and weather.
Seasons do not leap to life full-blown,
But flow serenely, year on year together
Down the centuries. There is a day
For planting, and a day for harvesting.
God takes His time, we do not need to pray
For sun, or for the silver rain of Spring.
Inevitable, as the reluctant sea
That beats, and beats, and beats upon the sand,
The cycle bears us forward timelessly
The old and faithful children of the land.
We are blessed, and fated in our birth
To the slow and lovely rhythm of the earth.

NEW ENGLAND

Ella Forbes

Here are both grace and beauty, hand in hand
They wander by the sea,
Or strolling inland, through the wooded ways
Robed in the vibrant glory of their days,
They weave a tapestry
Of shining lakes and mountains climbing far,
Under the genial sun and kindly star.
Here is the guarantee of God's good land;
The fragrant savor of a wholesome earth,
Which, of its substance yields, as He had planned,
That there be no unfruitfulness; no dearth.

Lured by her spell, encouraged by her smile,
I am of those who linger at her door,
And, with her permit, roam along her shore,
While beauty walks beside me mile on mile.
Here would I bide till, dusk enfolding me,
Night calls to slumber both the land and sea.

NEW ENGLAND LANDSCAPE

Eleanor Alletta Chaffee

Here, in the country's heart,
A man may find his rest.
Here were the earliest roots
Into the rich soil pressed.

His father's father fashioned
With patient hands the wall
Where lie the leaves, forgotten,
Of many a crimson fall.

Here man forgets an hour
All else save that this hill
Holds in its breast the secret
Of dreaming and of will.

At night he will awake
Within the city fast,
Knowing himself a prisoner
Forever to his past.

NEW ENGLAND CHURCHYARD

Marguerite Janvrin Adams

Mathilda, spouse of Ephraim, mother of seven stalwart sons,
Sleeps in the quiet of her grave beside her well-beloved ones.
"Seventeen Hundred Eighty-Seven"—the lichened stone records the
year
Of her ripe passing, and the verse absolves her from all earthly fear.
To have borne sons and have them there beside her, all the turmoil
over,
To have them and her husband near under the wayward grass and
clover,
Her sleep must be a rest unstirred by any loneliness now known
To them who bear the weight of loss, feeling the weight of alien
stone.
Mathilda, spouse of Ephraim, mother of seven stalwart sons,
You are the fortunate, the proud, and we the inconsolable ones.

GREEN MOUNTAIN LATITUDES

Frances Frost

Halfway between the Equator and the Pole,
Vermont wears the forty-fourth parallel around her meadow-and-moun-
  tain middle, and her soul is well aware of her divided ground.
Who lives Up-state beneath the Northern Lights is apt to be looked
  at wearily by Down.
While neither is averse to love or fights,
Down-state, of course, is nearer Boston Town and closer to temptation
  than the north.
But let a York State or New Hampshire man question a citizen's
  or acre's worth, he'll learn there is no latitude which can divide
  Vermonters about their sovereign state.
They'll declare war on a nation across the ocean; or independent as
  a hog on ice, talk straight and secede from the Union—if they take
  the notion.

LULLABY FOR A VERMONT TOWN

Frances Frost

With your wineglass elms
and your maple trees,
sleep, little town,
at the mountain's knees.

Gold in the hollow
of hills, your lights
are a handful of stars
to the nighthawk's flight.

Your square white houses,
your tall white spire,
dream in the rust
of the old moon's fire.

Sleep, little town,
while the night goes by,
until your sleepers
turn and sigh,

knowing all's well
and the hour late
by the homing cry
of the northbound freight.

NEW HAMPSHIRE MOON

Frances Frost

Above the heat-blue hills the high
Hawk drifts lazily down the sky.

Cloudy galleons cross the day
To guard the tides of Portsmouth Bay.

Rivers with Indian names dream through
White towns that feathered warriors knew.

On tall, red barns gold weathervanes
Veer lightly toward the hint of rains.

Farmers and boys in dungarees
Wade through flowers to their knees.

Indian-colored, back and breast,
They mow the red-top to its rest.

I keep New Hampshire green and fine
Inside my heart's own boundry line.

RETURN TO THE FARM

Mary Atwater Taylor

We who traveled every road to Rome,
And roads to Carcassonne and Samarkand,
At last return again to our land—
    We have come home.

Here are the fields and brook we could not spare,
The plum-trees heavy with their ripening fruit,
The burnished grapevine with its knotted root—
    These breathe our air.

This is the land we loved and tended well,
Here we were born, here we shall someday die
    Contented if we finally may lie
      Asleep upon the hill.

THE HARNESS SHOP

Minnie Hite Moody

There was deep gloom inside, as the leather
Hung from the front-room walls, black as the bridles
Over the pegs that nestled there together.
Then I learned once again how sunlight sidles
Across a plank floor in late afternoon.
In the back room the windows were wide flung
To catch the Summer. My heart sang a tune
It used to sing when I was very young;
And on a stool the harness-maker sat,
Plying his awl; pausing sometimes to chuckle.
I thought: life still can be as good as that—
Joy stitched in with the setting of a buckle—
And zinnias outside, drinking yellow light,
And people walking home with thoughts of night.

IN THE BOSTON PUBLIC GARDEN

Saul Gottlieb

This Sunday summer air—this clear sunlight—
moves us on recaptured paths, as if
our childhood selves were real, and this place ours,
and we the children circling in our vision,
stepping on shadows of elms, lost
for the moment in the careful mottled maze
of lawns, ponds, bridges, people.

How slowly the swan boats describe their voyage
along the flowered shores of the pond,
moved by that easy power of paddles,
by footloose, sitting college boys, trailed
by real ducks and drakes, ducklings, swans,
the passengers all still and smiling,
in clothes the colors of Seurat.

It's like a dream or memory
confined to a pleasant, silly place
like this lacework bridge the boys cross
laughing, crying us on to the swan-boat pier,
their voices bright bells sounded to charm us,
at which white pigeons flutter and coo,
weaving indolent love in circles of air.

As once before, we take a snapshot by the willow—
you in your starched deep-yellow frock—
then board the boat, beside aunts and nephews,
observe the duck's funny dive for nuts,
the baby's study of subtle swan-necks,
and debark to meet ourselves coming forward
from dark places edging the park.

FROM THE HARVARD YARD

Donald Hall

March twenty-first. I lean upon
The rail of Sever Hall,
Richardson's monument, and watch
Snow fall,

So thin it melts before it turns
The Yard a scrappy white;
First day of spring. Now seven years
Are light.

Late March, a freshman then (and now
Returned from years away)
I saw snow fail at wintering
This day.

Emerging then from Sever, I
Paused to consider Man
In terms of snow that fell without
A Plan.

The poem was no good. And yet,
Today I fail to see
Snow with a single thin response
In me.

Who can be sure his growing grows
Up and not down or out?
Growth is a word that dignifies
The stout.

MAZDA MIRACLE

Carl John Bostelmann

Not even Troy in all its fatal splendor
Could lift a skyline with so swift a fire
As sweeps Manhattan when the day's surrender
Illumines tier on tier of city spire
From Woolworth down to Whitehall!
Wrought from dream,
This radiance of iridescent walls
Ignites our island mirrored in this stream
That silhouettes the darkness as it falls.

Each dusk we watch and always wonder more
To know what wizard's magic words are spoken
To bring forth beauty high above the shore;
When we should know in crossing to Hoboken,
This mighty triumph which subdues the dark
Was once a meager glow in Menlo Park.

METROMANIA

Berton Braley

New Yorkers are people of very queer habits
Who, native and foreign,
Are packed in a warren
Like hordes of uncountable rabbits
With off, unaccountable ways
For instance, their days
Are fevered with hurries and rushes,
Jams, squeezes and crushes,

In subways and busses, and struggles with bunches
Of other cosmopolites, gobbling their lunches—
And so you would think that New Yorkers would say
Come nighttime—"Enough of that stuff for today."
> Yet the saps take no naps
> But are off where the crowd is
> Nor care if the mob's
> Made of ruffians and rowdies
> Or schemers and snobs.

New Yorkers are people whose notions are queer.
They love being given a kick in the rear,
They love being bullied and robbed of their jack
> By busboys and waiters
> Nightclub operators
> And fight speculators
> And clerks in the-yators
The more they are stepped on the more they come back.

New Yorkers are people who don't look at stars;
The signs that bedizen the city horizon,
> The glitter of chromium bars,
> Are things that they prize
Above any natural light in the skies.

New Yorkers are people whose attitude's curious,
People who relish the phony and spurious,
People who live in a town perpendicular
Tearing around to no place in particular.
Always in haste, but with leisure to waste
> Watching steel-riggers
> And foundation diggers
And fakers who peddle automaton figgers.

New Yorkers are lacking in privacy, peace,
Neighbors and time and apartments to lease;
In fact they are people who—taking the run of them—
Live terrible lives and it's fun to be one of them.

LOVE IN A CITY IN SPRING

Alice Duer Miller

Love in a city in spring,
Not so divine a thing
As love the poet dreams—
Meadows and brimming streams,
Yet there is much to say
For love in New York in May—
Parks set in tulip beds,
Yellows and whites and reds,
Japanese plums in flower
And that wisteria bower
Dripping its blossoms sweet
Over a rustic seat
Where tramps and nursemaids meet . . .

New York in early May
Breaks out in awnings gay;
Daisies and ivy trailing
From every window railing.
And at this time of year
Strange open hacks appear,
Shabby and old and low
Wherein strange couples go
Generally after dark,
Clop-clopping round the park.
And with it all, the loud,
Noisy, indifferent crowd
Offers to lovers shrewd
Infinite solitude.

TO AN ABSENT VIRGINIAN

K. H. Peatross

Have you forgotten how the shadows quiver
  Across the ruddy waters of the James,
Or how the sunset, low across the river
  Strikes all the shining ripples into flames?
Do you remember mountains, gently rising
  From lovely valleys, lower, friendly hills,
Edged by red roads, their color more surprising
  In contrast to green fields and silver rills?

Those August afternoons (do you remember?)
  Lying at ease beneath the locust trees,
When goldenrod, the herald of September,
  Engaged the close attention of the bees,
We smelt the fragrance of the grapes and apples,
  Beneath our hands the earth was warm and dry,
Upon the grass the sunlight lay in dapples,
  And looking up, we saw a cloudless sky.

The drowsy clack of mowers in the meadows,
  The curve of some almost forgotten road,
The coolness of a millpond in the shadows,
  The thrill of riding a haywagon's load;
Late roses blooming in an ancient garden,
  The smell of boxwood in the rain and wet,
Remember these? Oh, grant me peace and pardon,
  I know—I know that you will not forget.

CHARLESTON—POST CONFEDERATE

Alston Deas

Listen against this shell. There lingers still
The far, faint echo of a distant sea
Whose swift tides knew the depths of good and ill,
And clamorous tempests struggled ragingly,
Where, for a little space, a people passed,
Quitting a haven sheltered and secure
To prove a resolute faith; and sunk at last
Perishing gladly, since their souls were pure.

Have done with sadness;—but the teardrops start.
Traveller, there is much to understand.
See how it falls about us, and apart,
The light that never was on sea or land,
And sparkles upon my City, and my heart,
And on this shell that trembles to your hand!

LOUISIANA PURCHASE

Badger Clark

"Old Tom Jefferson, what do you mean,
Buying up land that we've never seen,
All Louisiana for a whopping sum,
From the Mississippi River to Kingdom Come?
And we only know that there's rain and snow
And grass and Injuns and buffalo.

Old Tom Jefferson, what's it worth,
A desert half-way around the earth,
A thousand miles from a road or track?
How do you get there and how get back?
Your horse might skip and your keelboat zip
But you'd still grow old and die on the trip.

Old Tom Jefferson, it's too far away.
Only miracles could make it pay—
Ships that sail against a river's power,
Wagons that go twenty miles an hour—
And the pioneers on our old frontiers
Won't get it settled in a thousand years.

Old Tom Jefferson, I tell you what,
Little New Orleans was all you got—
Fifteen million for that soggy port
And the rest thrown in for a bit of sport.
The Frenchies knew when the deal went through
That Napoleon had bamboozled you.

Old Tom Jefferson, we'll never see
Your wild Stony Mountains, wherever they be,
And your buffalo pastures may just do
For a place to banish our rascals to.
You've paid a lot for we don't know what,
And our fifteen million has gone to pot.

Old Tom Jefferson, once you shone,
Jarred the footings of the British throne,
Shaped the Declaration with your hand,
Trumpeted the liberty through the land,
So for old times' sake, in this big mistake,
We'll forgive a good man one bad break."

IN TEXAS

May Sarton

In Texas the lid blew off the sky a long time ago,
So there's nothing to keep the wind from blowing
And it blows all the time. Everywhere is far to go,
So there's no hurry at all and no reason for going.
In Texas there's so much space words have a way
Of getting lost in silence before they're spoken,
So people hang on a long time to what they have to say
And when they say it the silence is not broken.
But it absorbs the words and slowly gives them
Over to miles of white-gold plains and gray-green hills
And they are back in that silence that outlives them.
Nothing moves fast in Texas except the windmills
And the hawk that rises up with a clatter of wings.

(Nothing more startling here than sudden motion,
Everything is so still.) But the earth slowly swings
In time like a great swelling never-ending ocean,
And the houses that ride the tawny waves get smaller
As you get near them because you see them then
Under the whole sky, and the whole sky is so much taller
With the lid off than a million towers built by men.

After a while you can only see what's at horizon's edge,
And you are stretched with looking so far instead of near,
So you jump, you are startled by a blown piece of sedge,
You feel wide-eyed and ruminative as ponderous steer.
In Texas you look at America with a patient eye.
You want everything to be sure and slow and set in relation
To immense skies and earth that never ends. You wonder why
People must talk and strain so much about a nation
That lives in spaces vaster than a man's dream, can go
Five hundred miles through wilderness meeting only the hawk

And the dead rabbit on the road. What happens must be slow,
Must go deeper even than hand's work or tongue's talk,
Must rise out of the flesh like sweat after a hard day,
Must come slowly in its own time, in its own way.

TEXAS BUS RIDE

Kenneth Porter

We left San Antone and passed through the post-oak region,
    through the neat white towns where the names over shops are German,
    or possibly Czech, and grass and flowers are religion—
    Schulenberg, Weimar—each one a Lutheran sermon.

Then suddenly it was Deep South—
    trees dark with Spanish moss, unpainted shacks, Negroes with fishing-poles,
    brown water and steaming herbage—
    mildew and tarnish;
    the cotton hung in stringy rain-beaten bolls.

The Brazos behind, we were out among grazing cattle
    and ripening rice, the flat green coastal plain;
    We knew the ocean was near, we could see the little
    white herons flapping and flying through the thin soft rain.

Houston was west; the land grew wilder and wetter,
    We saw oil derricks, piled timber; at last we came
    To grey-bearded fishers—trees knee-deep in water.
    Here was Louisiana—except for the name.

SCENIC

John Updike

O when in San Francisco do
As natives do; they sit and stare
And smile and stare again. The view
Is visible from anywhere.

Here hills are white with houses whence,
Across a multitude of sills,
The owners, lucky residents,
See other houses, other hills.

And every San Franciscan knows,
No matter where his past has been,
There are a thousand patios
Whose view he is included in.

The Golden Gate, the cable cars,
Twin Peaks, the Spreckels habitat,
The local ocean, sun, and stars—
When fog falls, one admires *that*.

The homes are stacked in such a way
That every picture window has
An unmarred prospect of the Bay
And, in its center, Alcatraz.

RAINBOW ISLANDS

Don Blanding

Nature's a daring colorist
Here in Hawaii. She loves to use
Raw vermilion and amethyst
Massed on purple and burning blues;
Velvet mountains of varied green
Set in a sea of silk and jade.
Spanned by an arch of brilliant sheen
That the sun and sea and sky have made.

TAXCO, MEXICO

M. E. Uschold

A clear, thin dawn absorbs the velvet tones
Of bells, as night dissolves from winding street
And plaza, and constricted cobblestones
Resound unhurriedly to donkeys' feet.
The pulse of living strengthens as a flow
Of tourists siphons between climbing walls,
And gray antiquity reflects a glow
Of pale, cool silver and a blaze of shawls.

HOME THOUGHTS FROM ABROAD

Robert Browning

Oh, to be in England,
Now that April's there,
And whoever wakes in England
Sees, some morning, unaware,
That the lowest boughs and the brushwood sheaf
Round the elm-tree bole are in tiny leaf,
While the chaffinch sings on the orchard bough
In England—now!

And after April, when May follows,
And the whitethroat builds, and all the swallows!
Hark, where my blossomed pear tree in the hedge
Leans to the field and scatters on the clover
Blossoms and dewdrops—at the bent spray's edge—
That's the wise thrush; he sings each song twice over,
Lest you think he never could recapture
That first fine careless rapture!
And though the fields look rough with hoary dew,
All will be gay when noontide wakes anew.
The buttercups, the little children's dower—
Far brighter than this gaudy melon-flower!

EVENING IN ENGLAND

Raymond Hosken

Here in this quiet harbor past the light
Blinking its urgent message from the shore,
Our transport has dropped anchor for the night.
Gulls in the fading daylight wheel and soar,

Each clean wing, coral in the lingered gleam,
Beats an ascending pattern in the air.
The snowclad shore lies still as any dream:
No person stirs, no smoke lifts anywhere.

The evening deepens past the wooded hills
As lemon-colored lights show from the vale.
Slow, gradual dusk the waiting harbor fills;
And all night long, the code winks without fail.

WESTMINSTER BRIDGE

William Wordsworth

Earth has not anything to show more fair;
Dull would he be of soul who could pass by
A sight so touching in its majesty;
This city now doth, like a garment, wear
The beauty of the morning; silent, bare,
Ships, towers, domes, theatres and temples lie
Open unto the fields, and to the sky—
All bright and glittering in the smokeless air.
Never did sun more beautifully steep
In his first splendor, valley, rock or hill;
Ne'er saw I, never felt, a calm so deep!
The river glideth at his own sweet will.
Dear God! the very houses seem asleep;
And all that mighty heart is lying still!

THE MAP OF FRANCE

R. L. Duffus

Shut your eyes,
Now let me guide your finger
On the map.
It's alive, isn't it?
It's beating like a pulse.
It's warm with men's lives.

It doesn't matter where:
Nancy, Chalons, Dunkerque:
Mons, where the British saw the angels
In the older war;
Armenteers—that's Mam'selle's town;
Arras, where the old merchants
Spread their goods;
Valenceens—they made lace there;
Ameens, where the statue leaned
Above the ruins—
They didn't shoot Him down
In that war.

There's Rouen, that's where
They burned Joan of Arc.
She saved France, though.
If you don't believe it
Ask at Domremy, where they know.
They say some of the Frenchies—
The Stukas had been after them, and maybe
They saw things that weren't there—
Saw Joan the other night, in smoke and thunder.
She was dressed in steel, and crying,
But her sword was drawn.
Pity was in her eyes, and anger.

All along the line the dead were rising:
Light shone on Wipers and on Noove Chapelle;
The English dead were storming Vimy Ridge.
There was Verdoon and the Frenchies standing;
"Detoor!" was what they said,
"Road closed! No thoroughfare!"
The marines were back at Chateau Teery,
And in the Argonne Forest
Fritz's sewing-machines cost twenty Yanks apiece.
But they were paying what it cost.

Glory!
Tell that to the dead marines.
Glory stinks.
Glory has cooties in its shirt.
Glory lies in a hole
With a hunk of shell in its guts,
Yelling for water—
And there isn't any water.

It wasn't glory Joan was thinking of.
It was France.
This is the map of France.
It's alive, isn't it?
It's beating like a pulse.
It's warm with men's lives.

Not glory—something further.
They've been here a long time, these Frenchies
You see their churches
Against the sky.
Big ones, that pray in stone:
Reems and Chartres,
Notre Dame and Sainte Chapelle,
Ameens and Orleens.
They took a long time to build.

You see their roads,
Old roads with trees along them,

Straight roads, going places.
Julius Caesar came this way,
And here Joan rode her big white horse.
And here came the French,
Drunk with liberty,
Singing the Marseillaise,
To save the young Republic
At a place called Valmy.

You see their houses—
Old houses, dingy old houses,
Old villages,
Cobbled streets,
Worn by the feet of generations,
Old taverns,
Where men have talked on quiet nights
For half a thousand years.

They've got roots, these Frenchmen.
This is their land.
Havre and Compiegne,
Nancy and Laon,
Beauvais and Epernay,
Paris and Bordeaux,
Nantes,
Marseilles,
A thousand little towns—
They made them
A long time ago.

They made other things:
They made books and songs,
Pictures and statues;
They made ideas,
Ever hear of
Liberty,
Equality,
Fraternity?
They invented them.

The tanks break through.
There swoop the Stukas.
Hitler's on the march,
Into a land not his,
Into a land he cannot understand
And therefore would destroy.
The smoke rolls
In the Place de la Concorde.
The city's ringed with fire.
Maybe Hitler's right.
Maybe it's hell and damnation
And the world's end.
Maybe liberty won't work,
Maybe equality can't fight,
Maybe fraternity can't knock a tank out.

And maybe not.
The map says not.
Verdoon and Chateau Teery say not.
Notre Dame and Chartres say not.
The faces of Frenchmen,
The old houses,
The books,
The songs,
The streams, the rivers, the mountains,
The army of those who died for liberty,
Say not.

This is the map of France.
It's alive.
It's beating like a pulse.
It's warm with men's lives.
It's been ploughed in blood
And fertilized with bones.
But it will not die.
They say some beaten troops
Saw Joan the other night.
She wept but her sword was flaming.
This is the map of France.

PARIS

Alan Seeger

First, London, for its myriads; for its height,
Manhattan heaped in towering stalagmite;
But Paris for the smoothness of the paths
That lead the heart unto the heart's delight. . . .

Fair loiterer on the threshold of those days
When there's no lovelier prize the world displays
Than, having beauty and your twenty years,
You have the means to conquer and the ways,

And coming where the crossroads separate
And down each vista glories and wonders wait,
Crowning each path with pinnacles so fair
You know not which to choose, and hesitate—

Oh, go to Paris. . . . In the midday gloom
Of some old quarter take a little room
That looks off over Paris and its towers
From Saint Gervais round to the Emperor's Tomb,—

So high that you can hear a mating dove
Croon down the chimney from the roof above
See Notre Dame and know how sweet it is
To wake between Our Lady and our love.

And have a little balcony to bring
Fair plants to fill with verdure and blossoming,
That sparrows seek, to feed from pretty hands,
And swallows circle over in the Spring.

There of an evening you shall sit at ease
In the sweet month of flowering chestnut-trees,
There with your little darling in your arms,
Your pretty dark-eyed Manon or Louise.

And looking out over the domes and towers
That chime the fleeting quarters and the hours,
While the bright clouds banked eastward back of them
Blush in the sunset, pink as hawthorn flowers,

You cannot fail to think, as I have done,
Some of life's ends attained, so you be one
Who measures life's attainment by the hours
That Joy has rescued from oblivion.

A BOUQUET OF VERSES FOR PARIS
IN THE SPRING

Milton Bracker

LE PRINTEMPS

Hail to the months of *mai* and *juin*—
 Pull the cork and pour the vin!

Once you have a place to stay,
Orly, jail, or Le Bourget;
Hail the boat-train, hail the *gare*,
Hail a cab at St. Lazare.
Hail the banks, both left and right,
Hail the lovers, day and night;
Hail the bookstalls on the Seine
And the columned Madeleine.
Hail the fountains at Versailles
And the Boulevard Raspail
And the Place des Pyramides

And the Pont des Invalides
And the hospital at Neuilly
And the Métro stop at Reuilly
And old St. Germain des Prés
   And the île de la Cité
     And *la femme du boulanger*
      On the Rue St. Honoré.
Hail, in fact, all friendly *rues*—
May they soon be *avenues!*
Vive, for one, La Rue Richepance—
Vive, of course, *la différence.*
Hail the fleas, and hail the market,
Hire a car, and try to park it;
Hail Le Dôme, in Montparnasse
And the characters who pass;
Hail each artist and his palette
And each sculptor and his mallet.
Hail the *mode* and hail the *chic*
And the Opéra-Comique
And the Comédie Français
And the stirring Marseillaise
And the old francs, and the new francs
And each time you save a few francs.
Hail the office, far behind you,
   And the boss, who cannot find you,
     And the family ties that bind you,
      And the kids, who will not mind you.

Pull the cork and pour the vin;
Let not age or care embarrass
You; it's *mai* and will be *juin*—
   This is spring, and you're in Paris!

LE GRAND LUXE

   A traveler whose bankroll fits
   The bills presented by the Ritz
   May call the Place Vendôme
   Home.

LE SIGHTSEEING

The Vista that is most Parisian
Is along the *Champs* Elysian,
In the daytime, in the dark,
Toward or from the famous Arc.
Though your mood be glum and beefy,
It will make it green and leafy;
It will make your footsteps springy
And your shoulder blades feel wingy
And will lift you up with lightness
And will fill your eyes with brightness.
It will make a man breathe deeper,
An insomniac, a sleeper
And a guy who cannot smile,
A gay-hearted francophile
   Who will kiss his wife and then—
   Vive la vie parisienne!

LA PLACE DE LA CONCORDE

This is where the Reign of Terror
Killed a lot of folks in error
But Louis XVI might not be dead
If he hadn't lost his head.

LA BALLADE

(On the virtual inescapability of French fried potatoes in France)

I take off my hat to Parisian cuisine—
   The hat that I doff is in fact a beret;
An *haricot vert* is the favorite bean
   Of one who considers himself a gourmet.
   Garçon, l'addition! I am happy to pay—
The pâtisserie was the ultimate treat—
   But why, in the name of the Chef, *s'il vous plait,*
Must the land of the French be the home of the *frite?*

Farewell to my distant domestic routine;
   No chicken for me when I crave *le poulet*;
No fish, when I order *la truite amandine*—
   Nor can I resist any *crêpe* that's *flambée*.
The time at the table ennobles the day;
This Châteaubriand is an honor to eat—
   But what are these slivers I see on the tray?
Must the land of the French be the home of the *frite?*

No maître is wily, no waiter is mean;
   I've come for a month but I wish I could stay;
I dine like a King and my wife like a Queen
   Or maybe *un roi et une reine*, I should say.
And yet, as we sit at a sidewalk café,
We ask every (bilingual) native we meet:
   Forgive us for asking, but why is it, pray?
Must the land of the French be the home of the *frite?*

L'ENVOI

Oh, bring me an Idaho, hi-de-ho, hey,
Serve it with jacket and butter, complete!
   NO baked and NO mashed? *Inventez* a new way!
MUST THE LAND OF THE FRENCH BE THE HOME OF
THE FRITE?

LE BOIS

The Bois de Boulogne is like Central Park
Except that it's safer after dark.

LE TELEPHONE

According to a friend of mine,
Ne quittez pas means hold the line;
The only thing he didn't say
Was that it sometimes means, all day.

LA JOCONDE

The Mona Lisa
Is a tease, a
   Little like
The Tower of Pisa.
Has she fallen?
   Will it fall?
I can't make
   Them out at all.

As she hangs there,
   Subtly glowing,
Is she yes-ing?
   Is she no-ing?
If da Vinci
   Knew this baby,
It's a cinch she
   Told him Maybe!

LA LANGUE FRANÇAISE

The French all speak it* much too fast
   And if, on rare occasion,
I spot one word, it hurries past
Pursued by others, till at last
   They all sound Greek or Asian.

LES ARBRES

Not all the trees are chestnut trees;
Among the ones a tourist sees
   Are simply scores
   Of sycamores.

But there's no cause to fret, or mind
   Distinctions so pedantic
Because in Paris, you will find
   A *plane* tree is romantic.

LE BOUL' MICH'

Students in the Latin Quarter
Need a generous supporter
Nor does fellowship or grant
Match a very wealthy aunt.

* And the meanest thing, just *entre nous*—
They've taught their children to speak it, too.

LE THÉÂTRE

Although back home in Texas you're
   the owner of a gusher,
Your stock will fall in Paris if
   you fail to tip the usher.

LE BON MARCHE

(A rondeau)

In Paris, France, when spring is near,
I share a kind of reckless cheer;
   Between the counters, row on row,
   My love and I are wont to go,
Her hope untrammeled by my fear.

Not all the things she seeks are dear;
Not all the French eludes her ear
   And yet, a shopping tour is slow
     In Paris, France.

An objet d'art strikes me as queer—
My love's convinced it hath no peer.
   We spend. I watch our baggage grow.
   We spend—more than we should, I know,
And yet, I'd love to spend a year
     In Paris, France.

RETURN TO CHARTRES

May Sarton

We came to Chartres, riding the green plain,
The spear of hope, the incorruptible towers,
Stone upon stone, leaf upon leaf,
The great tree rooted in the heart of France
Blazing eternally with sacred flowers.
We came to Chartres, the house without a stain,
The mastery of passion by belief,
With all its aspiration held in balance,
We came to Chartres, the magic spear of grain,
The spear of wheat, forever nourishing,
The never-wasted stalk, the ever-blessing.

And there we meditated on our tragic age,
At the heart, flowering without a stem,
For we are barren men, haunted by rage
Who cannot find our hope here though we came,
Now all the hope we have is human love:
Passion without belief destroys our love.

MONT-SAINT-MICHEL

Charles Wharton Stork

Wide, level sands to the far edge of the sea.
Alone you rear your tawny pyramid might.
You are the archangel militant,
Though to the casual eye you seem to be—
So proudly dominant,
With lifted spear—an ancient Norman knight.

Fearless against the clouds you rise.
Nine desolating centuries
Have left you undiminished, undismayed.
Your silence is a shout
To put the armies of the Fiend to rout.
Man may have dreamed you; it was God who made.

FISH OUT OF WATER

Margaret Fishback

Beside the Adriatic Sea
They lunch at two, and sleep from three
To five. Then slowly wakes the land
Again, to loll upon the sand.

The cooks, at six, relinquish shore
To mold the pasta shells once more,
Their respite in the beach chairs done,
As sinks the hot, persistent sun.

The water's warm and gently wet—
I struggle to do nothing, yet
My conscience, from another clime,
Keeps prodding me: "What day?" "What time?"

It is an art to idle so—
I should have started long ago!
I can't, in peace, lay down my head
Until the sun has gone to bed . . .

But then, of course, it's nearly nine,
And everyone must dress and dine
And talk, till twelve or one or two,
Then sleep the lovely morning through.

SIENA, FROM A NORTHERN SLOPE

John Ackerson

We pause in the dusk, survey the battlement
Contoured upon the hill, and upward spring
White marble towers, wide and rich ascent,
While dulcet voices of the bells take wing;
All glisten with the recent rain, are flushed
With sunset, as the ancient evening dims,
Etruscan, Rome's; the legion's ranks are hushed,
And pass to pealing of the vesper hymns;
Fire-new, this sleek red sport car whips in, fast
As grey scud of the imminent storm, while heaves
The breast with surging memories of the past,
Feet crackle on the withered chestnut leaves,
On tombs—as if a rigorous nightfall quells
Fixed radiance in the message of the bells!

A NIGHT IN PERUGIA

Richard Church

Among the Tuscan towns I know,
Perugia, frowning at the sun,
Captures my ruminating mind
More than those queens, Florence, Siena,
Pisa, famous for their beauty.

All men who love what man has made
In high civility, from stone
And chosen wood, shaping cities,
Must think of those in Tuscany
And the marble slopes of Umbria
As of a necklace round the throat
Of that beloved woman who makes
The wilderness of earth a garden
Where peace lingers, and love rests.

Thus I recall them. All the more strange
Therefore, that I should recall them
Only when Perugia, persistent
And ever first, has been dismissed.
Why is this? She is a town that glooms
On the mountainside, over the sunny
Umbrian plain, where the strips of corn
Burn like bars of purged gold.
She offers no gracious invitation
To the stranger seeking comity
And symbols of those public graces
That make a city and an age.
Perugia lies for ever unfinished;
A piazza and precipitous streets

Of stone and savagely weathered brick.
The gaunt cathedral, that should gleam
Like intelligence within the eye,
Looms like a rustic barn, which storm
And poverty have joined to batter.
Seen from without, it's little more
Than a mound of scars. Above the streets
Swallows, grieving on the wing,
Seek what they never find. Their cry
Takes hold upon the shrinking nerves
Of the newcomer, imploring him
To save himself while yet there's time.

Whenever, through Lombard plain
Thunder-clouds threaten, they will gather
Unerringly about Perugia
And let the deluge down. Then gloom
Exceeds its omen; what the swallows
Foretold in their shrill oracle,
Fills the steep pavements and the streets
Of stone cauterised by time. Like wounds
That ache in winter, the cold nerves
Of the city shudder as only stone
Can shudder. Perugia under rain
Is a threat fulfilled and in fulfilment
Doubled. All that is sinister
In history, out of a savage past,
Gleams in the stone, a sweat of hatred.
Buildings half derelict in the sun
Take on a senile beauty, leer
And snarl behind the welkin's malice.
Yet it is Perugia I see
In the mind's eye, when I hear talk
Of Tuscany and the Umbrian hills
Where the vines outline the corn
And white oxen pull the plough.

I think of all that she refuses
To yield to my imagination,
And in her obstinacy I trace
The tale that from Etruscan seed
Broke through the centuries and bloomed
For Rome to cull. Such flowers as this
Yield a dangerous juice. I fear
That I'll return to Perugia
As the poppy-addict to his drug,
Knowing my folly, yet in faith
Prepared to squander all the rest
Because of something I have dreamed
Under this influence of a town
No Florentine would deign to visit.

ONE MAN, ONE MAN ALONE (ITALY, 1941)

Edward Hutton

Let Virgil speak, not thou, for Italy;
Or Dante: shall no longer Dante plead
In her defence? nor Beauty in her need?
Nor that majestic sadness not take flame,
To brand the Clown who trafficks in her name?
Let Dante speak, not thou, for Italy.

Or Gregory, he who in exile died,
Yet not in exile—and on Justice cried.
"Upon the Asp and Basilisk thou shalt go."
'Twas done at high Canossa in the snow:
Let Gregory speak, not thou, for Italy.

Or him who from Carrara's marble breast
Hewed those dread Forms of Slavery and Unrest,
Dark Day, dire Night: and with a brush of fire
Judgment proclaimed on man and man's desire:
Let Buonarroti speak, not thou, for Italy.

Or him whose notes to mortal hearts still bring
Our Lord enthroned with Seraphs on the wing,
Whose winding voices, linked in ecstasy,
Draw heaven to earth, when earth to heaven would fly.
Let Palestrina speak, not thou, for Italy.

Or the sad Tuscan, who with optic glass,
Exalted, saw the Constellations pass;
Along what paths the wandering Planets run,
And Earth obedient to the parent Sun,
Let Galileo speak, not thou, for Italy.

Or let the Soldier speak, for soldiers should
Have the last word in this, for ill or good,—
Yes, let the Soldier speak, who fought and bled
For Her: and left his Curse upon thy head.
Let Garibaldi speak, not thou, for Italy.

And if all these be dumb? Oh, living still
His voice shall rise from Umbrian vale and hill,
And Francis speak, not thou, for Italy.*

* The poem is addressed to Benito Mussolini, then Fascist Premier of Italy.

EL ARCHIVO GENERAL DE INDIAS

Irene Aloha Wright

These are the Archives of the Indies!
Here—in these tall cases, built from marble floor
Toward domed, arched ceiling—
Here are stored, in blue-wrapped bundles, pack on pack,
The papers passed between old Spain and her far colonies.
These are the records of their government
From days when they were conquered, one by one,
In revolution they wrote "Finis" at the close
Of these colonial records.
These are the Archives of the Indies!

Patronato, Descubrimientos, Descripciones . . .

Here are the records of discovery . . .
Out of the waters rise two continents and countless isles,
Taking slow shape through tales of strange adventurings.
Here gleam the phantom walls of Cibola,
And here, the Gilded Man who never was.
Yonder flows on without restraint Juan Ponce's spring of youth.
Here fancy finds a northwest passage through
To mines, spice isles, and monstrous mysteries.
These are the Archives of the enchanted lands
That lay beyond the Ocean Sea of prose reality.

Flotas Y Armadas

Fleets and Armadas . . .
Here—within these packs of yellowed papers,
Written neat, or scrawled "Off Cape Saint Vincent" as she rolled
On surges that have broken since upon the shores of bleak eternity,
Or done in the trim numerals of a cipher used—
Here are confined in this small space
The winds that swept the Spanish main, the broad South Sea—

The winds that blew from Cadiz to the Philippines
Through four long centuries!
Here never set the suns that shone,
The moons that shimmered white
Among the islets of the Caribbes.
Here howls the fierce typhoon—
The hurricane roars hoarse through chartless channels,
Thundering south, from Jacan to the Name of God,
A-shriek amid the cordage of lost galleons, ballasted with gold
And emeralds, pearls and dyewood from
Peru and Margarite and Mexico.
"May God be pleased to bring them safe to port
As your Majesty desires and Christendom hath need!"
Candles and prayers at vanished altars spent for goods and men
Rocked in the bottom of Old Ocean
Lo! These past four hundred years!
Here—the voice of guns!
Hawkins' and Drake's and doughty Baskerville's!
Pater's and Heyn's!
With Don Fadrique and a host
Of captains-general, admirals, and crews,
Avellaneda and that bold, fanatic, honest Astur, who
Slit Ribaut's throat in Florida: Pedro Menéndez!
How they sail yet upon this troubled sea
Of finite History!
How brave they sail!
How brave they sail through these old papers here preserved!
These are the Archives of the Indies! These!

> *Audiencia De Santo Domingo,*
> *Florida Y Luisiana.*

Letters of Governors, Accountants, Priests,
Of Captains, Indian Chieftains, Wives!
Who reads these records through sees north to Canada—
That "Frozen Land"—and finds Marquette, canoeing south
On mighty waters of an unknown stream.
Port Royal, Charleston, Jamestown, Augustine—
Here their beginning's told.

Half hid in sand, there lies
The wreck of La Salle's ship.
Who reads, hears arrows whistle, feels the whir
Of good Toledo steel; sees Indian skulk,
Creeping at dawn to storm the palisades
Of unremembered posts on river routes and shores:
"My Governor, send help! We are surrounded,
Our munitions gone. Send help."—
Sweated and torn, it lay against the heart
Of a bold friar, acting courier—
A scrap of paper here, that cry
Rings down the centuries: "Send help! Send help!"
These are the Archives of the Indies.

Audiencia De Mexico, Santa Fe, etc.

Look South!
How pale against the dawning sixteenth century arise
The sacrificial smoke wreaths o'er those piles
Of Aztec shrines and Inca palaces!
See yonder west coast sweeping on
From Darien to the Horn,
The flames around the funeral pyre of martyr-missionaries sink
To glow of furnaces at copper mines.
Amid the jungle see those clearings spread—cane and tobacco,
Bait for pirate ships!
On plains above the coastal fringe
Horned cattle graze, and sheep.
Two continents and countless, nameless isles
In fabled seas.
That acrid smoke? Borne from the guns, I think,
That Dewey fired . . . Sampson and Schley, at Santiago.
These are the Archives of the Indies! These—
Ashes of empire!
Worthless! Bale on bale!
So much old paper—tied with dirty string!

SOME CITIES OF SPAIN

Frances Parkinson Keyes

MADRID

Madrid is luncheon in the Ritz garden on a sunny day
And luncheon at Horscher's Restaurant on a rainy day,
And luncheon with pleasant friends in their pleasant apartments on
any kind of a day.
It is eating too much, on such occasions, but rising from table
With a wonderful sense of well-being and good fellowship
And the conviction that it does not matter whether or not you do any-
thing else that day.
Madrid is late mass at San Geronimo's and an hour at the Prado after
that
And before going on to one of those soothing and satisfying luncheons.
It is choosing beforehand in whose company you will spend that hour:
Velasquez and his royalty and warriors?
Goya and his immortal duchess?
El Greco and his ascetic saints?
Murillo and his mystic madonnas?
Nowhere in the world will you have greater variety of choice in the
matter of goodly company,
Either in the gallery or at luncheon afterward.

Madrid is the Gran'Via crowded with traffic at dusk,
Strident with sound and suddenly blooming with lights.
It is a narrow street of the quiet old city
Thronged with a procession honoring San Isidro,
The good laborer who is the city's patron,
And whom the city honors on his feast day
With a parade in which laborers young and old take part,
And a pontifical mass at the cathedral,
Which all the great of Madrid honor with their presence,
Knowing Isidro was greater than any of them.

Madrid is the beautiful dresses shown by great couturiers in their
salons—

Dresses which set the fashion for day after tomorrow—
And the medieval costumes worn by the guards at El Retiro—
Costumes which have never changed since the Middle Ages,
When El Retiro was a private pleasure ground,
And not a great park where prince and peasant alike
Could spend their hours of ease and of freedom;
Solace their ailments in its beneficent sunshine;
Seek the seclusion of its shadowy allées;
Breathe in the scent of its multitudinous flowers;
Watch the swift rise and fall of its glittering fountains;
Ponder the script on the base of the towering statues—
Statues which tell the story of Spain through its heroes;
Pause by the pools which reflect these embellishments,
And, through reflection, double their loveliness;
Feel kinship alike with the nursemaids, the children, the students, the
lovers—
The happy, carefree people who throng El Retiro—
Kinship, too, with the crippled, the aged, the homeless,
The people who have so little cause to be happy,
And yet, somehow, find happiness here.

Madrid is the portico of the Church of San Francisco,
On the Sunday when the animals are brought there to be blessed:
The Sunday when hucksters bring their donkeys, draymen their
horses,
Small boys their dogs and little girls their kittens,
And old ladies the cages containing their lovebirds
Whose twittering is the only love song they hear nowadays.
The good priest comes out of the church with his Holy Water
And sprinkles it over them all as he blesses them all and smiles at them
all.
Afterward the hucksters and draymen adjust the ornaments on their
donkeys and horses and pace off proudly,
The boys run away merrily, whistling to their dogs,
The little girls cuddle their kittens against their shoulders and whisper
to each other as they leave,
But the old ladies linger a little. Some of them are blind. They must
wait to be led.

Madrid is the focal point for all sorts of excursions.
You can go to Toledo or Segovia or even Avila and come back the
same day if you are in a hurry,
But it is a great mistake to spend your time in Spain hurrying around.
It is better to go to the Royal Golf Club where you watch polo instead
of playing golf,
And sit on the terrace gazing out at the mountains,
Until the shadows have engulfed all their lovely verdure;
Or to Alcala de Henares, the city of Cervantes,
To eat a leisurely supper at La Hosteria del Estudiante,
In a raftered room where your drink is drawn from great wineskins
And the pottery is inscribed with ancient mottoes,
And Sancho Panza seems to be serving at table,
And Cervantes there with you telling his tall tales,
And the erstwhile students your fellow listeners.
And again, you have the feeling of good fellowship.

SEGOVIA

Segovia is a mighty aqueduct,
Towering, three tiered, above a quiet city,
As strong, as stately, as indomitable,
As when the Romans built it, and conveyed
The water that they needed, from the fields
Into their houses and their bathing pools.

Segovia is a tiny restaurant,
Tucked in among the arches of those tiers,
Reached by steep stairs, low studded, heavy beamed,
With little tables set so close together
That every guest is neighbor to the next.
Great loaves of bread and earthen jugs of wine
Are amicably passed from hand to hand,
And gossip flows with equal unrestraint.
Then suddenly, there comes a hush because
A buxom waitress, bearing a great platter,
Edges her way amongst the crowded tables,
And proudly starts to carve a suckling pig.

Segovia is an *antiquario's* shop,
Tucked, hole in wall, upon a winding hill
Where scurrying cars sweep by with heedless haste,
So only wayfarers discover it.
Amongst the worthless piles of dusty trash,
Of battered furniture and broken metal,
Moth-eaten fabrics and worm-eaten books,
Are tarnished treasures lovely to behold
And precious to possess.
"You like this fan? Well, I am very pleased.
That crucifix? Yes, that would be a gem
In anyone's collection. La Granja glass?
Alas! Señora, I have none of that.
But I will search and when you come again next year
I shall have some to show you."
Apparently it never crossed his mind
That with the coming of another summer
The customer would not come too; for wreathed in smiles
He greeted her, the day of her return,
And proudly pointed to some lovely goblets,
Set safe and high upon a narrow shelf.
"You see, Señora, I did not forget," and she was very glad
That she had not forgotten, either.

Segovia is the ornate sepulchre
Of that most lowly and most fervent saint
Who sang because he suffered, and whose mysticism
Was tinged with kindness and with single-heartedness:
John of the Cross, whose life was bare and sad,
Whose bride was poverty, whose bed was stone,
And who was used so cruelly on earth
One marvels that he could have kept his belief of heaven.
I do not know why afterward, men chose
To place his quiet body in a tomb
So rich and gilded and elaborate
That it seems out of keeping with his life.
But after all, it does not matter much.
His monument is not in marble anyway,
But in the songs he sang because he suffered.

Segovia is that wonderful *alcázar*
Breathtaking whenever and however seen,
But seen best from below, at eventide,
When sunset glows behind it, or when stars
Begin to thicken in a darkening sky
And a triumphant moon swings into sight.
Then it stands out
Set in the glory of God's handiwork
As a great tribute to the work of man.
So have I seen it often. But the time
That I remember best is when I stood
On the small bridge that spans the little stream,
Curving around the hill the fortress crowns.
Beggars came crowding in upon the friends
Who stood there with me and upon me, too.
We bade them all begone; they spoiled the scene
Where there was nought but beauty otherwise,
Telling ourselves that we were right to do so,
Because you should not give to beggars anyway.
But one, an aged man, clad in soiled rags,
Leaning upon a cane, besought me, saying,
"Lady, I am poor and I am sick and I am old."
I wish I had not turned this man away,
That I had spoken to him softly, given him alms,
Whether it is best to give to beggars or not.
For I know
That as I myself grow poorer and feebler and older
This man will haunt me and I shall deserve it.

SALAMANCA

Salamanca is a city of many glories,
Tawny of color, intricate of carving,
Lavishly offered to the errant stranger.

One of these is her plaza, certainly the largest
And just as surely the most beautiful in Spain.
Another is the grooved and fluted wonder
Known as the House of Shells. And still another

The twin cathedrals, linked so close together,
That they seem indivisible,
Though one is called the old and one the new.

Wideset they stand within this spacious city,
Their glory unobscured by crowding roofs,
And chief among them is that seat of learning
Which was already old before the Pilgrims
And Puritans of sober Massachusetts
Bethought them of a university,
So that their ministry might be literate.
Fray Luis de León presides here still;
His statue dominates a noble square,
And in the classroom where he taught, the same rude benches
Stand, row on row, beneath a carven lectern
Which never will seem empty, for his spirit
Pervades the atmosphere and always will.
(Do you remember—it is not a legend—
That the familiars of the Inquisition
Came here one day when he was lecturing
And took him off to prison. Five years later,
The students sitting on those rough-hewn benches
Were suddenly aware he was among them.
Again they felt the power of his presence,
Though he returned to them unheralded.
With noiseless tread and unperturbed expression
Once more he mounted to his carven lectern,
And, in a gentle voice, said quietly,
"Well, gentlemen, as I was saying yesterday . . . .")

I love to linger in that ancient classroom,
And long I felt considerable self-pity
Because the nearby library, rich in treasure,
Was closed when I was in the splendid city,
And I could neither browse nor study there.
Another stranger, thwarted like myself,
Turned to me in the cloister and remarked,
"I wanted most of all to see that book
Written in blood." . . . . "Written in blood?" I asked.

"Yes—when he had no ink, the priestly author
Drew what he needed from his own pricked veins."
Over and over since then, I have cross-examined
Spanish scholars, asking about this book.
Some say there is none like it in existence,
Others that it was only signed in blood;
Some that they would seek for information
When it was possible to do so—and forgetting,
Have promised and forgotten once again;
But none has said that someday I might see it.
Well, I have grieved and grieved because this marvel
Was hidden from my eyes and from my ken.
But I have ceased to grieve. What does it matter
That this one book is hidden from my sight
When I, a writer, know past all misgiving
That every book which lasts was writ in blood?

AVILA

Avila is a city of matchless walls and many names.

It has been called the City of Knights—and why not?
Knights without number have gone forth from there,
To conquer continents and spread the Faith.

It has been called the City of Kings—and why not?
Avila gave a viceroy to Peru;
It was from Avila that Henry VIII,
Surrounded by the knights of Avila,
Went forth to war against the Musselmen.
It was in Avila, Alfonso XI
Found refuge from his furious enemies;
It was to Avila the Empress Isabella
Brought Philip, her small son, for princely ceremonies;
Later, the Emperor Charles came too. And on and on
The roster of these regal names continues.

It has been called the Land of Stones and Saints—and why not?
Within its gates are only narrow streets,

Winding their hard paved way between the walls
Of convents and of churches, carved and cold.
Its battlements and its cathedrals tower
Above a bleak and rock-strewn countryside,
Where little verdure thrives and few flocks feed.
Yet this forbidding city, these barren fields
Brought forth such miracles of sanctity
That all the world has bowed in awesome wonder.
The great Teresa leads the godly group,
But all are worthy of their mighty leader.

It has been called the city nearest heaven—and why not?
Its builders chose for it a high plateau
Far, far above the plains of Old Castile,
And from these heights its turrets rise farther still
Against the blue of the Castilian sky.
But it is not alone this lofty stature,
That brings it close to heaven. A nun of Avila
Has told me that Our Lord has shown Himself
To mortal beings here on more occasions
Than are recorded elsewhere in this world
And by His presence drew it to Himself.
I do not doubt her word.

The great Teresa,
In writing of His frequent revelations
Has told us that at first she only saw
His holy hands—and then His countenance—
And then at last His whole and glorious being,
And thus, by slow degrees, she came to know Him.

I believe the same is true of Avila.
We see it as the City of the Knights—
The City of the Kings—the barren land
That brought forth stones—
But also brought forth saints;
And then at last we see it close to heaven
Transfigured by the presence of Our Lord.

VALENCIA

Valencia is "the city of fertility"—
So I was told before I ever saw it
And, while beholding, did so with delight.
Mile upon mile of irrigated land
Surrounds it, for a network of canals
Waters this *Huerta*, and transfigures
An arid countryside into a garden,
Infallible and beautiful and vast.
Thus, the city—
Set in the midst of glossy orange groves
And humid fields of rice, ripening from verdure
Into a golden harvest—
Luxuriates in such fertility.
Even the gold forming the splendid ceilings
Of the Provincial Capital—treasure brought
Back from the new found world in caravels,
To ornament the *Generalidad*—
Has no such value
As the *Huerta's* gold.

Small wonder that you feast as nowhere else
Upon the produce of this fecund land!
Great earthen jugs of foaming orange juice
Empty their contents in your lifted glass
To quench your thirst, and you can drink your fill
And still the jug will never be half emptied.
Then when you sit at table,
First will appear the wonderful *gazpacho,*
That "liquid salad" served to you as soup.
Tomatoes, cucumbers and onions,
Green peppers, vinegar and olive oil,
Garlic, paprika, kummel seeds and breadcrumbs—
All these have first been pounded to a pulp
And then passed through a sieve to form a purée
Before the chilling process which completes
The preparation of this pleasing soup.

And, when you feel agreeably refreshed,
An iron skillet, hissing with such heat
That you are puzzled how it ever could have reached
Your plate so quickly, since it left the fire,
Is set before you, piled with saffron rice,
And beautified with scarlet pimiento.
Embedded in the rice are shrimp and clams,
Morsels of chicken, scraps of beef and pork,
Green peas, fresh parsley, hearts of artichokes,
Well oiled, well seasoned, skillfully combined
To form a perfect blending with the rice.
Paella of Valencia, all hail!
A nobler dish has never been devised,
Either in this city of fertility,
Or in the world that lies beyond its vale.

Valencia is the city of democracy—
And this is something no one ever told me,
But which I learned with wonderment and joy,
While viewing the Tribunal of the Waters:
That unique court, consisting of eight men,
Who, once a week, assemble just outside
The great Cathedral portal called the Gate
Of the Apostles, there to pass
Upon all problems of the *Huerta.*
More than a thousand years have come and gone,
Since first a group of farmers, all elected
By fellow farmers, each one representing
A portion of the land, canal controlled,
Foregathered here upon the stroke of twelve.
Kingdoms have also come and gone, and revolutions,
And fratricidal wars have rent the land,
And still the court
Has all the time remained inviolate.
Patient and attentive, these plain countrymen
Listen to every case that comes before them,
Before they render judgment,
But from their verdict there is no appeal.
Together, the accusers and the accused

Are brought before them by a functionary
Who has just set his mace upon a standard
Marking a semi-circle which a railing
Serves to divide the pavement in two parts,
One for the court, one for the populace
Who throng the sidewalks and the street as well,
For all are free to listen and behold,
And all who feel they have a just complaint
Are given time to tell their grievances,
And all who would deny responsibility
For doing harm, may speak in their defense.
This man opened a dyke, flooding the crops
Which had been nurtured by a neighbor?
Well, that was bad. This one has failed
To keep an outlet clean—
Water could not flow through?
Why, even worse! But where is the defendant
For this strange case? Not there?
It is dismissed,
And in another, evidence is lacking
Of any negligence or crime committed.
(Fines are imposed in pounds, because the pound
Was standard currency when first the court
Began to function, but the culprits may
Now pay in *pesetas* at their convenience.)
No other cases to come up today? Very well,
Until next Thursday at the stroke of twelve. . . .

The smock clad men rise from their chairs—
Only their president wears formal dress; the others
Come just as they are clad for working days—
And vanish through the Gate of the Apostles.
The mace bearer takes down
His mighty standard,
The iron railing opens, and the people
Who thronged the pavement and the street beyond,
Go quietly away, well satisfied
That the Tribunal once again has acted
To guard their rights, and with their rights, their city.

This is democracy in action, not in words.
Like a Town Meeting in New England, here we see
A form of simple rural government,
Created by and of and for the people—
God grant that it may never vanish from the earth!
Valencia is a city of Divinity—
And this is something that I do not know,
But that I can believe because I feel it.
When the Cathedral door has closed upon
The traveler, and he remains inside,
He may walk on between the battered columns
And gaping walls that bear such tragic witness
To civil war, until at last he reaches
A tiny chapel leading from the nave,
Whose Gothic arches still curve up toward Heaven
In all their pristine beauty. Even at high noon
Twilight pervades this place, but for one beam
Directed towards a small secluded niche,
Where flowing radiance is concentrated
Upon the Holy Grail. . . .

Valencianos relay the story—
Quoting from many wise historians—
Of how the Master of the Cenacle,
Our Lord's Apostles, and the early Christians
All guarded this most rare and precious relic
With the same zealous care that they bestowed
Upon the crown of thorns and holy shroud;
Of how this cup was later brought to Rome
By the Great Fisherman; how afterward
It was the chalice used by many Popes
In celebrating Mass, and finally sent,
By him who served as Papal Treasurer,
For hiding in the village of his birth—
The humble little town of Huesca—
Until Valerian, the emperor,
Should cease to persecute the Holy City.
Since then it has been hidden many times,
By many persons and in many places

But always there has been a careful record
Of how and why and when such things were done,
And now it has emerged triumphantly
From hiding and has been enshrined
In this dim chapel, where the only light
Is that which glorifies the sacred cup.
All this Valencianos firmly believe,
And who am I to doubt their scholarship,
Their earnestness and their sincerity?
I believe, with them, that they possess the Grail.
But should this firm belief be all unfounded
On anything but legend, still the humblest vessel—
From this great moment of the Consecration—
Becomes the undisputed replica
Of that which Jesus held, saying to His Disciples,
"This is my blood—drink ye all of this."
Hence, kindled by the radiance of the light
Which streams, effulgent, from Valencia's chalice,
Our faith becomes a thing of vital glory
Because we too have heeded His command.

SEVILLA

Sevilla is the scent of orange blossoms
Along the streets and wafted through the windows;
It's trellises and arbors wreathed in roses,
It's most of all the favorite—carnations:
In bright bouquets sent to a welcome traveler,
In mourning sheaves to decorate the tombs;
Snow white or shell pink on the Virgin's *pasos,*
Deep crimson, banked around the crucifixes,
Or nestling close between the glossy tresses
And high combs of the *señoritas*
(Dressed all in black, fingering their rosaries,
Veiled, but with gossamer lightness, by mantillas,
Meant to enhance but not to hide their charms)
Who, arm in arm with brother or with *novio,*
Walk up and down and round and round the city,

From Holy Thursday morning through Good Friday,
Not merrymaking, but not grieving, either.

Seville is an old-fashioned victoria hitched to a drooping horse
Whose feet go clop-clopping over the pavements day and night
And whose unshaven driver is cheerful and chatty.
It is a smart turnout with two men on the box and a crest on the door;
It is a carryall drawn by six tasseled mules.
Seville is the tomb of Columbus
Supported on the shoulders of four kings,
In the dim transept of the great Cathedral.
It is Murillo's statue in a sunny garden,
It is Carmen's moated cigarette factory changed into a university,
And Teresa's sequestered convent, unchanged through the centuries.
Seville is a sunset seen across the Guadalquivir,
And moonlight above the Alcázar.
It is blue tiles and slitlike streets—one that winds like a serpent—
It is parks that resound to the laughter of children
And shelter countless lovers in their lanes.
It is monumental archives and flowerpots strung along the steep sides
of a house;
It is white walls and carven doorways,
And patios so freely shown through iron grillework
That it is hard to recognize seclusion
As their outstanding attribute. And yet
If you should try to penetrate within them,
You would find out that they are subtly secret,
Even while thus hidden. The Sevillaño
Is courteous, but he is unlike the Madrileño,
Who, saying, "This is your house," means what he says.

Sevilla is a *Feria* which started
Long, long ago just as a cattle fair,
And came to be the city's chief fiesta,
Bustling and crowded and hilarious,
Noisy with cries of vendors and with shouts of children.
Gay with festoons of light and blinking signs.
Broad avenues are lined with striped pavilions,
Tentlike in form and fabric, because people

Have not forgotten all about the cattle fair.
But otherwise these festival pavilions,
Wide open to the avenues they line—
Lace curtained, flower wreathed, illuminated,
Crowded with dancers, ringing with music,
And called *casetas* now—bear no resemblance
To the small striped tents of long ago.
The girls who dance are clad in ruffled dresses—
Flamenco costumes—quaint and multicolored—
And girls not dancing in the bright *casetas*
Are strolling in the crowded street, or sitting,
Their ruffled skirts spread fanlike all around them,
Atop the folded covers of victorias
Or on the benches of the carryalls.
Tireless, night and day these Sevillanas
Chatter and laugh and click their castanets
Whether they dance or not. Others ride pillion
Behind their sleek and slender cavaliers.
Still others, instead of ruffled dresses,
Wear riding habits, cut with such perfection
That these seem moulded to the graceful forms
Of the incomparable equestriennes
Who ride alone, nor need a cavalier
To make their beauty seem desirable.

Sevilla is the dance of the *seises* before a golden altar on Corpus
Christi and the Feast of the Immaculate Conception
Little boys who carry castanets in their hands and sing sweetly before
they begin to move with precision
In the same figures that their ancestors were taught hundreds of years
ago, and wearing the same costumes,
Striped doublets, white knee breeches, plumed hats, nothing is altered.
Once Rome decreed that these dances must cease, then relented, saying
They might continue as long as the costumes were wearable, for
otherwise waste would ensue.
So through the centuries somehow the costumes have lasted,
Doubtless due to some miracle—or to very skilled needlework,
Quietly done by very great ladies.

Sevilla is the sound of the *saetas*—
Sad songs that echo through Semana Santa—
The gleam of candles and the flash of jewels
That light the image of the Macarena.
Blazing with countless gems, she leaves her church,
Her *paso* borne aloft by fifty men—
Dockhands who trudge beneath the panoply
Of her magnificence, bearing their load
With patient pride. Meanwhile, before her go
The censer bearers, acolytes and priests,
The masked *confradias* in their peaked hoods,
Fathers and sons, down to the smallest child
Whose heritage is this fraternity.
And when the heavy doors that guard her shrine
Are opened, and the waiting multitude
Sees her emerge, serene and glorious,
A cry goes up that reaches to high heaven,
And there are some who weep and some who pray,
And all are certain that the Macarena
Hears cries and prayers alike, and that the tears
Which have been shed for her will soon be dried.
She is the people's Mother, too, as well as Christ's,
Their darling and their refuge and their queen.

There is an ancient saying which tells you,
"Seville will drive you away or swallow you up."
Perhaps. But if you are so driven,
I believe you will come back, begging more tender treatment,
And, if deserved, that you may have it. While, if swallowed,
I believe you will rejoice in such engulfment.
For there's another saying, too, about a window,
That lets you look toward heaven from Seville,
And later on a second, that lets you look from heaven toward Seville.
I have had my glimpse of heaven from Seville,
So now I hope that midst the "many mansions"
Which we are promised, I may find a window
Where I can look down on the bright carnations,
The azure-colored tiles and secret patios,
The slitlike streets and sunny open parks.

I hope that mingled with the heavenly music
I still shall hear the Sevillanos singing
And most of all I hope the Macarena
Will not live far from my celestial mansion.
A far greater writer than I has said that the most wonderful building in
        Spain is a tomb and the most wonderful painting a burial scene,
But I do not think so.
It was a foreign writer who said that and I like much better what a
        Spanish writer has said,
"There is one thing more sacred than a tomb: a cradle. There is one
        greater than the past: the future."
There are many cradles in Spain and its future stretches out to a
        limitless and glowing horizon.

THE ISLES OF GREECE

Lord Byron

The isles of Greece, the isles of Greece!
   Where burning Sappho loved and sung,
Where grew the arts of war and peace,
   Where Delos rose, and Phoebus sprung!
Eternal summer gilds them yet,
But all except their sun is set.

The mountains look on Marathon,
   And Marathon looks on the sea;
And, musing there an hour alone,
   I dreamed that Greece might still be free;
For, standing on the Persian's grave,
I could not *deem* myself a slave.

A king sate on the rocky brow
    Which looks o'er sea-born Salamis;
And ships by thousands lay below,
    And men in nations—all were his!
He counted them at break of day,
And when the sun set, where were they?

And where are they, and where art thou,
    My country? On thy voiceless shore
The heroic lay is tuneless now,
    The heroic bosom beats no more!
And must thy lyre, so long divine,
Degenerate into hands like mine?

'Tis something in the dearth of fame,
    Though linked among a fettered race,
To feel at least a patriot's shame,
    Even as I sing, suffuse my face;
For what is left the poet here?
For Greeks a blush, for Greece a tear!

Must we but weep o'er days more blest?
    Must we but blush? Our fathers bled.
Earth! render back from out thy breast
    A remnant of our Spartan dead!
Of the three hundred grant but three,
To make a new Thermopylae!

What, silent still? and silent all?
    Ah! no: the voices of the dead
Sound like a distant torrent's fall,
    And answer, "Let one living head,
But one arise—we come, we come!"
'Tis but the living who are dumb.

18

HOUSES

Even more than cities and villages, fascinating as many of these are to me, dear as are many others, houses individually rather than collectively have special meanings for me.

This is no doubt partly because from infancy the houses in which I have lived have been in some way, and occasionally in several ways —architecturally, historically and artistically—important. I was born in James Monroe's house at the University of Virginia. My paternal grandmother, with whom I often stayed, lived in the house that had been built for Count Rumford at North Woburn, Massachusetts. My mother inherited from her paternal great-grandfather a house of early American design in Newbury, Vermont, which had never gone out of the family then and has not done so since. At the impressionable age of ten, I spent an autumn at Fontainebleau in a house that had been a *dépendence* of Madame Pompadour; and as a no less impressionable woman in her sixties, I kept house for two summers in the Montefrio Palacete at Avila. Somewhere between the two I bought and restored a house in Alexandria, Virginia, which had numbered Washingtons and Lees among its previous owners, and lived there very happily for five years. I left it with regret, when my work seemed to indicate that Louisiana rather than Virginia should be my writing center during the winters. But now that I have had the great privilege of restoring and living in the beautiful and historic Beauregard House, I can no longer regret my move.

Perhaps these examples, which are by no means all-inclusive, will suffice to show why houses, as such, have come to have a special appeal for me and why poems about them almost invariably catch my

eye and—if they have any merit whatsoever—hold my attention. Wher
they have charm and distinction as well they are fondly treasured. I
believe those I have chosen for this section of the Anthology all have
the two latter characteristics.

NEW HOUSE

Bessie Glen Buchanan

No one has come to live here yet,
but the road ends in open ground
and the foundation stones are set,
Tomorrow there will be the sound

of saws and hammers pushing back
the silence. Lumber, brick and sand
will reach this leafy cul-de-sac,
fall ready to the builder's hand.

Who brought a dream to this obscure
abode? Neighbors far away—
who made its shaping doubly sure?
No sign of tenantry can say.

Perhaps the sunset's burning gold
flashed from a window still not there,
and hilltop quietness foretold
what busy towns refuse to share.

Deeper into the wilderness
The dream goes on, the search fulfilled.
And who shall ever dispossess
those who had faith enough to build!

NEW ENGLAND FARMHOUSES

Roselle Mercier Montgomery

They stand forth frankly to the world—four square
And solid, plain, disdaining ornament,
Their barns and woodsheds quite as prominent
As porch or parlor is! They have the air
Of having been designed for work or wear—
To beauty they appear indifferent,
Like homely women, worthy, excellent
Who scorn the vanities of ladies fair!

Such houses, unaware of coquetry,
Have no small balconies, no inglenooks,
No dear retreats for which a lover looks—
They have not learned the lure of mystery,
Yet they achieve a beauty none denies—
One looks at them—as in a mother's eyes.

VICTORIAN PARLOR

Elizabeth Bohm

Let hands be gentle when they part the curtain
Whose foliage and flowers of gold brocade
Protect this place. Here everything is certain
Forever, though stars fade.

When it is time for tea the sunset blazes
Red dew upon the crystal chandelier,
The mirror fills and flows with forest hazes:
Let hands be folded here.

Far from the world of bare and plushless noises,
The other planes of streamlines raw in brass,
Let hands learn peace where on the mantel poises
A shepherd of white glass.

INMATE

Leslie Nelson Jennings

Behind those prim lace curtains there was no
Ancestral ghost who wandered through the night,
Rehearsing what had happened long ago,
Drifting down stairways, luminous and white.
Still flesh and blood, the inmate of that place
Sat in the parlor as she had for years,
A look of strange withdrawal on her face,
Hands folded laxly, eyes too old for tears.

Houses aren't always haunted by the dead.
Such presences can pass through any door
Into the past, and so be comforted.
Here was a living shadow even more
Pitiful than those misty shapes for whom
Remembrance lingers in an empty room.

THE HOUSE

E. M. Almedingen

Here, by this fireplace, in candlelight, they said:
"Bastille has fallen . . ." "The King of France is dead . . ."
"If Boney comes . . ." and later "Waterloo!"
Here they read The Times, the Post and Galignani,
And shrugged at Europe's madness. They were sane
Busied with sport, accounts, farming; duly loyal
To Morning Prayer read by a younger son
Within the walls raised by a Norman hand.

Here Adams, Kaufmann, Nash and Canaletto
Once pleased their will, and home from a Grand Tour,
They stood and watched the wrappings fall
Off painted canvas, porcelain, chiselled marble,
And said: "Carpaccio and Giorgione
Into the gallery, and this Van Dyck had best
Be in the library, yes, close to the door—
With Lely, Romney, Kneller for his neighbours."
Here their possessions calmly possessed them.

And up the inlaid treads of wing-like stairs,
Within the curtained rooms, women in lawn and lace
Listened to gossip, prayed, dreamt, bore their children,
Read "Rasselas," "Clarissa,"
Wept over "Childe Harold" and "Giaour,"
Learnt of Shelley's death, and fell in love
With Mr. Darcy.

Here, from the arms of nurses, children went
To play with hoop and ball, to learn their letters,
To serve the world. From these formal doors
They went, and the intolerable skies
Of India, South Africa, New Zealand

Observed their dreams of quiet English shade,
Of hours browsed away by river banks
When accents of a tranced first love
Were whispered with a hawthorn for a witness.

Here, by this window framed in sea-green silk,
They stood and watched the bonfires leap
Which told the Midland skies
That God had saved the Queen for fifty generous years.

Here, fold on fold, still lives
The richly woven chronicle
Of pleasure, duty, passion, occupation—
All framed within their privilege
So difficult and sharp in its demands
(Accorded grace here met grace unaccorded
But stumbled on).

Things owned in pride and love
Still keep the touch of fingers lost in dust;
Things once looked upon enclose the secrets
Of eyes which see no more.

Come back, come back at night,
With oak and beech and cedar in the dark
True to their truest shape.

Come back
To hear the heartbeat of the old grey stone,
Yourself a ghost commanding ghostly treasure,
An intimate of high noon and of night,
At ease in love and hate of yesterday.
They lived and felt and loved. They were,
And they still are. The house is their home,
Warmly expectant in the leaf-thin trance
Which spills its light across the old spinet,
And from the light comes faint a lovers' minuet.

And turn away from all imagined loss
Until within your thought, upon your pulse,
Yesterday and to-day come to their marriage-bed,
And bid you accept to-morrow's dole.
The cedars say: "Be reconciled without, within,
For death in life and life in death are one,
Continuous, woven together, as, lip to lip
Are lovers' mouths."

                    Now let us go
And watch the swans glide on towards the Severn.

INCORPORATE

Mazie V. Caruthers

Who with an old house lives, becomes at last
A part and parcel of his own estate—
Sensitive to its moods, initiate
In all the joys and sorrows of its past;

Wainscoted walls and creaking stairs could tell
Strange tales, and—if so be one's listening—
Often the rooms seem stirred by whispering.
Thus, does an ancient homestead weave its spell.

Then, as relentlessly the years haste by,
And they who have loved the place pass through its door
In solemn state, to come again no more—
He who has ears, may hear the old house sigh.

OLD THINGS

Dorothy Quick

Old things have peace which they have earned
By centuries of standing fast.
Within them all that they have learned
Is stored, so that the present, past
Are merged into one entity.
Those who are sensitive can reach
Far back through time's periphery
And know what ancient things can teach.

ON RESTORING AN OLD HOUSE

Ethel deLiesseline

O Lord, walk through my house and make it Thine,
For it is old and leans like a broken tree;
But there is more to it than floors of pine
And ceilings high, for there is memory
That comes through folding doors of yester sons
With courageous hearts, who gave it castle form;
And I am here descendent of the ones
Who had the will to work till evening storm!
O Lord, walk through my heart and make it strong.
And give me fires ablaze to dream beside;
Hallow halls and stairs, and lend a song
To help me to restore the dreams that died.
O Lord, walk through the house I hold in trust,
And be with those who come when I am dust!

CLOSED HOUSE

Robert P. Tristram Coffin

He could not go there summers, but his house
Holds only sunshine all the summer through,
The whippoorwill sings on the lilac bush
Surprised to find an empty house so new.

The clapboards are snow white, and all the blinds
Are opened wide as if the house were filled
With many faces drinking light and air,
But all the light on emptiness is spilled.

The lilac is kept back and not permitted
To notify by bloom the house is lost;
The place seems open to callers of all kinds
Except the careless ones, the rain and frost.

It looks as though before you passed the slope
Of the outside cellar-door, the low
Door would rise up and let out a man,
And he would sing out with a bright hello.

The owner takes good care his house shall look
Decent to the people going by.
He owes it to himself, for this house is
The place where he was born and he will die.

WINTERPROOF

Arthur Guiterman

The pipes are drained, the furnace flame has died,
The rooms are all in order, every chair
Correctly covered: we have closed and tied
The shutters that the windows shall not stare
Forlornly. So, we lock the door: Dear house
Good night, and may no storms that round you sweep,
No pert, intrusive chipmunk, nibbling mouse,
Nor squirrel, scampering, disturb your sleep.
While earth is hard with frost and drifts enfold
Your garden beds, but late so gay with flowers,
Rest well, beloved home, and safely hold
Our precious memories of happy hours
To greet us, like returning bluebirds, when
We light the fire upon your hearth again!

A TRAVELER DEPARTS

W. H. Gerry

My benediction now, beloved host,
On this your house wherein I have been fed,
Not commonly, but on the spitted roast,
The wine, the leavened loaf of life instead.
I know my welcome; but the selfsame road
Which wound me to you tugs me on once more,
And something deep inside like a small goad
Pricks this contentment as always before.

Where this road leads, or what will nearer show
Beyond the blurred blue hills slow leagues away,
I cannot answer, as I cannot know
Why I must learn, or why I must not stay.
I have been cursed or blessed with restless feet;
For me no more than pause, and no retreat.

THE WANDERER

Inez Clark Thorson

He may have crossed a continent to see
Exotic blooms the sun may not behold,
Or mountaintops that never are set free
From snow that falls deep fold on deeper fold.

Then he one day may hear a lone bird call
Or see a strippled leaf drift toward the ground,
Nostalgic, he will turn his back on all
That lured him far . . . he would be homeward bound.

The distant vistas are no longer green,
And now disquieted he cannot wait
To cross the miles that lift like walls between
Him and a long-unopened picket gate.

19

NATURE

In this section the poems which mean the most to me personally are those about hills, which I might even have placed in the section on courage rather than in the one on nature. The poem which begins, "For me the hills", and ends, "My feet are bruised, but I have climbed today", I have often quoted at the close of a speech, when lecturing was a regular part of my work. (Another poem with which I often closed a speech was Henry van Dyke's "Work", which I have included in the section, *Prayers*.) I believe that anyone who has had to contend with severe physical handicaps will readily understand my feelings for these poems, and, in like measure, that anyone who owns land, above all inherited land, will find a special message in the poem about this. But why pick and choose? If I did not believe that every one of these poems had a special message for someone, I would not have included it in this Anthology.

STOPPING BY WOODS ON A SNOWY EVENING

Robert Frost

Whose woods these are I think I know.
His house is in the village though;
He will not see me stopping here
To watch his woods fill up with snow.

My little horse must think it queer
To stop without a farmhouse near
Between the woods and frozen lake
The darkest evening of the year.

He gives his harness bells a shake
To ask if there is some mistake.
The only other sound's the sweep
Of easy wind and downy flake.

The woods are lovely, dark and deep,
But I have promises to keep,
And miles to go before I sleep,
And miles to go before I sleep.

A BOUNDLESS MOMENT

Robert Frost

He halted in the wind, and—what was that
Far in the maples, pale, but not a ghost?
He stood there bringing March against his thought,
And yet too ready to believe the most.

"Oh, that's the Paradise-in-bloom," I said;
And truly it was fair enough for flowers
Had we but in us to assume in March
Such white luxuriance of May for ours.

We stood a moment so in a strange world,
Myself as one his own pretense deceives;
And then I said the truth (and we moved on).
A young beech clinging to its last year's leaves.

I GATHERED STARS

Raymond Kresensky

The night I gathered stars and pressed
Them lightly in my opened hands,
The moon was there, a thought of rest,
And kind as one who understands.

I did not see the earth, or care;
It was so lonely, dead and still.
I trod with God the rising stair,
My feet upon a moonlit hill.

But suddenly the moon went down
And silhouetted tree and spire.
I felt the shadows of the town
Dispelling my age-old desire.

That night I gathered stars. I hurled
Them far and wide, and saw them fall
Against the hardness of the world,
Shedding a brightness over all.

OLD GARDEN

Edith Tatum

The years have left their mark upon the house,
It stands dejected midst the ancient trees;
The tangled garden that surrounds it, still
Is full of charm and wind-blown mysteries.
It must have been a woman, long ago,
Who planned and planted it, who loved the earth,
The changing seasons and the sun and rain;
Watched them in rhythmic unison give birth
To beauty that refreshed her heart and soul
And brought them order and serenity.
It seems to hold the blossoming of dreams,
The fragrance of a deathless memory.
I wonder was her life a happy one,
Or did her garden give some deep hurt ease?
I think that when the silvered moon is low
She walks in peace through spicy shrubberies.

GHOST CHURCH

Herbert Elliott

The church went back to the wild, for men
Left it to ruin and dark decay.
The sun and moon peer through the roof.
The weather and wind come in to stay.

At the broken door a slender birch
Pauses as if to enter in,
Like a maid in first communion dress,
Pure and free from sin.

The ancient churchyard across the way
Has taken the wild rose to its breast.
The slate slabs echo the hymn of the thrush
When the day sinks burning in the west.

In utter peace the doe and fawn
Come here to feed in the dying light,
The wind blows with an organ tone
And stars march up the aisles of night.

COUNTRY WOMAN

Beren Van Slyke

Have you picked up a quince to smell it
And thought of grape jam on cellar shelves,
Of honey, brown eggs in water glass,
Of the braided bulbs of garlic and onion
Hung from the rafter?

There is sage and bay in the autumn wind,
There are apples that have not dropped from the bough,
Red withering brown in the smoke and the haze.
The cows are slow to pull at the frost-grey grass;
There was ice on the pond last night.

The city is miles away.
The quince in your hand
Is warm as a grandmother's cheek.

HELD BY THE LAND

Christina Rainsford

Compact of courage, stubbornness and hope
Is that deep urge that holds man to his land
Dares him to build on a volcano's slope
Whose plume of smoke can turn to burning brand,
To put down roots along a river side,
Tempting the water's fury when in spate
It sweeps the shore in a tumultuous tide
And he is left—homeless and desolate.
Men have returned from war to farms they own
To find the buildings burned, the cattle dead,
Rebuilt a homestead painful stone on stone,
Steered rusty plow through fields unharvested.
From primal sources scarcely understood
Springs love of land—potent as ties of blood.

ANSWER

Dorothy Quick

What have men gained? Their loss is easier said:
No more are they akin with tree and leaf,
No longer from the land will they earn bread,
Since their communion with the sod is brief.
The cities offer riches with new creeds—
The land retains God's answer to men's needs.

FED

Elspeth Bragdon

Of trees and water the heart has need:
Trees for shelter and shade and sound.
On blowing green the heart can feed
When feet are weary of touching ground.
Their wet black trunks in the windy rain
Are cool and sweet to the finger's touch,
And silver leaves are a cure of pain
That comes from wanting the sky too much.
Water will echo a changing mood
With sun and shadow, ripple and calm.
Thirst and hunger find drink and food
In water cupped in the aching palm.
    Trees and water, water and trees. . . .
    The heart can live for long on these!

THE RED WOODS

Dorothy Quick

Here is eternity made manifest
With dignity of timeless years,
The stalwart answer to man's quest,
The calming of his present fears.

BENEDICTION

Angela Morgan

Hills are earth's longing to commune with God;
Mountains, her great Amen; and trees,
Loved of the sky, though wedded to the sod . . .
Life has no truer worshippers than these.

HILLS

Arthur Guiterman

I never loved your plains!—
Your gentle valleys,
Your drowsy country lanes
And pleached alleys.

I want my hills!—the trail
That scorns the hollow.—
Up, up the ragged shale
Where few will follow,

Up, over wooded crest
And mossy boulder
With strong thigh, heaving chest,
And swinging shoulder,

So let me hold my way,
By nothing halted,
Until, at close of day,
I stand, exalted,

High on my hills of dream—
Dear hills that know me!
And then, how fair will seem
The lands below,

How pure, at vesper-time,
The far bells chiming—
God, give me hills to climb,
And strength for climbing!

FOR ME THE HILLS

Helen Truesdell Koch

For me the hills—no winding valley ways
Hemming me in and sheltering my days;
For me the effort, the vast, farflung goal,
Great draughts of beauty for my thirsting soul.

Far from above, the mists that drift below
Drown in soft azure beauty sin and woe;
And oh, the joy of conquest, looking back to say:
"My feet are bruised, but I have climbed today!"

EVENING AFTER RAIN

Edith Tatum

Long lacy fronds of the mimosa tree
Are studded with small diamonds of the rain;
Honeysuckle fragrance stirs memory
From dreamy summer sleep to life again.
New bathed crape myrtles gleam with rosy flame,
And through the air comes sound of silken wings
Seeking a hidden nest. A lovely name
The red-bird calls from where he sits and sings.

The wind-stirred trees are fluid, a green wave
That flows with melody across the day,
Mingling with silver mists of rain to lave
From earth-bound things the dust and heat away;
While liquid flute notes of the woodland thrush
Send a hymn of peace through the evening hush.

THE SACRAMENT OF FIRE

John Oxenham

Kneel always when you light a fire!
Kneel reverently, and thankful be
For God's unfailing charity,
And on the ascending flame inspire
A little prayer, that shall upbear
The incense of your thankfulness
For this sweet grace
Of warmth and light!
For here again is sacrifice
For your delight.

Within the wood
That lived a joyous life
Through sunny days and rainy days
And Winter storms and strife;
Within the peat
That drank the moorland sweet
Of bracken, whin, and sweet bell-heather,
And all the joy of gold gorse feather
Flaming like Love in wintriest weather,
While snug below, in sun and snow,
Peat heard the beat of the padding feet
Of foal and dam, and ewe and lamb,
And the stamp of old bell-wether;
Within the coal,
Where forests lie entombed,
Oak, elm, and chestnut, beech and red pine bole,
God shrined His sunshine, and enwombed
For you these stores of light and heat,
Your life-joys to complete.
These all have died that you might live;
Yours now and high prerogative

To loose their long captivities,
To give them new sweet span of life
And fresh activities.
Kneel always when you light a fire!
Kneel reverently,
And grateful be
To God for His unfailing charity!

LIGHTNING OVER A CALM SEA

May Williams Ward

Water is my brother
Fire my enemy.
Do not ask me whether
In each, high-handedly
I ignore another
And opposite quality.

As of now, sea is brother
Predictable and dear;
The threatening fiery other
Has lineaments of fear.
And relationship of both to me?
Too near.

STILL THERE IS PEACE

Leslie Savage Clark

It is not lost, the peace we long have sought,
Earth holds it safe in spite of blustering man,
In spite of wars and all the boundaries bought
With terror, blood and tears since time began.
No vaunted missile yet has range to mar
The vibrant color harps of Northern Lights,
The afterglow of setting sun, or bar
Orion's tranquil march across the nights.
Still there are hillsides where the maple burns
And hemlock trails the deer and foxes know,
Still there are purple grapes as fall returns
And boughs of golden apples hanging low.
Twilight and crescent moon, these shall not cease
Though rulers rise and fall—still there is peace.

20

SEASONS AND FLOWERS

I am aware that I have included three poems about lilacs in this section. No one who has lived in rural New England will need to be told why, just as no one who has lived in the Deep South will need to be told why, with many other flowers omitted for lack of space, I have included the only poem I could find about crape myrtle! The reasons will probably be more obvious than those about Texas in the section devoted to *Places*.

Though it was originally planned to have separate sections for *Seasons* and for *Flowers*, this schedule was changed. After all, is there any better way to interpret the seasons than through flowers in the months when we have them? In the Deep South that means all the months; in the freezing North scarlet-leaved trees and fluffy snowflakes take their places!

SPRING

From Pippa Passes

Robert Browning

The year's at the spring,
The day's at the morn,
Morning's at seven,
The hillside's dew-pearled.

The lark's on the wing,
The snail's on the thorn,
God's in His heaven,
All's right with the world!

THE DAFFODILS

William Wordsworth

I wandered lonely as a cloud
That floats on high o'er vales and hills,
When all at once I saw a crowd,
A host of golden daffodils;
Beside the lake, beneath the trees,
Fluttering and dancing in the breeze.

Continuous as the stars that shine
And twinkle in the Milky Way,
They stretched in never-ending line
Along the margin of a bay:
Ten thousand saw I at a glance,
Tossing their heads in sprightly dance.

The waves beside them danced; but they
Out-did the sparkling waves in glee:
A poet could not but be gay
In such a jocund company:
I gazed—and gazed—but little thought
What wealth to me the show had brought:

For often, when on my couch I lie
In vacant or in pensive mood,
They flash upon that inward eye
Which is the bliss of solitude;
And then my heart with rapture thrills,
And dances with the daffodils.

TULIP BEDS IN HOLLAND

Angela Morgan

I used to wonder where the rainbow went
After its hour was spent.
I used to think
The sunset poured its colors, gold and pink
And lavish purple, somewhere on the ground;
That dawn's vermilion and the stupendous blue
Of daylight's coming, too,
Might all be found
Hoarded upon the palette of the artist earth
To give new paintings birth.
Holland, I saw your tulip gardens giving all
Their tides of color to the Spring's call,
Spilling their splendor in one mighty overflow . . .
And now I know!

SPRING LILACS

Mona Moulton

When lilacs blow along an old stone wall
To spill their essence from a tiny cup,
When all the air is lilac full and all
The lilac time comes back, my heart fills up
With a long remembering loveliness
There is no space in time to measure this
A hundred years of beauty or one hour
'Tis heaven that's near whenever lilacs flower.

AS LILACS SPEAK

Frances De Vliegar Anderson

Listen! The lilacs speak with rain-sped scent
And the heart, again, persuaded you are near;
For true and false are now so subtly blent,
Under the lilacs' voice your own rings clear
And the hour strange and lilac-eloquent;
Here reason sleeps. Once more, the heart will hear
Other words than speech of lilac-cry;
Blossom-sweet they fall and falling, lie.

Yet, if they lie, they voice a gentle wrong—
A welcome fiction, surely one most kind;
How else could you return except in song
Of May? How else, this miracle defined?
Let reason doze his little hour—not long,
Until the treasure-delving bees have mines;
How else could you return and speak again,
Except you speak as lilacs speak, in rain . . . ?

GEOGRAPHY OF LILACS

Frances Frost

I have a map of old New England roads
drawn with a blunt blue pencil on my heart,
the roads where lilac bushes can be found
by white doors in Vermont, by a haying cart
rain faded near a red New Hampshire barn.
The lilac roads twist seaward down in Maine,
Massachusetts hides them by a pond,
Rhode Island reels with lilacs in the rain,
and Connecticut cellar-holes let foxes live
under the clustered spires. However deep
the night, I could follow lilac backroads home,
I could find New England even in my sleep.

CALLA LILIES IN THE DUSK

William Struthers

Be these the phantoms of fair souls, astray—
Souls who, by earth unsullied, passed away?
So pure, mayhap, were they that, in his might,
Death did relent and bid them take mute flight
Back to the borderland of sunlit day—
Ghost-pale for having seen the King of Night.

From THE VISION OF SIR LAUNFAL

James Russell Lowell

And what is so rare as a day in June?
Then, if ever, come perfect days;
Then Heaven tries earth if it be in tune,
And over it softly her warm ear lays;
Whether we look or whether we listen,
We hear life murmur, and see it glisten;
Every clod feels a stir of might,
An instinct within it that reaches and towers,
And, groping blindly above it for light,
Climbs to a soul in grass and flowers;
The flush of life may well be seen
Thrilling back over hills and valleys;
The cowslip startles in meadows green,
The buttercup catches the sun in its chalice,
And there's never a leaf nor a blade too mean
To be some happy creature's palace;
The little bird sits at his door in the sun,
Atilt like a blossom among the leaves,
And lets his illumined being o'errun
With the deluge of summer it receives;
His mate feels the eggs beneath her wings,
And the heart in her dumb breast flutters and sings;
He sings to the wide world, and she to her nest,—
In the nice ear of Nature which song is the best?

YELLOW ROSE

Minnie Case Hopkins

There is not anything that grows
More lovely than a yellow rose:
A rose that speaks of sun and moon,
Of candles lit and golden June.

KINSHIP

Marion Doyle

Green candles lit
In a lovely room
Are magic to banish
The deepest gloom.

A yellow rose
Upon its stem
Is the only
Kin to them.

CRAPE MYRTLES IN THE SOUTH

Edith Tatum

The summer finds them in old pleasure gardens,
Where they are massed with stateliness and grace,
Or giving solace to small Negro cabins,
Roots deeply sunk into a barren place.

Red banners high, some march down city streets
Triumphantly, bright petals on the grass;
While others hover near a village church
In robes of white like brides who go to mass.

In lavender, beside a quiet grave,
Pale shattered blossoms drifting like slow tears
Of sympathy; or near green sheltered spot
A rosy glow seems to forbid chill fears.

Here in the Southland, these crape myrtle trees
Bring gladness to our hearts the summer long,
Demanding little for the joy they give,
They are a living sermon, prayer and song.

WILD BRIAR-ROSES

Robert P. Tristram Coffin

Sweet from the rock, honey from hateful places,
Tenderness opening among the thorns,
Wild briar-roses scent the heedless ocean,
Willfuler, wilder than unicorns.

Shyer than partridges, these roses never
Endure captivity when taken indoors
But fold their willful beauty up and scatter
Petals like broken hearts upon the floors.

Blown on the ledges in the time of gales
They waste their hues on clouds, die in an hour;
They live to burn their loveliest unseen
Where winds cry saddest, there they flower.

These roses are not for use, for comfort,
Look not for them in happiness tomorrow,
These hearts interlocked are hearts of the north,
Their other names are lonelinesses, sorrow.

PASTORAL

Viney Wilder

Summer is standing still along this road
Where wild blackberries hang from dusty vines,
An ancient wagon creaking with its load
Complains to distant hills and towering pines.

Time stops for just a moment to record
Tranquility against some future day.
A reservoir of peace that can be stored
And drawn upon when summer slips away.

BEAUTY ONCE SHARED

Helen Tappan

Close fast the door upon the lovely night,
Until the high, full, summer moon shall pass;
Shut out old apple trees in silvered grass
And muted paths where heliotrope gleams white.
Forget the lemon lily and pale phlox,
The rosy, bending lithrum, ghostly sweet,
Where shadowed lawn and shadowed orchard meet;
Forget the glow of opened hollyhocks.
Light all the lamps and keep them blazing high,
And call the neighbors in with laughing talk;
Forget the mystery of the garden walk,
Beneath the tender, sad, moon-ridden sky.
For well I know, being a woman grown,
Beauty once shared cannot be borne alone.

NOW IS THE TIME

Minnie Hite Moody

Now is the time once more of Roman candles,
Of fireflies, watermelons, crowded beaches,
Of small boys fretting at lawn mower handles,
Of Independence Day and fervent speeches;
A time of layer cakes, fried chicken, thunder
Suddenly bursting with the picnic spread;
A time for singing and for preaching under
Camp-meeting tents . . . a time when overhead
The falling stars plunge awesomely; a time
For combines in the wheat fields of the nation,
A time for drinks with lemon and with lime,
A time for ice cream, ice cubes, perspiration,
Baseball and laughter and a blazing sky—
Ladies and gentlemen, we have July!

END OF SUMMER, GEORGIA

Anderson M. Scruggs

Mark now the weariness of leaves
Toward August's end, with summer done;
Though rich and full, the woods yet show
The gradual lessening of the sun.

Now, imperceptibly, each day
The blood and warmth of leaf and stem
Will vanish in the thinning air,
Till nothing more remains of them.

Mark too such sadness in our hearts:
We who are neither young nor old,
Now in our rich full-seasoned love,
Sense vaguely winter's coming cold.

SEASON OF AMBER

Dorothy Quick

September writes long shadows on the lawn,
Slanting grotesquely in the afternoon;
There is an earlier, more salient dawn
Where sandals follow the reluctant moon.
Her thirty silvered days will quickly pass
Golden with sunshine and with ripened grain.
A deeper greenness is upon the grass,
Flowers bloom now that will not bud again.
Here air is cooler, yet it holds no chill,
The curve of sky is brighter, without glare.
There is a deeper lassitude, a still
And lovely connaisance that lingers where
Sunset and moonlight mingle to recall
The end of summer and the start of fall.

WORDS FROM ENGLAND

Donald Hall

The maples of Connecticut
In dry October breezes flare
All shades of orange, shades of red.
There is my home, but I have not
For two Octobers rested there,
Nor the red maples visited.

The English autumn pales the trees
With yellow fog to ornament
This island jewel of a Queen.
As morbid as a slow disease,
October makes its faint descent
Toward winter's rainy quarantine.

Another year and I will be
Returned to where the seasons are,
Each delicate compartment shut.
Then I will watch the truthful tree
That tells position like a star,
A maple in Connecticut.

INDIAN SUMMER

Margery Mansfield

Uphill, because the sky is blue
And climbing clouds have topped the wood,
I will be going uphill, too,
Lost in an Indian summer mood,
How clear an ax rings through the air,
A power-saw drones a mile away.
I walk with autumn till I hear
A child that laughs at play.
I see a farmhouse round the bend
And hear the cattle low.
And there I'll stop. To find a friend
Is far enough to go.

BUTTERNUTS

Elizabeth Jane Astley

There's more than red fox and brown deer
In Vermont woods this time of the year,
There's a shower of butternuts at dawn
That frost has sharpened its scissors on.
The nuts are velvet and green brown
So much like leaves that they hardly show,
With a shell like the granite underground
From which the nut trees grow.
A tree itself could cover a field
With saplings from its butternut yield
But there'll be none when the autumn's done

For chipmunks gather them one by one
And people getting their hands all black
Crowd the nuts in a gunny sack
Knowing a cure for the agues of winter
Is the sound of butternuts under a hammer.

HARVEST

Alice Hartich

Now apples redden and grapes are clouded
With silver mist; the barns are crowded
With grain, and summer's languid haze
Gives way to brisk September days.

The local school house, swept and dusted,
Re-assumes the task entrusted
To its arms: the education
Of a new world's generation.

Lord, bless the harvest with service using
Man's kindest ways, his wisest choosing,
That gratitude may magnify
The gracious Source of our supply.

And bless the schools that truth may nourish
The seeds of growth till wisdom flourish
And faith and love become the core
Of this, our greatest harvest store.

NEW ENGLAND NOVEMBER

Donald Hall

In that New Haven house
Where laughing relatives
Perform the family jokes
And all the family lives,

Where turkey roasted whole,
Potatoes, turnips, peas,
Onions and Brussels sprouts,
And globes of Holland cheese,

Where pumpkin, apple, mince
And seven kinds of pie,
Plum pudding, cake and nuts,
Fill up the family eye;

Or in that northern house
Where two old people stay,
Valley'd between red hills
That burn the sky away,

And stuff their cellar full
Of food won by the hand
In years of labouring
On the New Hampshire land;

That country now is full
Of fire and plenteousness,
And pride blesses the land;
The land that comes back to bless.

NOVEMBER

Gertrude Hahn

November has a nunlike mien;
The sober colors of her scene,
The whispering of withered leaves,
Like swishing habit-skirts and sleeves.

The gravity of graying skies,
Like calmly contemplative eyes;
The hush that hovers in the air,
Like perfect peace that follows prayer.

Still scarlet-leaved, one slender tree
Bears beauty with the dignity
Of kneeling novices who take
The vestal veil for Christ's dear sake.

FIRST SNOW

Frances Frost

The first snow, soft as a kitten's paw,
skitters across the woodshed eaves,
skips to the crimson barberry haw,
shyly clips the crabapple trees.

The first snow, white as a blue-eyed kitten,
pats withered grass and Queen Anne's lace,
humps with a sly and silver mitten
and gives me a flurry full in the face.

21

ENVOI

I hope the reader who has read this far is not going to feel that I have shown presumption in dividing the section entitled *Envoi* between Kipling and Keyes, to the exclusion of all other authors who have written about leave-taking.

Kipling's "L'Envoi" was of course a natural for a book of this type. The verses written by my son Henry and chosen among many that were submitted for the so-called *Sophomore Blue Book* at Harvard, are included not because the poem was written by a member of my family but because it seems to me to express so movingly the feelings and ideals of many earnest young men who are hopefully searching and not yet finding their life work. As to my own verses, "God Has Been Good to Me", they are included at the special request of the Editor. I would not have done so on my own initiative, but I am glad he wanted them. How could I close a book more fittingly than with such an expression of deep conviction?

EPILOGUE

Henry W. Keyes, Jr.

Two years have passed. And now we must look back
And see where wandering footsteps left the track
    Mapped out by our ambitions and ideals.
When young and joyous we first entered here
We all had rosy dreams of how each year
    Would answer all our prayers and our appeals.

In this short time—this truly tiny space—
We thought to resolutely run a race
    Toward things more manly than our early deeds.
Some strove their hardest; though they could not reach
The goals they set themselves, yet they could teach
    Their backward brothers struggling through dark needs.

In this glad season nature turns away
From winter's storms and troubles, and is gay
    Anticipating summer warm and bright.
Let us, though we learn lessons from the past,
Go bravely forward, hoping to the last
    That each day's work will bring us nearer light.

L'ENVOI

Rudyard Kipling

When Earth's last picture is painted, and the tubes are twisted
and dried,
When the oldest colours have faded, and the youngest critic has
died,
We shall rest, and, faith, we shall need it—lie down for an aeon
or two,
Till the Master of All Good Workmen shall set us to work anew!

And those that were good shall be happy: they shall sit in a golden
chair;
They shall splash at a ten-league canvas with brushes of comets'
hair;
They shall find real saints to draw from—Magdalene, Peter, and
Paul;
They shall work for an age at a sitting and never be tired at all!

And only the Master shall praise us, and only the Master shall
blame;
And no one shall work for money, and no one shall work for fame;
But each for the joy of the working, and each, in his separate star,
Shall draw the Thing as he sees It for the God of Things as They
Are!

GOD HAS BEEN GOOD TO ME

Frances Parkinson Keyes

God has been good to me, for I have sailed,
Into the Golden Horn—and through the Straits
Magellan glorified—and where the veiled
Harbor of Rio gleams and radiates.

God has been good to me, for I have stood
In the Red Square when it was white with snow—
And at the edge of a dark Chilean wood
When Aconcagua burned with Andean glow.

God has been good to me, for I have lingered
In the Alhambra when the moon was bright—
And in Damascus, dazzled, as I fingered
The brilliant wares spread out for my delight.

God has been good to me, for I have dwelt
Above the parapet at Carcassonne—
And on the pampas, where the shadows melt
Into mirage—and by the Rubicon.

God has been good to me, for I have tasted
Hymettus honey and Formosa tea—
Isfahan melons—and the rare, unwasted
Vintage of Jerez and of Hungary.

God has been good to me, for I have smelled
Night-blooming cereus on starlit hedges—
And waxen-white gardenias, which swelled
With fragrance, blossoming on window-ledges.

God has been good to me, for I have heard
The crush of Arctic ice around a boat
Jammed in the Neva River—and a bird
Piercing the Persian twilight with its note.

God has been good to me, for I have felt
His glory all about me as I gazed
Upon Gethsemane—and as I knelt
In Chartres Cathedral, overwhelmed and dazed.

God has been good to me, for I have known
All these His Wonders—and when He shall send
Me on the Last Great Enterprise, His own
Beatitude shall crown my journey's end.

INDEX OF AUTHORS

[1] Translator

[1] Translator

INDEX OF POEM TITLES

INDEX OF FIRST LINES

THE AUTHOR AND
HER BOOK

Frances Parkinson Keyes, *whose books have been best-sellers almost every year since 1936 and are published simultaneously in England and the United States and in as many as twelve foreign languages, was born at the University of Virginia, where her father,
John Henry Wheeler, a Bostonian transplanted to the South, was head
of the Greek department. Her mother was Louise Fuller Johnson, a
New Yorker who had earlier moved to Newbury, Vermont. After
Dr. Wheeler's death, Frances and her mother spent their summers in
Newbury, Vermont, and their winters in Boston, a city which was to
become the scene of* Joy Street *(Messner, 1950), a bestseller of
1950–51. As a girl, she studied in Geneva and Berlin, as well as Boston, and with a governess. She speaks four languages and even today
spends much time in travel. She was married at eighteen to Henry
Wilder Keyes, whose home, Pine Grove Farm, near Haverhill, New
Hampshire, was just across the river from Newbury, Vermont. In
1917 he became governor of New Hampshire. In 1919 he was elected
to the United States Senate and served three terms, during which
Mrs. Keyes divided her time between her family of three sons and
the beginning of a literary career, initiated with articles in the Atlantic
Monthly and a novel,* The Old Gray Homestead *(Houghton Mifflin,
1919). Her interest in her husband's Washington career led her to
depict Washington political life in a series of letters to American
women which became a* Good Housekeeping *running feature entitled* The Letters from a Senator's Wife *and was later published in
book form by Appleton in 1924. In 1923 she began a novel set in
Washington which appeared in 1930 as* Queen Anne's Lace *(Liveright, 1930). From 1923 to 1935 she was an associate editor of* Good
Housekeeping *and from 1937 to 1939 editor of the National Historical Magazine. Mrs. Keyes has spent much time in France, which led
to the biography of St. Therese,* Written in Heaven *(Messner, 1937)
and the life of St. Bernadette of Lourdes,* The Sublime Shepherdess
(Messner, 1940), and a more personal record, Along a Little Way

(new and revised edition, Hawthorn, 1962). In 1940 she visited Mexico to write The Grace of Guadalupe *(Messner, 1941). Mrs. Keyes holds degrees of Litt.D. from Bates College and George Washington University, and in 1951 received the degree of Doctor of Humane Letters from the University of New Hampshire "as a distinguished author, ambassador of good will, and interpreter of American life." In 1946 she received the Siena Medal awarded annually to "The outstanding Catholic woman in the United States"; in 1950 the Silver Medal of French Recognition for her aid in reconstructing the Abbaye of the Benedictines at Lisieux; and in 1959 she was decorated with the Order of Isabella the Catholic in recognition of her work in Spain. She still retains her ownership of the Oxbow, her ancestral homestead at Newbury, Vermont, and her legal residence is still at Pine Grove Farm, the Keyes' family home at North Haverhill, New Hampshire; but in the winter she uses the historic Beauregard House in New Orleans, which she has restored, as her writing center. Among her books besides those previously mentioned are:* The Career of David Noble *(Frederick Stokes, 1921)*, Silver Seas and Golden Cities *(Liveright, 1931)*, Lady Blanche Farm *(Liveright, 1931)*, Senator Marlowe's Daughter *(Messner, 1933)*, The Safe Bridge *(Messner, 1934)*, The Happy Wanderer *(Messner, 1935)*, Honor Bright *(Messner, 1936)*, Capital Kaleidoscope *(1937)*, Parts Unknown *(Messner, 1938)*, The Great Tradition *(Messner, 1939)*, Fielding's Folly *(Messner, 1940)*, All That Glitters *(Messner, 1941)*, Crescent Carnival *(Messner, 1942)*, Also the Hills *(Messner, 1942)*, The River Road *(Messner, 1945)*, Once on Esplanade *(Dodd, Mead, 1947)*, Came a Cavalier *(Messner, 1947)*, Dinner at Antoine's *(Messner, 1948)*, Therese: Saint of a Little Way *(Hawthorn, 1962)*, All This Is Louisiana *(Harper Bros., 1950)*, The Cost of a Best Seller *(Messner, 1950)*, Steamboat Gothic *(Messner, 1952)*, Bernadette of Lourdes *(Messner, 1953)*, The Royal Box *(Messner, 1954)*, The Frances Parkinson Keyes Cookbook *(Doubleday, 1955)*, Blue Camellia *(Messner, 1957)*, The Land of Stones and Saints *(Doubleday, 1957)*, Victorine *(Messner, 1958)*, Station Wagon in Spain *(Farrar, Straus & Cudahy, 1959)*, Frances Parkinson Keyes' Christmas Gift *(Hawthorn, 1959)*, Mother Cabrini: Missionary to the World *(Vision Books, 1959)*, The Third Mystic of Avila *(Farrar, Straus & Cudahy, 1960)*, Roses in December *(Doubleday & Co., 1960)*, The

Chess Players (*Farrar, Straus & Cudahy, 1960*), The Rose and the Lily (*Hawthorn, 1961*), Madame Castel's Lodger (*Farrar, Straus, 1962*), St Anne, Grandmother of Our Saviour (*new and revised edition, Hawthorn, 1962*).

A TREASURY OF FAVORITE POEMS (Hawthorn, 1963) was completely manufactured by Doubleday & Co., Hanover, Pennsylvania. The text and extracts are set in Fairfield, with headings in Garamond Bold.

A HAWTHORN BOOK